Proud to be a Swan

The History of Swansea City AFC

Proud to be a Swan

The History of Swansea City AFC

1912 – 2012

Geraint H. Jenkins

y Lolfa

First impression: 2012

The publishers wish to acknowledge the support of
Cyngor Llyfrau Cymru

Cover design: Y Lolfa
Cover photograph: Swansea City win the
Championship play-off final at Wembley, May 2011
(courtesy of Swansea City AFC)

ISBN: 978 184771 481 7

FSC

Published and printed in Wales
on paper from well maintained forests by
Y Lolfa Cyf., Talybont, Ceredigion SY24 5HE
website www.ylolfa.com
e-mail ylolfa@ylolfa.com
tel 01970 832 304
fax 832 782

For Ann

Contents

Foreword

IT GIVES ME great pleasure as Chairman of Swansea City AFC to write the foreword for this long-awaited publication that charts the history of this proud football club. Its release comes at a time when the club is enjoying life in the best league in the world, namely the Barclays Premier League. We've been in the top flight before when the remarkable feats of manager John Toshack took the club from the old Division Four to the top of Division One back in the early 1980s.

It was a roller-coaster ride that saw the Swans grace the top division for a brief two-year spell before slipping back down into the basement again. But that's probably been the story of

Swansea City over the last hundred years – a roller-coaster ride that has seen a number of highs and, as our fans will tell you, too many lows along the way.

That's why it's such a pleasure to see the launch of this superbly researched and written book while the club is flying high in its centenary year.

The Swans went global during their first season in the Premier League and the media revelled in the tale of the club's rapid rise, especially over the last ten years when at one stage it was one game away from losing Football League status altogether. Now we're playing our attractive brand of football to a world audience on a weekly basis. The lovely, ugly Vetch Field, home to so many great stories, heroes and zeros, has been replaced by a modern and impressive Liberty Stadium that is now sold-out for every game.

But, as Chairman of an ambitious and hard-working Board of Directors, each and every one a Swansea fan, we are all aware that football has a habit of kicking you hard the moment you take your eye off the ball. So, after 100 years of hard work, on and off the field, with so many people playing their own special part, it's important that we continue to enhance the good name of Swansea City for future generations of Swans fans everywhere. As far as I'm concerned, we've got the best fans in the land, and nobody deserves success more than the growing Jack Army.

Enjoy the book – and here's to another 100 glorious years.

Huw Jenkins
Chairman
Swansea City AFC

Preface

THERE WAS A festive air around the Liberty Stadium on Sunday, 13 May 2012, the last fixture in Swansea City's first season in the Premier League. At the bidding of the manager Brendan Rodgers, large numbers of supporters added to the gaiety of the occasion by wearing Elvis Presley costumes and masks in a very public riposte to those pre-season pundits who had declared that there was more likelihood of Elvis appearing than of little old Swansea avoiding the relegation trapdoor. The illustrious visitors were Liverpool and, to the delight of the capacity crowd, the mighty Reds were confounded by the possession-based passing game, zonal pressing and work rate of a rampant Swansea team. A delightful 86th-minute goal by Danny Graham brought a richly deserved victory which took the club to eleventh place in the wealthiest and most demanding league in the world. By any measure, it had been a fabulous achievement. Following the final whistle the weary but jubilant players, accompanied by their besuited colleagues and members of the back-room staff, set off on a leisurely lap of honour. Emphasizing the family nature of the club, several players carried babies (stars of the future) and Ángel Rangel's delightful toddler Isabella Rose caught the eye as she cavorted happily on the sacred turf. Basking in the warm sunshine, the Jack Army roundly cheered their favourites and chanted 'We love our manager' in heartfelt homage to the man who had inspired and guided the team to success. How fitting that the Swans should have capped 100 years of history by opening a glorious new chapter in the Premiership.

How fitting also, given the unpredictable history of the

club, that within a matter of weeks the celebrations had turned to lamentations. In early June Brendan Rodgers became the third Swansea manager in four seasons to desert his post. His departure to Liverpool, greeted with dismay by the supporters, provided further proof that loyalty among managers and players within the Premier League has become an unfashionable, even alien, concept. Undaunted by this setback, however, chairman Huw Jenkins worked his magic once more and the arrival of Michael Laudrup provided the players and supporters with a powerful psychological boost. As the club enters its centennial season there is every reason to believe that the 'beautiful football' to which the Jack Army has become accustomed will flourish as never before.

Swansea's much admired former goalkeeper Roger Freestone once maintained that there was never a dull moment at the club, and in writing its centenary history I often found myself clinging on for dear life as the roller-coaster ride gathered pace and oscillated between breathtaking success, decent achievements, near-misses, ineptitude, tragicomedy and despair. I hope I have done justice to this multi-layered saga and that the curiously compulsive task of chronicling relegation dogfights and possible financial meltdown has not deflected attention from the exhilarating examples of free-flowing, attractive football, played with style and panache in 'the Swansea way', under managers like Joe Bradshaw, Billy McCandless, John Toshack, Roberto Martínez and Brendan Rodgers. At this historic juncture we remember most of all the high drama of the great games and the skill and creativity of past and present players whose feats have gladdened our hearts and made us proud to be a Swan.

In researching and writing this book I have incurred many debts. The bulk of the research was undertaken at the National Library of Wales in Aberystwyth and at the West Glamorgan Archives Service in Swansea, and I'm most grateful to the staff of those institutions for providing for my needs and for their courtesy and support. I readily acknowledge my debt to the late David Farmer and to Colin Jones whose tireless researches have provided me with a robust and accurate factual and statistical base for my work. Brian Lile very kindly allowed me to read his excellent unpublished essay on the early history of soccer in Swansea and John Jenkins supplied me with a constant flow of references, both weird and wonderful, relating to the fortunes of the club and football in general. It was a particular pleasure to consult the profuse material assembled by Gwyn Rees at his home in Townhill and to share his memories of players and matches. Gwyn Davies was most helpful at Swansea Public Library and I'm grateful to Phil Sumbler and Huw Cooze for patiently answering my queries regarding the Supporters Trust. The richest source for match reports and photographs is the *South Wales Evening Post* and I'm indebted to the editor Spencer Feeney and to Patricia Jones for their generous assistance and genuine interest in this book.

I have also benefited greatly from conducting interviews with several key figures associated with the recent history of the club. In writing an earlier book in 1976–7, I was fortunate to interview two princes of Welsh football – Ivor Allchurch and John Charles – and, thanks to Huw Bowen, I have also derived material from his interviews with John Conibear, Tom Kiley and Gordon Daniels. I learned a good deal through conversations with Glenda Charles, Malcolm Charles, Mel Charles, Alan Curtis, Chris Davies, Huw Jenkins, Cliff Jones, Garry Monk, Mel Nurse, Colin Pascoe, Brendan Rodgers and Paulo Sousa, and I thank them most warmly for sharing their experiences and thoughts with me.

The club itself has given me unstinting support and I have nothing but admiration for the way in which the current directors, under the wise guidance of the chairman Huw Jenkins, have stabilized matters both on and off the field and provided a clear and decisive strategy for the future. Jonathan Wilsher, Media and Communications Manager at the club, has not only been a constant pillar of support but has also taken a lively interest in the progress of the book. His colleague Chris Barney has also been most helpful.

The keen observer may have noticed that a small but companionable group of supporters congregate on match days alongside Ivor Allchurch's statue at the Liberty Stadium. Semi-affectionately referred to as the 'Academic Jacks', they speak of Ivor in awed tones and discuss the past and present fortunes of the Swans with lively and sometimes disputatious zeal. I count myself fortunate to be one of them, not least because the likes of John Conibear, Ann Ffrancon, Gwenno Ffrancon, Martin Johnes, Huw Richards, Peter Stead and Steven Thompson have given me every encouragement in writing this book. My greatest debt, however, is to Huw Bowen, the convener of these pre-match huddles. He kindly shared with me the fruits of his researches into the inter-war history of the club and, most of all, willingly undertook the chore of reading a draft of the entire manuscript and improving it beyond measure. I gratefully acknowledge his generosity and friendship.

I owe sincere thanks to the publishers Y Lolfa and particularly to Lefi Gruffudd and Eirian Jones for supporting this enterprise with the genuine enthusiasm that diehard Swansea supporters will immediately recognize. I'm also grateful to William Howells for kindly taking the time and trouble to prepare the index. My wife Ann and daughters Gwenno, Angharad and Rhiannon know better than anyone how much affectionate care I have devoted to the writing of this book, and my debt to them for their love and support over the years is irredeemable.

Finally, it has been a particular privilege to support this mercurial club for nearly half the period covered in this book and I hope those who buy, borrow or steal a copy enjoy it as much as I enjoyed writing it.

Geraint H. Jenkins
July 2012

1

The Formative Years

ALDERMAN EDWARD GEORGE Protheroe, mayor of the Borough of Swansea in 1911–12, was a jolly character with a great sense of fun. He was something of a prankster and he enjoyed relaying gossip. It amused him to make facetious comments during tedious Council proceedings and his constituents loved him as much for his irreverent ways as for his concern for their needs and aspirations. A tailor by trade, he was a natty dresser who habitually wore a navy blue suit with stiff shirt cuffs which he pushed back into his sleeves. Aware that rain was prone to fall on most days of the year in Swansea, he always carried an umbrella. Every dog has his day and Ted Protheroe was fortunate to have two glorious days in 1912. The first came on 20 June when he was privileged to confer the Freedom of the Borough of Swansea on the exotic operatic diva Madame Adelina Patti of Craig-y-nos. The second occurred on Saturday, 7 September, when the first official fixture of Swansea Town as a professional football club in Division Two of the Southern League was held. Even though the sun shone brightly on the appointed day, Protheroe carried his trusty umbrella with him as well as a straw hat. His sturdy footwear stood him in good stead as he negotiated a posse of photographers before duly declaring the Vetch Field open by toe-poking the leather match ball to set proceedings in motion. He then scuttled off the pressed clinker pitch to reflect on his moment of sporting glory, leaving the two sides to entertain a noisy and excited crowd of over 8,000 people. By a curious stroke of fate, given the mutual loathing which unites the rival fans in our day, Swansea's first opponents were Cardiff City. The game – a vibrant occasion in many respects – marked a turning point in the sporting history of the town. The Jacks were given their first taste of the beautiful game, played by professionals on a ground which was to enter the annals of Welsh sporting folklore.

It should not have come as a surprise to anyone that a town like Swansea had established its own professional soccer club. Momentous changes had occurred in its size and influence, and it was ideally placed to host the dribbling code as a major spectator sport. Those who lived to be a hundred in 1918 would have witnessed a town swelling from less than 5,000 acres in the early 19th century to over 24,000 acres. Its population of 151,025 in 1911 made it the second largest urban conurbation in Wales and it was growing swiftly. In an introduction to a pamphlet entitled *A Greater Swansea* (1912), no less a person than Lloyd George declared that 'Swansea has important work awaiting it'. But there appeared to be several Swanseas, each of which was seen in a different light. Romantic enthusiasts, mindful of the town's magnificent coastline and bathing facilities, still felt twinges of nostalgia for the halcyon days when Georgians dubbed it 'the Brighton of Wales'. This was all very well, but it did not please those scientists, engineers and chemists who, embarrassed by the previous depiction, preferred to think of it as 'an intelligent town', home of the Royal Institution of South Wales and the oldest museum in Wales, and peopled by active, respectable citizens who reckoned that knowledge was power. But Swansea's international reputation and its claims (until it was overtaken in size by Cardiff in the 1870s) to be 'the Welsh metropolis' were unquestionably based on its industrial and commercial traditions.

The first industrialized region in Wales, Swansea became known as Copperopolis, a world-leading producer of copper in the Lower Swansea Valley, and it is entirely fitting that when the club forsook the much-loved Vetch Field in 2005 its handsome new stadium should have been located on the site of the White Rock copper works, on the west bank of the river Tawe. Although Iolo Morganwg, a tireless anti-slave trade campaigner in the 1790s, despised Swansea's 'war-whooping commerce', its thriving copper trade undoubtedly brought international fame to the town. The influential Vivian family dominated the industry and their labour force, who toiled away manfully in the polluted, sulphur-laden copperworks, created the wealth which sustained them. Once copper was knocked off its perch in the 1890s, the tinplate industry took over and outpaced its rivals throughout the world in the Edwardian period. By 1913 commercial exports from the bustling port of Swansea had reached record levels by exceeding six million tons. The town was bursting with confidence and vitality. To the poet Edward Thomas, who was killed at Arras in 1917, it was a fascinating and irritating place, shameless and unpretentious in equal measure, and clearly determined to bulge out of its boundaries: 'it swarms about the Tawe, climbs over the hill with inconsiderate vitality'. The more famous poet Dylan Thomas, who knew his Swansea, remained torn between the ugliness and loveliness of the town, and had he been a soccer fan he would have witnessed both traits in abundance on the Vetch Field.

By the booming years of the Edwardian era, therefore, Swansea was clearly sufficiently large and successful to sustain a professional soccer club and to promote in the town and region what the matchless 'Welsh Wizard' Billy Meredith called 'a noble and manly game'. On the face of it, the circumstances appeared to be extremely favourable. By 1911 two of every three persons in Wales were living in Glamorgan, and many of them were besotted with sport. Those who disliked team sports found pleasure in cycling, whippet-racing, foot-running and especially boxing. Tiny fighters like Jim Driscoll, Jimmy Wilde and Freddie Welsh were household names and national heroes in the world of boxing. Of the team sports, none could match rugby, a game which could boast glittering achievements in the annals of Welsh sport. In the never-to-be-forgotten year of 1905

Wales conquered the powerful All Blacks and over the course of eleven years it captured six triple crowns. At St Helen's, iconic international rugby players like Billy Bancroft, Dicky Owen and Billy Trew were excellent role models for the young in their 'All White' colours. Indeed, Swansea Rugby Football Club still basked in its reputation as 'the Invincibles' and as a nursery for players of exceptional prowess. In Swansea Town's inaugural season at the Vetch Field, the town's rugby side were crowned Welsh club champions and claimed a famous victory over the mighty Springboks on Boxing Day. To knock such a long-established and popular game off its pedestal was a daunting challenge for the Johnny-come-latelys who favoured the round ball. But it was very clear by this stage that the appetite for soccer, among players and spectators, had sharpened so appreciably that the handling code was already in danger of losing its primacy in Swansea. Indeed, soccer mania had become deeply entrenched and tensions between both codes were more pronounced in south Wales than in any other part of Britain. A good deal of friction emerged as representatives of both sports sought to gain the upper hand.

Curiously, however, association football in Wales had first taken root in the north-east. The pioneers were based in Wrexham, where the Football Association of Wales was founded in 1876. Clubs like Chirk, Druids and Wrexham were a powerful force in Welsh soccer and not until Cardiff City broke their monopoly in 1912 was the Welsh Cup whisked off to south Wales. Players from north Wales staffed the national side and were inspired by the legendary goalkeeper Leigh Richmond Roose and the quicksilver winger Billy Meredith, both of whom were dazzlingly eccentric showmen of the highest class. But demographic changes meant that soccer was also swiftly becoming a popular recreation in south Wales. In-migration from rural parts of Wales and a particularly large influx of thousands of working people from the West Country from the 1890s onwards transformed the prospects of the round-ball game. A substantial soccer culture blossomed for the first time in south Wales. Resentful of the ascendancy of the north and the way in which the governors of the Welsh FA excluded players from the south from the national team, the soccer-loving proletariat in the towns, valleys and coastal plains of Glamorgan and Monmouthshire were determined to promote 'the people's game' at all levels in their neck of the woods. The South Wales and Monmouthshire Football Association was established in 1893 and thereafter local leagues sprang up like mushrooms after summer rain. Once soccer had taken root, it proved impossible to contain, though no one at the time had any inkling that it would conquer the world.

As far as the Swansea region itself was concerned, some form of rough and ready competitive soccer, as opposed to the rowdy melees of pre-industrial times, had been played since the mid-1860s. However, the first soccer match of any real significance played in the town was the international match between Wales and Ireland, generously hosted by St Helen's, where a crowd of 10,000 watched Wales win a fast, open game 4–1 in February 1893. To have penetrated this citadel of rugby was no small achievement and 'Soccerites', as the press often called them, spoke optimistically of a bright future. A bewildering number of leagues – among them the Swansea Schools League (1898), the Swansea Junior League (1901), and the Swansea and District League (1901) – enjoyed fluctuating fortunes, and the expansion of organized soccer, sustained by the local press, became a lively topic of conversation in schools, pubs and clubs as well as in the workplace. By the Edwardian years the *South Wales Daily Post* was confidently predicting that some of the most forceful personalities in the game in the south were no longer prepared to be 'bossed from Wrexham' and were looking for an opportunity to strike out on their own. Visits to Swansea by famous teams like Preston North End and Derby County attracted enormous interest and the clamour for a professional club began to grow. Amateur clubs calling themselves Swansea Town and Swansea East Side (later Swansea United) became arch-rivals in 1906–7 and vied for supremacy in the hope that some day soon they would enter the professional world. Their success was also a visible warning to rugby followers that soccer meant business. Year by year it assembled a loyal following, many of whom were convinced that the time was ripe to create a team that would represent the town at a professional level. By 1911 the Swansea and District League had the best part of 2,500 players on its books and, even more significantly, by 1914 there were 431 professional soccer players registered in Wales, most of them in the southern industrial belt and the coastal towns.

Champions of the handling code were not best pleased by these developments and viewed soccer upstarts with a mixture of superiority, suspicion and loathing. Some of them were gripped by a sense of dread. Could this effete round-ball game, clearly designed for softies, undermine the rugged, manly sport which God had given to the Welsh? As it still does in our times, the *Western Mail* fuelled the myth that rugby was the authentic national game, that it was classless and democratic, and that it best expressed the cult of manliness and the ethics of sportsmanship. Its columns bore lurid headlines such as 'Soccer's Menace to the Rugby Game' and rugby supporters were warned to take the threat very seriously. Further west, 'Ajax', the soccer correspondent of the *Cambria Daily Leader*, rubbed his hands with glee as he witnessed the discomfiture of his rivals. The oval-ball game, he maintained, was a torpid spectacle, full of slow-moving scrums, ponderous kicking and ill-tempered brawls. Moreover, its image was tarnished by its public-school origins and its shamateurism. Clearly, he declared provocatively, rugby's days were numbered, whereas soccer's popularity among discerning working-class people was soaring. Much more heat than light was generated by these exchanges and the truth is that both codes had become an integral and popular part of the recreational life of Swansea.

Meanwhile, standards were rising and soccer matches were becoming increasingly competitive on the fields of Swansea. Interested observers noted that it was in more robust health than ever before. One of them was Harry Bradshaw, formerly a successful manager at Burnley, Woolwich Arsenal and Fulham, and a stout advocate of flowing football, dribbling skills and passing. Having turned three clubs into major footballing forces, Bradshaw became secretary of the Southern League which, following its foundation in 1894, had become the dominant competition for professional clubs, outside the Football League, in the south of England and the Midlands. Intrigued by the spectacular progress of soccer in the industrial valleys and towns of south Wales, Bradshaw cast his beady eye over facilities in Swansea. On 21 January 1912 he met interested parties in the town and convinced them that there was no good reason why Wales's second largest town could not form a first-class professional football club which could hold its own against rivals in the Second Division of the Southern League. His words were greeted with unbridled enthusiasm and events moved swiftly from then on. On 2 May four Welsh clubs – Swansea, Llanelli, Newport and Mid-Rhondda (Cardiff had already joined a year earlier) – were unanimously elected members of the Southern League.

The next priority was to invite a shrewd administrator to assemble a consortium of well-to-do investors to put the infant club on a secure financial footing. The opportunity of founding a professional soccer club was an enticing prospect, especially for those who craved social status and perhaps enjoyed giving rugby administrators a bloody nose. The prospects were bright when John William Thorpe, a Swansea solicitor and sometime clerk to the Pontardawe magistrates bench, emerged as the principal driving force. A Lancastrian, Jack Thorpe had been articled as a solicitor to the footballing fanatic Llewelyn Kenrick, clerk to the magistrates of Ruabon and the founding father of the Football Association of Wales. Thorpe had played for Druids and had captained Ruabon's amateur team before moving to Swansea, where he became an avid supporter of local soccer and a keen cricketer. He readily agreed to set the organizational wheels in motion. At a meeting hurriedly arranged for 14 June and held at the Royal Hotel, Swansea, it was unanimously resolved to establish a new club. Thorpe was elected chairman and his right-hand man as part-time secretary was S. B. (Sam) Williams, a lugubrious figure who resembled a monk who had just broken his vows. Nicknamed 'Hail, Smiling Morn', he went on to serve the club unstintingly for 35 years. But Thorpe was the pacesetter. A forthright, no-nonsense leader, he had a clear, legalistic mind which enabled him to make swift and sometimes ruthless decisions. The 'strong whiff of Micawberism' which the historian Tony Mason detected in the boardrooms of many professional clubs at this time was not apparent in Swansea, and Thorpe shaped and moulded the club swiftly and effectively. Although little money was to be made by investing in the club, he knew that local manufacturers, financiers and traders, who were proud of the town and eager to enhance its prestige, would be happy to dip into their pockets. In no time at all, a coal exporter, a fish merchant, an insurance inspector, a hotel proprietor and two licensed victuallers had rallied to the cause by becoming the club's first directors, and by 25 July Swansea Town AFC Ltd, a limited liability company with a capital of £2,000, had been officially registered.

Another long-standing problem – the need to acquire a centrally-placed ground – was also solved. The favoured site was popularly known as the Vetch Field, which had derived its name from the time in the mid-19th century when a contractor sowed the refuse-littered meadow with a cabbage-like plant known as vetch, which was then used to feed cows. But the field soon fell into disrepair as the town corporation mindlessly tipped ashes and refuse on to it. In April 1891, however, two wily local entrepreneurs, William Teague and Henry Bowen Jenkins, unveiled plans to transform it into the Swansea Athletic Ground. Very soon spectators were gawping at trotting matches, bicycle races, foot races and even balloon ascents and parachute descents. When Sanger's circus came to town the Vetch hosted a battle scene in the Sudan which included dashing horsemen, marauding tribesmen, mules and camels, and deafening cannon fire. Undeterred by these exotic distractions, players signed by the newly-formed soccer club, Swansea AFC, trained at the stadium and made their debut on the ground on 17 March 1893. Thereafter the Vetch Field became inextricably associated in people's minds with the dribbling code. Yet its future was far from secure. It had been a target for developers since the early 1890s and in 1899 it was bought by the Swansea Gaslight Company, which inconveniently dumped materials and equipment willy-nilly on the ground and left the playing surface to deteriorate. The Company had plans to build on the site but, fortunately, it failed to gain Parliamentary permission to go ahead. Much to the relief of the inhabitants of the Sandfields and every soccer lover in the town, in 1912 the newly-formed senior club was able to take out a seven-year lease on the ground for £75 per year.

In the event, the club made the 'Vetch' its long-term physical and spiritual home by remaining there for 93 years. It is difficult to overstate the symbolic importance to a football club of having a much-loved sporting arena. For all its faults, the Vetch Field captured the imagination of all those who were Swansea to the marrow, and even the most cynical fans have been known to succumb to dewy-eyed sentimentalism in recalling their own experiences of games watched at the ground. Over more than nine decades the Vetch bore witness to the twists and turns of the club's turbulent history. It provided unforgettable moments of high drama and celebration, but also a series of humiliations too numerous to mention and often too painful to recall.

When Jack Thorpe and his fellow directors snapped up the site on a favourable lease there were sighs of relief all round. Having a home, conveniently located in the centre of the town, helped to create among supporters a special sense of place and identity. Over the years 'Down the Vetch' became a catchphrase and one of the enduring fascinations of the ground was its piecemeal development into a decidedly bizarre, lopsided array of terraces and stands, with awkward access points, inferior parking facilities, foul-smelling urinals and unappetizing meat pies. Nestling precariously among rows of terraced working-class housing and, appropriately some would say, overlooked by the county prison, it most certainly did not lack character. From the outset supporters got used to jostling vainly for an unimpeded view and coping with either squalls of driving rain or persistent drizzle which often turned the pitch into a strength-sapping quagmire. The historian Huw Bowen has memorably likened the experience of supporting the Swans at the Vetch to watching matches through 'a watery curtain'.

Yet, a football ground is primarily 'a landscape of pleasure'. Over the years there were many moments to savour even whilst peering into the miasmic gloom, for key matches at the Vetch had the uncanny knack of stirring the soul, as giants like Blackburn, Arsenal and West Ham United can readily confirm. The club's finest players could count on the undiluted loyalty of thousands of supporters in this very special setting, none more so than Ivor Allchurch, the 'Golden Boy' who remains the enduring hero of all true fans of the Swans. Who would ever forget seeing him in his pomp at the Vetch? Ivor – the surname has become redundant to all who worshipped him – embodied everything that is admirable in football, and it is fitting that his wondrous presence is commemorated in a life-size bronze statue by Michael Field, which was unveiled outside the Liberty Stadium in October 2005. Before each home game, many of those who were privileged to see Ivor grace the game caress his boots before entering the stadium. The ritual is deeply reassuring.

Songs as well as illustrious players also express the sense of affinity, even the kinship, which exists between supporters and the Vetch. The club song, which became hugely popular during John Toshack's golden era in the early 1980s and is still sung loudly in the new stadium, is inextricably associated in people's minds with the club's first home:

Swansea, oh Swansea,
Oh City, said I,
I'll stand there on the North Bank,
Until the day I die.
Take me to the Vetch Field,
Way down by the sea,
Where I will follow Swansea – Swansea City!

When plans were first laid to transfer the club to a new location in the Swansea Valley, they were met with incredulity and anger for the simple reason that they violated the supporters' sense of place. In terms of financial and business logic, the club's removal to the Liberty Stadium and its vastly improved facilities made excellent sense, but diehard fans could not help but feel that it was an act of betrayal. Anyone who would like to evoke the spirit of the Vetch could do no better than to read *The Vetch Field: A People's History*, published in 2005, a labour of love which admirably succeeded in commemorating 'a ground that has a place in all our hearts'.

All this of course lay far in the future, but it bears repeating that, even though the Vetch Field left a good deal to be desired from an aesthetic and playing point of view, it was a focus of intense parochial loyalties. In the summer of 1912, however, it was a case of all hands on deck as the founders strove to ensure that the pitch and its immediate environs were rendered fit for purpose. Speed was of the essence. Bands of perspiring workers were hired to remove the boulders, rubble, ashtips and firebricks which disfigured the Vetch and bring the ground up to the required standard. Only so much proved possible within two months and preparing a turfed surface was out of the question. Players in the Southern League were almost certainly familiar with playing on hard, gritty surfaces on urban waste grounds, but they were soon to discover that the unforgiving rolled ash and cinder surface at the Vetch was no place to be diving into reckless tackles. Nothing could have been further removed from the current brush-satin grass surface of the pitch at the Liberty Stadium. Small wonder that the newly-appointed player-manager, Walter Whittaker, who was placed in charge of overseeing the refurbishment of the ground, found it hard to live down the taunt that Swansea Town AFC was not a fit and proper club to take its place in the Southern League.

Many at the time must have questioned the wisdom of appointing a 34-year-old goalkeeper to be the first player-manager of the club. Goalkeepers, after all, are a breed apart and their ball-handling skills normally far exceed their footballing prowess. But Thorpe and his fellow directors had clearly taken advice and knew that the Mancunian had gained considerable experience and made valuable connections while playing for Grimsby, Blackburn, Derby, Reading, Brentford and Exeter. He knew the soccer world and was familiar with some of the rising talent and certainly the gnarled old pros in the lower divisions of the Football League. Moreover, standing at 6' 1" and weighing 14 st 8 lbs, he cut an impressive figure. By some distance he was bigger and taller than all the directors, as well as the players he recruited. A bear of a man, he oozed authority in the board room and dressing room. On the field he was dominant in the air, thriving on physical contact and, despite his brawny frame, proving as nimble as a cat. Swiftly introduced to the realities and hardships of managerial life, Whittaker's stentorian voice was soon ringing around the Vetch Field. He was expected to work wonders: with a tiny budget of £250 he was instructed to assemble a squad of 20 players within eight weeks. Although there was a genuine desire among supporters to see a Swansea-born team, everything had happened too quickly for Whittaker to be able to rely on home-bred players and there was clearly no time to train up callow youths. Nor did he have funds to sign dazzling stars. The traffic of Welsh-born soccer players was always in an easterly direction and there was no likelihood that a club like Swansea could attract a virtuoso like Billy Meredith or an expensive, if eye-catching, nomad like Leigh Richmond Roose.

But Whittaker chose well. Working within his means, he

signed seasoned, efficient journeymen rather than flamboyant stars, bread-and-butter players with a great heart and who knew that the financial rewards – up to £3 per week – were greater than those available in mines and factories. Such players also looked forward to the challenge involved and to the public acclaim and moments of glory which an ambitious new club had to offer. Hard-bitten professionals provided the fulcrum of the squad: Jock Hamilton, formerly of Brentford and Leeds, and a splendidly self-confident centre half, was recruited to lead the side. Arthur Cleverley (Brentford) and Jack Nicholas (Derby) were known to be a fiercely competitive pair of full backs, powerful in the tackle and relentless harriers. John Duffy and Sam Jepp at half back were unafraid of physical commitment and would provide a powerful engine room in midfield. Up front, swift forwards like Jimmy Swarbrick (Chelsea) and especially Billy Ball (Stoke), a startlingly quick centre forward capable of scoring from fractional opportunities, were expected to make their mark. It is worth emphasizing that this was a squad of white males, with no black or foreign-born players, let alone *galácticos*. When Northampton played at the Vetch in December 1912 the home supporters were distinctly surprised to find that the visitors had included a player 'of dusky hue' in their ranks. The only two Welshmen in the initial squad were Willie Messer, a local-born winger with genuine pace and determination to match, and William Thomas Havard, who later became the only soccer- and rugby-playing Welsh bishop to win a cap (in 1919) at rugby for Wales.

What sort of tactics and training methods did the first Swansea team adopt? Up until around 1930 teams in Britain, and Swansea was no exception, deployed the traditional pyramid (2–3–5) formation, consisting of two full backs, three half backs and five forwards. Training, both before and during the season, was mostly confined to repetitive morning sessions of running, skipping and gymnastic exercises. Little use was made of the ball, but since a laced-up leather football in the Edwardian age was large and heavy there was no likelihood that the players would fail to recognize it on Saturdays. Whittaker's tactics were based on a rock-solid defence, and the whole team was encouraged to be intensely hard-working, supportive of each other and more than ready to dole out harsh treatment when provoked. In short, the first Swansea team relied on grit, hard sweat and teamwork, a combination which would come to their rescue on many occasions during the coming season. Two warm-up friendly games – at Morriston and Merthyr – put the squad in good heart for some pretty competitive clashes in the Second Division of the Southern League and in the Welsh League. Everything was set fair for the first official fixture on 7 September 1912.

Although there was none of the razzmatazz and theatricality of modern times, there was still a festive air about the long-awaited first match against Cardiff City at the Vetch Field. At a time when it was extremely rare for clubs to wear matching shirts and shorts, Swansea bucked the trend by appearing in pristine white shirts, white shorts and black stockings. No numbers were allowed on shirts until 1939 and identifying visiting opponents was sometimes difficult for fans, if not the players. Players wore heavy shin guards and knee-pads as protection against the cinder surface. High-ankled, long-laced and toe-capped leather boots might not have made Whittaker's men the nimblest side ever to wear the Swansea colours, but they could tackle like tigers and wallop the ball long distances. Yet it promised to be no easy baptism. Reporting for the *Western Mail*, 'Citizen' fully expected Cardiff, who were the more experienced side and the holders of the Welsh Cup, to 'annex the points'.

Spurred on perhaps by the extraordinary success of two male voice choirs from the town at the National Eisteddfod at Wrexham the previous day, and also by the fervour of the 8,000-strong crowd who had swarmed on to the makeshift banks and mounds around the ground, Swansea surprised the visitors with the quality and speed of their play. With a stiff breeze and the sun at their backs, they tore into Cardiff, who suffered the early misfortune of being reduced to ten men when Croft was injured and forced to leave the field. Well marshalled by 'Wonderful Whittaker' in goal, the Swansea defence held firm while the forwards outplayed Cardiff for great swathes of the game. The elusive Billy Ball cleverly netted a rebound to put Swansea in front on the half hour, only for Jack Burton to equalize for the depleted visitors. Swansea spurned three glorious chances in the second half and, but for the agility of Jack Kneeshaw in the Cardiff goal, the home side would have claimed both points. 'Huge Crowd Witness Some Sparkling Football' ran a banner headline after the game, and even unreconstructed rugby fans who had turned up out of curiosity were glad to have seen a game bereft of 'interminable... scrimmages and general scramblings'. Whatever the shortcomings of the pitch, it was lightning fast and suited strong runners. Flushed with his club's success, a local reporter hailed the 'mushroom-like' emergence of a team which was already affectionately being referred to as 'the Swans'. Pleasingly, too, there was no sign of the partisanship and tribal rivalry which would later disfigure these local derbies.

Thereafter, inspired by the player-manager, the Swans went from strength to strength in their first season. The writer Nabokov once maintained that a goalkeeper who possessed 'an aura of singular glamour' was the key to success on any soccer field. Whittaker certainly had that aura about him and over the course of the season he made truly miraculous saves as well as rallying his troops in adversity. Cleverley and Nicholas were 'shining lights' in defence, the electrifying runs of Swarbrick and Messer caught the eye, and the impish opportunism of Ball made him a firm favourite with the home supporters. Against all the odds, Swansea came within a whisker of winning promotion to the First Division of the Southern League and deservedly won the Welsh League title and the Welsh Cup. The side's defensive solidity and its vigorous, competitive style were well suited to some of the wretched playing surfaces in south Wales. Time and again, 'Ajax' praised the 'rear division' for its valiant efforts during hard-fought cup matches and, in his usual provocative way, he claimed that such contests were infinitely superior to rugby even at its best. No better example could be cited than the 'Glorious Triumph' of the Swans in the Welsh Cup semi-final played at Ninian Park on 15 February 1913.

In a game of intense, prolonged excitement Cardiff were two goals ahead at the interval, only for Swansea, stung by harsh words from Whittaker, to stage an astonishing comeback. Although Cardiff were unfortunate to lose two players through injury, the Swansea players were so brilliant on the ball and so fleet of foot that the hosts were made to look slow and clumsy, so much so that they resorted to a crude and fruitless kick-and-rush style. Four goals in the second half, two of them by the effervescent Ball, sealed a memorable victory for the visitors. Pontypridd were the opponents in the final. A turgid draw at Cardiff led to a replay played on a wretched mud-heap at Tonypandy on 24 April, a game which proved to be more a test of stamina than of footballing skill. Nonetheless, a crowd of nearly 10,000 braved torrential rain to watch a dogged Swansea side, ankle-deep in sticky mud, gain the upper hand and victory by a single goal. By any standards, it had been an extraordinary season and Walter Whittaker had every reason to be proud of his achievement.

The player-manager would have been the first to acknowledge his debt to the supporters, who had shown the kind of passion and pride which in turn inspired the players. Although some support came from the leafy middle-class suburbs which snaked outwards towards Gower, the overwhelming bulk of the spectators were from working-class residential districts close to the Vetch and from high-density housing estates to the south and east of the town. The catchment area also included the Welsh-speaking industrial working-force and *gwerin* (peasantry) of the Swansea Valley, many of whom, as the Glais-born scholar T. J. Morgan put it, flocked to soccer matches in order to forget 'their bread-and-scrape lives' and immerse themselves in a world of exciting and uplifting deeds. Cloth-capped male adults for the most part, they readily parted with a hard-earned sixpence, and perhaps a penny for a programme, to stand on earthen mounds or banked terraces to cheer on their team. Crowds, of course, are never silent or passive, and the Swansea fans were well known for being vociferous, boisterous and partisan. Soccer offered them an escape from the drudgery and frustrations of work. It allowed them to let off steam by singing loudly, taunting rivals and barracking hapless referees. Mercifully, the age of the foul-mouthed chant and the obscene ditty had not yet dawned, and on the whole the atmosphere was good-natured, even when the home supporters bellowed their 'War Song' in a bid to intimidate visiting teams and supporters. As early as 1913 the fans had made this song, declaimed to the music hall tune 'Here Comes the Chocolate Major', their signature tune. Its chorus ran as follows:

> We are the Swans' supporters, we are the village boys,
> When our team is playing, hear us all hurrahing,
> Shouting, Coleman, now then, SHOOT for goal, man,
> Now, Bally, pass it to Swarby, Jimmy don't shoot too far;
> IT'S IN! (ha! ha!) we grin (ha! ha!)
> We make an awful din as we all shout HURRAH!

Fans bearing white rosettes and scarves, or waving white handkerchiefs, might not have been able to summon up an aria or two, but they certainly sang hymns with great passion. 'Calon Lân' and 'Cwm Rhondda' were favourite pieces and crowds in those days knew the words by heart. It is worth recalling that 28 per cent of the inhabitants of the County Borough of Swansea spoke Welsh in 1911 and that the proportions were much larger in the Swansea rural district (73 per cent) and Pontardawe rural district (83 per cent), where many soccer enthusiasts would never have thought of singing in any language other than Welsh. Of one thing we can be sure: teams from beyond Offa's Dyke that visited

Swansea were left in no doubt that they were playing in a different country.

Trouble involving spectators was common in Britain in the years before the Great War and it was not unusual for local rivalries to spill over spontaneously into violence, especially when crowds became incensed by constant barging, hacking and tripping or by other perceived injustices on the field. Remarkable as it may appear to us, however, there was a refreshing lack of animus against Cardiff City and its supporters at this time. For instance, during the exciting derby Welsh Cup match at Ninian Park in February 1913, the Cardiff fans actually cheered the four Swansea goals as loudly as those of their own team. If anything, bad feeling and thuggishness were more likely to occur when Swansea encountered some of the tougher, though technically inferior, valley teams. Following a fractious, hard-fought draw against Mond Nickel Works on 2 November 1912 several unpleasant altercations broke out between the players and visiting supporters. A week later, Swansea supporters were so incensed by the overly physical approach of the Pontypridd team that the Bristol-based referee felt obliged to caution the 22 players on the field. Whenever the Swans were at their most fluent and inventive, visiting teams often displayed a flagrant disregard for the laws of the game. Increasingly revelling in their partisanship, the Swansea supporters regularly turned up in their thousands to show their loyalty.

By the end of the 1912–13 season, gate receipts totalled £2,285, and the Supporters Club, which had organized its own sports paper called 'The World of Sport' as well as prize draws, smokers' evenings and trips to away fixtures, could boast 600 members, the largest of its kind in Wales. These, and many hundreds of other supporters, were present at the Royal Hotel, Swansea, on 24 April 1913 to greet the captain, Jock Hamilton, whose inspirational qualities had been the key to the team's success against Pontypridd in the Welsh Cup Final, and his colleagues. A booming brass band welcomed the open-air cavalcade and it was claimed, with pardonable exaggeration, that the King himself could not have received a more enthusiastic reception. In breaching the citadels of rugby in the town, the Swans had successfully mustered a passionate and determined army to lead the charge. Indeed, a correspondent who dubbed himself 'Pendragon' reckoned that the red-hot partisans at the Vetch Field were giving rugby notice to quit.

The achievements of the first season had far exceeded the expectations of the board of directors, the supporters and perhaps even the players themselves. The club had done wonderfully well and ambitious new targets were set for the second campaign. A newly grassed surface was greeted with joy by the players and a brand new grandstand with 1,100 seats offered dignitaries and the well-to-do shelter from the rain which seemed to fall in lashing torrents whenever a game was held at the Vetch. Although Walter Whittaker added a few fresh faces, he was generally content to rely on the group of honest players who had served him so well. His team might have lacked a dash of colour, but it was well-organized and resilient. Crowds continued to flock to the ground and among the highlights of the second season was the visit of Queens Park Rangers in the first round of the FA Cup on 9 January 1914. Even though many of the supporters were infuriated by the club's decision to double the price of admission to a shilling, over 18,000 attended the match. Disappointingly, the Swans inexplicably managed to snatch defeat out of the jaws of victory, and there was little to celebrate in the ensuing league games.

Whittaker's ultra-defensive tactics, not unlike those of Paulo Sousa nearly a hundred years later, meant that the increasingly frustrated Ball was often forced to toil alone in attack. Many disgruntled supporters criticized the directors for failing to sign bustling forwards and 'goal-getters'. True, the club eventually finished fourth in the Second Division of the Southern League, but this time it had no trophies to celebrate. It was all too foreseeable that a scapegoat would be found and, to general dismay, Walter Whittaker was dismissed at the end of the season. It transpired that some of the directors had been poking their noses into team affairs and refusing to act on his recommendations. When he voiced his objections, the club dispensed with his services. It was a sad moment for the supporters and sadder still for Whittaker himself to have to leave in such acrimonious circumstances a club he had moulded and cherished. He died, a broken man, at the age of 39, in June 1917.

New brooms were summoned to the Vetch and improvements were promised by the incoming chairman, Frank Newcombe, and by Whittaker's successor, John William Bartlett, formerly manager of Leicester Fosse. Jack Bartlett soon got into his stride and his blunt manner left the players in no doubt that he was a man who took decisions without fear or favour. He signed the Welsh international Tom Hewitt from South Liverpool FC and Fred Buck and Amos Lloyd, two quick and clever players, from West Bromwich Albion. There was every reason to believe that more expansive, attacking ploys would grace the Vetch under the new regime. Bartlett certainly enjoyed the confidence of his squad, but he suffered the misfortune of having to keep the ship afloat during the war years.

The declaration of war on Germany by Britain on 4 August 1914 ushered in a gloomy, unsettling period for everyone associated with sport. 'Business as Usual' was the government's mantra and the footballing authorities argued that soccer fixtures should continue because they were plainly good for morale. To their credit, clubs like Swansea 'did their bit' by encouraging players to hang up their boots temporarily and join the forces. Moreover, as news regularly filtered through of mounting casualties in the trenches, players preferred to fight for king and country than be labelled shirkers and cowards. Swayed eventually by overwhelming public opinion, on 3 July 1915 the Football League decided to suspend official soccer matches held under its aegis, while the Southern League committee simply left clubs to work out their own salvation.

For much of the war-torn years, therefore, soccer was played on an ad hoc basis, standards of play deteriorated and attendances fell. The financial implications for Swansea AFC were enormous.

Yet, paradoxically, it was during the war that Swansea experienced its finest hour in its formative years. On 9 January 1915 the team met a full-strength Blackburn Rovers in the first round proper of the FA Cup. Having won the Cup five times, Blackburn had a glorious history in the competition to add to their current status as League champions. Their talisman was Bob Crompton, the greatest of all their players, a seasoned international and one of the finest centre halves in the game. By contrast, Swansea had no one who enjoyed celebrity status, and the *Athletic News*, not unkindly, described the home team as a 'heterogeneous collection of players from all quarters'. The result was thought to be a foregone conclusion. But by reminding players at the Vetch of how Swansea supporters at the front were bravely confronting 'the heavy heel of the Germanic Jack-boot' and sending poignant letters wishing the team well in their forthcoming clash, local newspapers fortified their spirits. Bartlett opted for a blanket defence, urging his men to counter-attack whenever possible but to attend mainly to their defensive duties in order to keep the score fairly respectable. However rousing his team talk may have been, Swansea were by a considerable distance the underdogs. But soccer, as they say, is a funny old game, and much of its charm lies in its unpredictability, especially in games associated with the FA Cup.

On the day, a swaying, singing crowd of around 16,000 squeezed into the Vetch Field to cheer on their favourites. Unnerved by the Welsh *hwyl* and some tenacious tackling, the Lancastrians were initially thrown off their stride, But gradually they took control of the game, winning constant possession and forcing Swansea back with successive waves of attack. Brave hearts were required during the hurly-burly of the contest and none of the Swansea men shirked physical challenges.

Swansea's centre half, Joe Bulcock, an inspired recruit from Crystal Palace, stood out like a Colossus in the home defence and there were full-throated roars from the crowd whenever he and his colleagues thwarted their more skilful opponents. Then, out of the blue, came one of those moments which would live long in the memory of the home team and their supporters. Amos Lloyd set off down the right wing, shook off would-be tacklers, and crossed the ball into the penalty box where Ben Beynon, the only amateur in the Swansea side and one who had previously starred on the rugby field for the 'All Whites', deftly controlled it before sending a thunderous shot into the net. Ecstatic roars from the crowd were followed by hymns sung with even greater fervour than before. During the second half Blackburn redoubled their efforts to penetrate a packed and determined defence, but Bulcock and his men stood firm. Then, during almost unbearable tension, Blackburn were awarded a penalty. Up stepped Billy Bradshaw, an unerring penalty-taker who had scored from the penalty spot on 36 consecutive occasions. This time, however, his nerve failed him and he blazed his shot wide of the post. Thereafter the Swans held out superbly against incessant attacks. When the final whistle sounded the jubilant crowd swarmed on to the pitch and astonished football correspondents were uncharacteristically lost for words. ''Twas a glorious victory' was the best the *South Wales Daily Post* could muster and, although in the next round a home defeat at the second attempt against Newcastle United on a pitch described as 'a near relative to the cabbage patch' ended hopes of a lucrative run in the Cup, the day on which mighty Blackburn Rovers were humbled became part and parcel of Vetch Field folklore.

Although there was a huge sense of relief at the Vetch when peace returned in 1918, celebrations were muted. The chairman, Frank Newcombe, had died in the meantime and his successor, Ben Watts-Jones, a Swansea draper, strove manfully to guide the club through a period of deepening gloom and sadness, and to keep it solvent. He and his fellow directors were left to reflect on the events which had tragically cut short the lives of five Swansea players, among them Arthur Cleverley, the most reliable of full backs, Joe Bulcock, always a tower of strength at centre half, and Ted Mitchell, a gifted inside forward. Others who had experienced the horrors of trench warfare, and lived to tell the tale, would never be the same players again.

Following the travails of war, soccer experienced a boom period from 1919 onwards. Former soldiers who had escaped unscathed picked up the threads of their playing careers and there were new and exciting footballers to watch and admire in south Wales. There was an air of optimism at the Vetch when Joe Bradshaw, a dynamic young manager, took up the reins. Having worn the colours of Woolwich Arsenal, Fulham and Chelsea, and earned the unusual distinction of having played in every single position during his career, Bradshaw had made his managerial reputation by taking lowly Southend United to the First Division of the Southern League in his first season. By the time of his appointment on 5 May 1919, it had already been decided to expand the First Division to 22 clubs, of which Swansea would be one. The old stalwart Jack Nicholas was appointed player-coach and, to the delight of the supporters, a concerted effort was made to stiffen the side with Welsh-born and, even better, Swansea-born players.

The most ubiquitous of these was Ben Beynon, the amateur hero of the hour against Blackburn. Beynon had returned to St Helen's after the war to resume his rugby career, but he never settled. To the consternation of rugby followers, he then committed an act of unforgivable treachery by signing professional forms for the Swans. Worse still, he later struck a Faustian bargain with the devil by defecting to the murky world of rugby league. Fortunately, other recruits proved to be more dependable investments. Swansea-born Billy Hole, a startlingly fast outside right, became the first of a dynasty of gifted footballing Holes. He established a fruitful partnership with Ivor Jones (father of Bryn and Cliff), who was signed from Caerffili for £50 and became the first Swansea Town player to win a Welsh cap. These and others swiftly realized that Joe Bradshaw was an astute man-manager as well as being an excellent tactician. The welfare of his players mattered a good deal to him. In the most unfortunate circumstances imaginable, his skills were put to the test in December 1919 when David 'Tich' Evans, a clever left winger whom Tottenham Hotspur had been watching closely, cut his own throat under the main stand at the Vetch while suffering from depression following the tragic death of his young wife a fortnight earlier. There was a good deal of morale-building to be done afterwards and Bradshaw proved equal to the task. Ninth place in the First Division did not truly reflect the quality of Swansea's play in the higher division, but the prospects were promising.

A new and compelling chapter opened in May 1920 when the Football League decided to set up a Third Division, to which Swansea, Merthyr and Newport were admitted as founder members. That Swansea Town AFC was deemed worthy of moving up a grade bore witness to the exceptional progress that had been made over the previous eight years. Prophets of doom in rugby circles had been proved wrong and doubting Thomases on the terraces and in the press had been silenced. The playing staff was in good health under an extremely accomplished manager, the support had expanded hugely, and the general mood was bullishly optimistic. The club had survived its first test. Now the 'roaring twenties', to be followed by the 'locust years', beckoned.

2

Highs and Lows

SHORTLY BEFORE 1P.M. on Saturday, 8 January 1927, Thomas P. Ratcliffe, conductor of the Band of the Welsh Guards, stood on the touchline of the Vetch Field. Sniffing the wind, he buttoned up his tunic, hitched up his carefully pressed white flannels and, with all the dignity he could muster, marched across the rain-sodden turf to the centre-spot where he mounted a wooden platform and raised his baton. Enthusiastically welcomed by the milling crowd of supporters, the band struck up and, as one eloquent correspondent put it, 'the harmony and melody of community singing rose up on the fog-laden air'. The occasion was the third round of the FA Cup and the visitors were Bury, a powerful First Division side. Inspired by the community singing, however, Swansea made the illustrious 'Shakers' look like third-raters and swept them aside by hustling them off their game. A hat-trick by Len Thompson and a goal by Harry Deacon ensured a 4–1 victory which was duly acclaimed in the closing moments as the home supporters sang 'Cwm Rhondda' with spine-tingling fervour. 'How Bury were buried' was an apt banner headline for reporters. On the surface, all seemed to be well at the Vetch.

But for those with eyes to see, by 1927 the club had reached a critical watershed in its short history. Its successful manager, Joe Bradshaw, had resigned for personal reasons on 19 August 1926 and the board of directors, few of whom had ever kicked a ball in a straight line let alone in anger, had deluded themselves into believing that they were fully capable of selecting the team and determining tactics. Their head-in-the-sand refusal to make an immediate appointment was a serious error of judgement. Already there were signs of decay on the field. Several veteran players had seen much better days, defensive frailties were being exposed, and the fluid, uninhibited style, as well as the concentrated effort, of the Bradshaw era were fading swiftly. The woeful Bury side had been easy victims for Swansea and much tougher challenges lay ahead. Crowds were dwindling, especially for league matches, and the club had expected many more than the 20,000 who cheered them to the Cup victory against Bury. It was a sign of the times, too, that song-sheets for that occasion, sponsored by the *Daily Express*, had been distributed beforehand to ensure that Welsh hymns were sung with the kind of gusto that had previously been taken for granted. Lean years lay ahead and supporters understandably gazed back wistfully to the so-called 'golden age' (1919–26) under Joe Bradshaw.

From the moment Swansea Town was admitted into the Third Division of the Football League in 1920, Bradshaw had set himself the task of building an attractive, stylish team. Blessed with excellent first-hand knowledge of the game at a high level and acute analytical intelligence, he was well placed to assemble a team noted for its brains, skill and speed. From the outset, as befits an idealist, he placed a high premium on fine, delicate football. He had such a soft spot for the Corinthian toff William (Billy) Young Brown, a cultured, versatile amateur who was allowed to train at Chelsea, that he made him club captain. But the hub of the side was Ivor Jones ('Wee Ivor'), the tiny Merthyr-born maestro whose instinct for space, quicksilver feints, step-overs and sharp-shooting made him a firm favourite with the supporters. Every fan loves a player who can fire the imagination and whenever Ivor Jones was at his slick best there was simply no way of containing him. He was the first of a Merthyr dynasty of footballers and also the first of two unforgettable Ivors. Although he was often prone to over-elaborate, his mesmeric control and party tricks drew gasps of admiration and spontaneous applause even from visiting supporters. Another consummate master of his craft was Billy Hole, a local boy whose glorious body swerves and astonishing speed took him past flat-footed full backs and earned him nine Welsh caps. Crowds flocked to the Vetch Field during the initial post-war boom to watch these scintillating players and there was every reason to believe that Bradshaw's patient team-building would bring success. Finishing fifth in the first season in Division Three was a fine achievement in the 1920–1 season and over the next three seasons Swansea inched remorselessly towards the target of promotion.

That target might have been reached even sooner had not an alarming economic downturn occurred in 1921. Gates plummeted in the second season as thousands of working people in the valleys were made idle. In order to stave off possible bankruptcy, clubs in south Wales had little option but to transfer some of their best players or grant them free transfers in lieu of wages. To popular dismay, the board of directors decided to make the local idol, Ivor Jones, available for transfer. By April 1922 West Bromwich Albion had snapped him up for £2,500, a record fee. Infuriated supporters registered their disapproval by voting with their feet. At the following home game against Bristol Rovers, only 3,000 turned up to watch Swansea confound the visitors and their stay-away fans by scoring eight goals.

In a way, it could be argued that Ivor Jones's individual brilliance, tinged as it was with unhurried elegance, was a liability to the team. Over-elaboration and tip-tapping at the edge of the penalty box meant that only 39 goals were scored during the 1921–2 season and it may well be that Bradshaw had realized that Jones the individualist, who had so often played to the gallery, was hampering the progress of the team as a cohesive unit. But losing a star can be like a bereavement to loyal fans and the directors were pilloried for betraying the club. When the team finished the season in tenth position, directorial heads rolled. Jack Thorpe returned to take up the reins as chairman of a streamlined board of seven and promptly silenced the rising displeasure of the supporters by making funds available to Bradshaw to buy new players. Thorpe had complete faith in Bradshaw's gift for talent-spotting and his tactical ingenuity, and the manager relished the freedom to promote his long-term plans. Some diehards, however, continued to believe that the financial climate, not to mention the attitude of some bone-headed directors, were hardly conducive to hopes of promotion, while others still pined after Ivor Jones.

Determined to prove them wrong, Bradshaw entered the transfer market with a vengeance and also renewed the contracts of those whom he had identified as having a winning mentality. His goalkeeper was Jock Denoon, a taciturn Scot signed from Norwich City for £75. A former policeman, Denoon was not easily intimidated as he patrolled the penalty box. An agile beanpole of a man, he had startling reflexes and a strong competitive instinct. Even his own defenders lived in fear of his legendary tongue-lashings and by making many memorable saves during his 173 league appearances up to 1927 he became a firm favourite with the home supporters. Bradshaw's full backs were dour and uncompromising. Over seven seasons, Sketty-born Ernie Morley, a ferocious tackler, made 123 league appearances and won four Welsh caps. His partner was the legendary Wilfie Milne, a sturdy Tynesider who wore the Swansea colours a record 587 times between 1920 and 1937. Milne was as tough as old boots and his sliding tackle was the stuff of legend. The antithesis of the prima donna, he never thought of himself as being bigger than the club, and on one memorable occasion he was even drafted in at the eleventh hour to play in goal at Leicester. Jimmy Collins of Dundee proved to be a glutton for work at the heart of the defence and brought a certain steeliness which had been absent earlier. From Birmingham came Joe Roulson, a classy half back, and Harry Deacon, an accomplished goal-scoring inside forward whose gifts included playing second violin in the Swansea Philharmonic Orchestra. The diminutive Willie Davies, signed for 10s 6d from Rhymney (and later sold to Cardiff for £3,000) and Joe Spottiswood, signed for £500 from Chelsea, were swift and penetrating wingers, while Jack Smith from Queens Park Rangers and Len Thompson from Birmingham were prolific goal-scorers.

Painfully aware that a substantial bank loan had made this spending spree possible, Joe Bradshaw was determined to inspire the creative endeavour which would bring promotion. Local reporters had every faith in him: 'Mr Bradshaw knows his football from A to Z', wrote 'Cygnet' in the *Sporting News*, 'he has played in first-class football himself, and his sporting record demands respect.' Everything seemed to be falling into place in the bid for honours. A run of sparkling victories in the opening months of the 1922–3 campaign augured well. Swansea's home form was outstanding and the general consensus was that the team was playing as attractively as any side in the division. Supporters were electrified by the pace, accurate passing and clinical finishing of Bradshaw's team. Seventy-eight goals were scored over the season, more than any other club managed in the entire Football League. Only once – a severe 1–6 drubbing at Luton in January – did the team crumble under pressure, and but for an unfortunate spate of injuries Swansea might well have pipped the eventual champions, Bristol City. Although disappointed to have finished third, Bradshaw had created a happy environment at the Vetch and his shrewd tactics and attractive style of play had won him the total loyalty of the players.

The sense of anticipation at the beginning of the 1923–4 season was palpable. Owen Evans, a native of Newtown and a thoroughly sensible man, became chairman, and by the New Year the prospects were rosy. Perched on top of the table, the team had not conceded a point at home and were playing with spirit and determination. But then, unexpectedly, lamentable away form dashed hopes of promotion. Performances fell away badly following a 0–2 defeat against Aston Villa in the second round of the FA Cup in early February. Local correspondents were convinced that disharmony in the boardroom was having adverse effects. 'Harmony blooms at the Vetch, only to die in a night', wrote 'Rolande' on St David's Day 1924. How far boardroom interference and the 'childish and silly whims' of some directors affected performances on the field is hard to judge, but only four away victories in 21 matches told its own story. Frailties in defence and a goal drought meant that Swansea ended the season in fourth place. Would promotion ever come? Was Joe Bradshaw, for all his football knowledge and capacity to inspire players and spectators, the right man for the job?

But Bradshaw himself never lacked confidence in his own judgement. He had already taken steps to remedy the weaknesses. With the full support of Owen Evans, he added to the squad two players whose inspirational qualities would make them Swansea legends in due course. In late February 1924 he signed Jack Fowler, a Cardiff-born striker, from Plymouth Argyle for a record fee of £1,280. After an anxious period of transition, Fowler settled down and soon formed a special bond with the fans. There were no airs and graces about this veteran of the Great War. He simply rolled up his sleeves and gave of his best in every game. Barrel-chested, aggressive, strong with both feet, he had such an unerring eye for goal that he was one of those footballers who generated crackles of excitement on the terraces. His streak of meanness in the penalty box and fierce will to succeed were traits which Bradshaw had quickly recognized. During his career at the Vetch, Fowler scored 102 goals, including nine hat-tricks, and his five goals against Charlton remains a club record to this day. But statistics only tell part of the story. Apart perhaps from Lee Trundle, no striker in a Swansea shirt has scored so many extraordinary goals from unexpected positions. Newspaper reporters avidly sharpened their pencils when Fowler was on form and he was one of the few Swansea stars who was pictured on Player's cigarette cards. Paraphrasing a popular song, the home supporters would sing regularly, 'Fow, Fow, Fow, Fow, Fowler, score a little goal for me'. Seldom did he fail them.

Having plucked a proven goal-scorer from rivals Plymouth, in the summer Bradshaw persuaded Sheffield Wednesday to part with a fiercely competitive defender whose name would become synonymous with Swansea Town. Even at 26, Joe Sykes was a young man who combined footballing intelligence with a strong personal sense of duty. Able to play as a centre half or at half back, he was a tenacious tackler and, despite his relative smallness at 5' 9", he was also a powerful header of the ball. Calm under pressure and admired for his shrewdly angled 'carpet' passes, Sykes was such a good reader of the game that he always seemed to be in the right place at the right time. He was also a scrupulously fair player. Bradshaw wisely made him captain, knowing that he would instil into the players a wonderful team spirit and a readiness never to concede defeat until the final whistle. His totemic value to the team was immense. He made 312 appearances for the Swans and up until his death in 1974 this stout-hearted and loyal servant continued to fill the role of the ideal club man and was duly regarded with undimmed affection. In Bradshaw's day, just as Fred Keenor personified the spirit of Cardiff City, so did Sykes embody the ideals of Swansea Town. And as the manager established a special rapport with him, promotion appeared to be that much nearer.

Bradshaw added a few more faces to refresh the ranks. Lachlan Macpherson, a precursor of the revered 'Slim Jim' Baxter, the Rangers and Scotland wing half, brought a high degree of artistry and showmanship to the midfield, while by December Dai Nicholas, a stocky and nippy Aberdare-born winger, had come from Stoke City to stiffen the flanks. But the key figures were Sykes and Fowler. Their presence transformed the team into an effective unit without sacrificing the skilful creativity which had become its crowd-pleasing hallmark. Not even a 1–3 defeat to Aston Villa on a liberally sanded Vetch

Field in the second round of the FA Cup could dampen spirits. There was a general feeling that Bradshaw had completed his team-building successfully and that the directors were pulling together effectively.

In the event, as the season drew to a close, everything hinged on the results against two Devonshire rivals. Before a crowd of 30,700 at Plymouth on 25 April 1925, a free kick by Deacon was enough to secure a hard-fought draw. Having completed their fixtures Plymouth now had 56 points. Swansea, with 55 points and an inferior goal difference, needed to win their last game against Exeter City at the Vetch to claim the title. A cacophonous, swaying crowd of 24,400 packed into the ground on 2 May and goals by Fowler and Thompson, who had sparkled throughout the game, brought the crowd to the peak of euphoria on an afternoon of immeasurable joy and relief. When the exotically named referee Captain A. J. Prince-Cox blew the final whistle, 'the cheering, gesticulating and joy-maddened mob raced after their fleeting heroes'. 'Rolande' rhapsodized about the 'truly romantic rise of Swansea Town' and an immensely proud Joe Bradshaw looked forward to seeing his Swans 'flapping their wings' against the likes of Chelsea, Derby, Fulham and Preston in Division Two. At long last, the ghost of failure at the very last hurdle had been exorcized. To add to the celebrations, the club also made off with the Welsh League and Southern League titles. The chore of polishing silverware was a new experience for the backroom staff, but they set about it wreathed in smiles.

While preparing for the challenges ahead, the club was obliged to consider the likely consequences of the revision of the offside law, which was due to come into operation in the 1925–6 season. Unlike rugby football, which appears to change its rules and regulations with every passing phase of the moon, soccer has always been reluctant to change a broadly successful formula without good reason. But by the mid-1920s the offside law, which had remained unchanged since 1866, was in dire need of revision. As it stood, the law declared that a player was onside if, when the ball was played, there were three opponents (usually a goalkeeper and two defenders) between him and the opposing goal. Increasingly, however, savvy managers had been exploiting the rule by adopting the one-back game. This entailed moving one of the two full backs up the field and catching opposing attackers offside. For a short period, even Swansea exploited the rule in a negative way, though Bradshaw abandoned this ploy when it clearly ran counter to his liking for free-flowing play. The Vetch faithful also deplored the tactic: 'Play the game, Swans' was the cry from the popular banks and there was considerable relief when the new law reduced the number of players required to play a forward onside from three to two. This change transformed patterns of play and required both managers and players to adopt new tactics and methods.

No one welcomed the revision of the law more wholeheartedly than Jack Fowler, for the immediate effect was to improve goal-scoring rates appreciably. Goals flowed 'like clichés at a party conference' as play was no longer compressed into a narrow zone on either side of the halfway line. Soon afterwards, however, this change was nullified when Herbert Chapman, the new manager of Arsenal, converted his attacking centre half into a defensive third-back or 'stopper'. Others followed suit. As a result, the traditional 2–3–5 pyramid was transformed into a 3–2–2–3 formation, a profile known as WM. This system was the first to establish a numerical balance between defenders (five) and attackers (five). Many wondered at the time whether the Swansea style would continue to be just as imaginative and influential as before in this brave new world.

The likely effects of the new offside law was only one of the dilemmas facing the Swansea management team over the summer of 1925. Space was another. Plans were laid to increase the capacity of the Vetch to 31,000 in the coming season and to a breathtaking maximum of 58,000 in the long run. Such pipedreams at a time of financial uncertainty caused considerable head-shaking and improvements were usually undertaken piecemeal. But there was no doubting the mood of optimism and anticipation. As Owen Evans, chairman of the board, put it: 'The name of Swansea Town in the football world stands high for bright, clever football of the highest class.' Although competing in a higher division would inevitably impose new playing demands and financial strains, there was every reason to suppose that Bradshaw and his men would prove equal to the challenge of facing more experienced and robust opponents. As many as 10,000 fans attended a pre-season trial match in August and saw enough to convince them that Swansea would figure in the race for promotion to the First Division.

Early skirmishes in the 1925–6 season brought a rude awakening. A 1–2 defeat to South Shields in the opening game raised fears that the team would be out of its depth. But the players more than held their own over the course of the season and were entitled to bask in the glory of trouncing Fulham 6–0 and the 'Invincibles' of Preston 4–1 at the Vetch, and of delighting 2,300 travelling supporters who watched them beat Chelsea 3–1 at Stamford Bridge. Indeed, but for insufficient strength in the reserves, some unfortunate late-season injuries and a dollop of ill-luck, Swansea would have finished higher than fifth at the end of the league campaign. But the highlight of the season was undoubtedly the team's excellent cup run, which took them to the brink of a final at Wembley. Exeter, Watford and Blackpool were brushed aside in the early rounds and, on 30 January 1926, Stoke were routed 6–3 at the Vetch. In spite of the deplorable playing conditions, Fowler scored four memorable goals. Three weeks later, 8,000 home supporters travelled to Millwall where a splendid volley by Fowler prepared the way for a titanic sixth-round battle against Arsenal at the Vetch.

By the time of the game on 6 March 1926, Arsenal were on the road to becoming a major power in the land. Their manager, Herbert Chapman, wielded complete control over affairs and ruled the club like a grenadier. A shrewd tactician, he had introduced an innovative formation based on defence in depth and smash-and-grab counter-attacking raids. His star-studded side, led by Charles Buchan, who was as robust on the field as he was opinionated off it, were firm favourites. No cup tie had aroused as much interest since the defeat of Blackburn Rovers eleven years earlier. Far from being overawed, the Swansea players were determined to make the most of their day in the sun and to add another scalp to their conquests. The absence of their manager – Bradshaw was struck down by flu – made them all the more eager to win. From the directors' point of view, the only regret was that the Vetch was not twice its size. Nineteen special trains, all of them crowded to the doors, steamed into Swansea and dozens of queues had formed outside the ground by 11a.m. Buskers kept them entertained and mobile chip shops did a roaring trade.

Swansea colours were everywhere and, when the turnstiles stopped clicking, over 25,000 had been packed so tightly into the ground that stretcher-bearers were kept busy as fans fainted and were passed over the heads of standing spectators to the touchline. The crowd doffed their caps for 'Hen Wlad fy Nhadau', the respective captains Sykes and Buchan shook hands, and a pulsating contest began in uncharacteristically bright sunshine. The home supporters, keenly aware that an Arsenal spokesman had confessed beforehand that their players were unused to playing in cockpits where the crowd was within 'kissing and hissing range of the players', were at their most raucous. The ground echoed to the strains of Welsh hymns and, with Sykes and Fowler at their imperious best, levels of excitement on the popular banks reached fever pitch. To their credit, the Swans kept their cool, moving the ball around the field as they probed for openings. Rugged and uncompromising at the back, Arsenal held them at bay. Every Swansea attack was greeted with a deafening roar. Several crunching tackles and confrontations stoked passions and, shortly before the interval, the crowd erupted when Len Thompson seized on a partial clearance, strode into the penalty area and scored with a powerful right-footed shot. In the second half Arsenal wilted as Swansea attacked with whirlwind speed and deftness of touch. The crescendo of noise grew even louder when Fowler, Swansea's extraordinary goal-machine, broke through, bore down on goal, and shot unerringly past Harper in the Arsenal goal. The visitors then made desperate efforts to regain the initiative and scored a fortuitous goal. From his own half Alex Mackie lofted the ball high into the Swansea goalmouth where Denoon, leaping high, took his eye off the ball and allowed it to fall, second bounce, into the net. To the great relief and pleasure of the fans, however, Swansea held firm thereafter until the final whistle.

Not many readers of the local press could make head or tail of 'Rolande' when he described Swansea Town as 'the cynosure of all eyes in the football world', but they knew that the pilgrimage to Wembley was reaching its climax as the amount of media attention increased by the day. Bolton Wanderers presented the final hurdle in the semi-final. A large Welsh contingent, many of them festooned with ribbons, daffodils and leeks, made themselves heard in the 40,000-strong crowd at White Hart Lane. To their dismay, however, the players froze on the big day. Within 25 minutes Swansea had conceded three goals against their canny rivals from the First Division and, despite a spirited response in the second half, it was clear that the team had been overawed by the occasion. Ironically, their chief tormentor was the Welsh international left winger Ted Vizard, whose speed and trickery bamboozled Sam Langford, the normally tough-tackling and dependable full back whom Swansea had bought from Merthyr. The long and exhausting cup run had evidently taken its toll. It also adversely affected Swansea's challenge for promotion and played some part in the defeat at the hands of lowly Ebbw Vale in the Welsh Cup final. Yet, it was some consolation to the board that the total receipts of £33,769 for the season included the healthy sum of around £9,000 derived from the successful campaign in the FA Cup. For their part, the players could be extremely proud of having gone so far in the cup and also finishing fifth in the league (scoring 77 goals in the process).

Then, in the summer, came a bombshell. Joe Bradshaw resigned, citing family reasons for his decision to return to London to manage Fulham. Not until the sudden departure of Roberto Martínez in 2009 would Swansea supporters be as mortified as they were in 1926. Bradshaw's decision was a grievous blow to the directors and the players. He had presided over Swansea's first golden age and it had been widely believed that he had his eyes on securing even more glittering prizes for the Swans. He had moulded a team schooled in modern tactics and had nurtured what was called 'the Swansea way'. His players were skilful, swift and inventive, as well as being loyal to him and the club. The team was so attractive that it regularly won plaudits from visiting sides and their supporters. Unlike hidebound managers of the day, Bradshaw believed that there was a good deal to learn by venturing abroad, and he had been happy to take his squad on close-season tours to Denmark and Sweden, where his players showed a fine collective spirit and a high degree of skill. Always open to new ideas, Bradshaw had also broken with tradition by arranging for the players to spend a week training and relaxing at the spa town of Llandrindod Wells prior to key cup games. Nor did he dismiss out of hand some of the mysterious nostrums – never seen in any pharmacy – deployed by his trainer and assistant Ernie Edwards in healing or soothing the aches and pains of injured players. Bradshaw worked hard at man-management, at improving the skills and tactical awareness of players, and instilling in them the importance of acting as ambassadors for the club. His rapport with the supporters was also excellent. Such an intelligent and thoughtful manager would not be easy to replace.

In the event, the directors decided to postpone the appointment of a new manager and to shoulder the responsibilities themselves. The team was left rudderless for a whole season and it says much for the leadership of Joe Sykes that the players rallied and fought so well that the team finished in twelfth position. Chairman Owen Evans insisted that the club was still 'a happy family', but eventually the board relented in the face of growing criticism. On 31 March 1927 James (Jimmy) Hunter Thomson, a Scot, was appointed manager. Formerly a player with Hearts, Portsmouth and Bury, Thomson had served as secretary-cum-manager of Bury since 1923 and had guided the club to promotion into Division One in his first season as well as overseeing the massive redevelopment of the ground at Gigg Lane. A flamboyant dresser and something of a charmer, he was very different from Bradshaw. His arrival coincided with a close-season tour of Spain and Portugal, during which Swansea soundly drubbed a relatively unknown team called Real Madrid.

During his four-year stint at the Vetch, however, Thomson failed to distinguish himself. Lacking leadership qualities, too weak to withstand interference from the board, and distrustful of the press, he sometimes cut a hapless figure. The players swiftly lost faith in his flawed strategies and morale plummeted. In fairness to him, it would have taken an extraordinary manager to have injected new life into a club saddled with several ageing players and with hardly any funds to strengthen the ranks. Players who had thrived under Bradshaw were now a grizzled, battle-scarred force, and the likes of Fowler thus moved on. More worryingly, prize assets were sold between 1928 and 1930. The remarkably prolific goal-scorer Len Thompson was transferred to Arsenal for £4,000, while Wilf Lewis, a Welsh international, went to Huddersfield for £6,500. Right back Ben Williams, a talented Penrhiwceiber boy who had been signed by Bradshaw for just £25, went to Everton for £7,500 and the stylish halfback Lachlan Macpherson followed him for £6,000. Doubtless these transfers made good business sense, but it was dispiriting for supporters to discover that Thomson's replacements were obscure Scottish and English journeymen. Forced to wheel and deal the best he could, he was unfortunate to find himself at the helm during a period of severe and growing financial pressures.

On the field, defensive slackness, poor positional play and a reluctance to shoot on sight became the norm under Thomson's watch. Gone was the fast, skilful, passing play that had been Swansea's trademark, and criticism of the manager's 'helter-skelter, feverish' kick-and-rush style filled newspaper columns. Both in 1929 and 1930 relegation was avoided only by the narrowest margin and a year later the club was spared only because Bury beat Reading on the final day of the season. Disgruntled supporters accused the directors of selling off the family silver, failing to sign quality players, and neglecting to invest in home-based talent. But the plain truth is that the financial situation was so parlous that it was impossible to make lavish signings or pour money into developing local youth players. Income from falling gates did not come anywhere near to covering outgoings. It was hard to stem the tide of failure and Thomson's haggard expression told its own story. But for the fighting spirit of the evergreen Sykes, the determination of Harry Hanford, a muscular, lantern-jawed stopper from Blaengwynfi, and the infectious, if erratic, zeal of the Llansamlet-born centre forward Ronnie Williams, Swansea would not have escaped relegation during these dark years. Even in the twilight of his career, Sykes's boyish enthusiasm shone through, while the bulldozing Williams was such a great trier that the Vetch crowds readily forgave his bouts of recklessness and glaring misses in front of goal.

The economic and sporting malaise was not confined to Swansea and its environs. In the eastern valleys of Glamorgan the demise of King Coal meant that thousands of families were forced to pull hard at their bootstraps. Unemployment rates spiralled and 'life on the dole' was so miserable that feeding and clothing children became a daily struggle. In an article published in the *Athletic News* in August 1929, Ben

Watts-Jones, a long-serving member of the Swansea board, wrote: 'One of the mysteries of today is how the people there [in the Rhondda] exist, let alone how football clubs carry on.' By the end of the 1920s, in fact, several clubs in south-east Wales had already fallen victim to the economic blight. Cwmparc AFC was wound up in 1926 and Mid-Rhondda followed suit in 1928. Aberdare Athletic dropped out of the Football League in 1927 and, having successfully applied for re-election to the League on two previous occasions, Merthyr Town found the door slammed in its face in 1930. These were alarming developments and the loss of so many exciting and lucrative derby games had grave implications for both Swansea and Cardiff. Indeed, there were very real fears that Swansea Town would fall into this 'slough of despondency' and end up bankrupt.

In the circumstances, during Thomson's stay there were only few moments of joy for supporters to cherish. Loud and prolonged cheers marked Jack Fowler's hundredth goal for the club on 10 November 1928, disbelieving fans blinked hard as West Bromwich Albion were thumped 6–1 the following February, and tribal passions were nourished when Cardiff were beaten twice before crowds in excess of 20,000 in February 1929 and August 1930. Even hardcore supporters derived pleasure from seeing the swarthy Evertonian Dixie Dean score twice at the Vetch and the diminutive Alex James, in his flapping shirt and baggy shorts, display his 'fluttering foot' tricks in Preston's colours. But such unusual prowess served only to expose the poverty of their own team's performances. With calls for his resignation ringing in his ears, James Thomson decided to leave in July 1932. This time, no tears were shed on the departure of the manager.

Spurning the lessons of the past, however, the board once more refused to make an immediate appointment. Ignoring the pleas of outraged supporters, the directors believed that the managerial salary could be put to better use and that even they could improve on the performance of the wretched Thomson. Daily training routines were left to Ernie Edwards, while the board supplied what might charitably be called the 'collective wisdom' required to select the team. By this stage, old favourites like Fowler, Hole and Deacon had departed and the club, operating on a shoestring, had cut the playing resources to the bare minimum. In the circumstances, it is a miracle that relegation was avoided. During the self-imposed manager-free interregnum, the team finished fifteenth, tenth and nineteenth, which was marginally better than Thomson's record. But there were some deeply dispiriting defeats, none more so than the 0–7 debacle against Tottenham Hotspur on 3 December 1932. On countless occasions it was left to the veterans – Milne, Sykes and Hanford – to rally the troops in adversity, though a trinity of Celts – Lochore-born Alex Ferguson in goal, Penrhiwceiber-born Syd Lawrence at full back, and Glaswegian Jim Miller at wing half – proved to be reliable recruits. But the threat of relegation was staved off mainly as a result of the prowess of goal-poaching centre forwards. The first was Cyril Pearce. Tall, well built and technically more adroit than his partner Ronnie Williams, Pearce joined the club from Newport County in 1931, scored freely with both feet and proved to be a marvellous header of the ball. No other Swansea player has emulated his finishing power over the course of a season. He scored a staggering total of 35 league goals in the 1931–2 season before leaving for Charlton Athletic. His successor Tudor Martin, a Caerau product, was as strong as a bull and he, too, won the hearts of the fans by scoring freely over four seasons.

If strikers can raise spirits, so too can winning trophies. It was some consolation, given the gloom caused by falling gates and indifferent league results, for the club to win the Welsh Cup in May 1932. On a stormy night Swansea drew 1–1 with Wrexham at the Racecourse. With the crowd expecting extra time to be played, the Swansea players trooped off the pitch, insisting that a replay should be held at the Vetch. Astonishingly, following hasty deliberation, it was agreed to hold the replay on the following evening. A leg-weary Swansea won an exceptionally good game 2–0, but the festivities were muted since the home side were due to meet Bury in a league game on the following day. More important, certainly from a financial point of view, was how far the Swans could sustain a successful campaign in the FA Cup. Only in the 1933–4 season, however, did supporters briefly espy the glittering ramparts of Wembley. But their hopes were dashed in the fifth round when Portsmouth of the First Division outclassed the home side before a record crowd of 29,700, a gate which produced welcome receipts of £2,300.

Against all expectations, by gaining four points from the last three league games of the 1933–4 season, Swansea once again avoided relegation. At this point – and this may or may not have been associated with the departure of Ben Watts-Jones (he became secretary of Cardiff City, who were faring even worse than the Swans) – the directors came to their senses and agreed that appointing a qualified manager was not such a bad idea after all. Another Scot was appointed in June and there were a few sniggers when it transpired that manager Neil Harris's former post was with Belfast Distillery. Formerly on Newcastle's books, this Glaswegian had won a solitary cap for Scotland and was reputed to be a strict disciplinarian. His appointment, at least in the eyes of the fans, was distinctly underwhelming and Harris himself had no illusions about the task ahead. Falling gate receipts meant that the club was in no position to sign top-class players, and the need to balance the books led to the departure of stalwarts like Ronnie Williams and Harry Hanford. The irreplaceable Joe Sykes retired in 1935 and for the next four seasons the club hovered uncomfortably in the danger zone at the foot of the table. One possible means of salvation employed by Harris was snapping up affordable Welsh-born players (some of whom were internationals) from the valleys. Right half Jack Warner was a native of Tonyrefail and left winger George Lowrie came from Tonypandy. Tommy Olsen, a skilful inside forward of Danish descent, arrived from Tredegar and the burly Ebbw Vale-born centre forward Joe

Brain, formerly with Arsenal and Spurs, also came to ply his fading wares. Local boys like centre half Reuben Simons and the rugged Emmanuel brothers, Len and Tom from Treboeth, were thrown in at the deep end without any reliable lifelines. In desperation Harris even signed and played his own son John. Changes were rung frequently, with no tangible effects, and there was a deep sense of shame when, during the silver jubilee season in 1937–8, a shambolic performance at Fulham resulted in a 1–8 defeat. The Vetch faithful were torn between jeers, tears and hysterical laughter.

Even the much-vaunted cup-fighting spirit deserted the club. A meek exit 0–4 at the hands of Wolves in the third round of the FA Cup in early January 1938 caused widespread consternation, not least because of the lack of leadership both on and off the pitch. In successive seasons at the end of the decade, Swansea also suffered the indignity of losing in the final of the Welsh Cup to two decidedly inferior sides – Shrewsbury and Wellington – based in Shropshire. As the club's standards declined, slipping irrevocably into the relegation zone became an obsessive fear. Newspaper headlines such as 'Life and Death Struggle' and 'Why a Relegation Fight Each Year?' multiplied as the prophets of doom sharpened their pens. At his wits' end, Harris sought to stiffen the backbone of the side by signing wheezing veterans like Bill Imrie from Newcastle and Tommy Bamford from Manchester United, neither of whom made an appreciable difference to the club's dwindling fortunes. Time and again, supporters were left staring over the precipice as seasons drew to a close. Every point was deemed to be as precious as gold sovereigns, though it is hard not to chuckle – given the subsequent track record of the two teams – on reading the local newspaper headline on 16 April 1938: 'Swans drop a point to Manchester United'. Clearly the fate of the Swans was a serious business. 'Rolande' feared that relegation would prove a 'death-blow' to professional soccer in south-west Wales and, as the final fixtures loomed in the spring of 1939, the players were urged by the supporters to fight with every nerve and sinew to avoid the dreaded drop. Fortunately, fate smiled on the Swans. There were gasps of relief all around the town when, on 1 May 1939, Syd Lawrence saved the club's bacon by converting two penalties in a 2–2 draw against Bradford at the Vetch. The point was enough to keep Swansea in Division Two. By June, Harris had moved on. Even though the crippling financial circumstances of the times and the limited resources at his disposal had made his task extremely daunting and perhaps impossible, the plain fact is that Harris, like his predecessor, had failed miserably.

Over two decades, therefore, those associated with Swansea Town had witnessed euphoric joy followed by deep despair. The glowing record of achievement under Joe Bradshaw had been replaced by anxious, debt-laden years, mediocre performances on the pitch, and the constant fear of tumbling into the third tier of the Football League. How did these contrasting fortunes affect the loyalty and support of the fans? In such difficult times, supporters must have asked themselves whether they really could spare a shilling to watch their favourites. Would the team's performance at the Vetch justify making that sacrifice? Was it worth risking pneumonia by venturing out on a rain-soaked afternoon? Would a major cup tie, with its built-in promise of a high-profile scalp, be worth attending, given that much of the action was obscured by the jostling, swaying crowd on the North Bank? In the 1920s the answers to these questions were generally affirmative. During the Bradshaw era, the support grew incrementally as the prospects of promotion fired the imagination of the public. By the mid-1920s league gates usually ranged from 12,000 to 15,000. Cup ties and derbies were always better attended, often to the point of overspill, and the arrival of glamorous visitors and star names added to the thrills. Over-ambitious plans were often brought forward to increase capacity at the Vetch, but common sense prevailed and the supporters had to be content with a new double-decker grandstand, seating over 2,000 spectators and a further 4,000 standing fans, designed by the local architect Sidney R. Crocker. When it was officially opened on 17 September 1927 the Swans raised their game and thrashed Wolves 6–0. But further building plans were set aside as the economic depression brought hardship and distress. Gate receipts slumped alarmingly during the so-called 'locust years' of the 1930s. The club not only fought an annual battle against the threat of relegation but also of bankruptcy. On average league attendances fell below 10,000, club membership plummeted, and by the end of the 1936–7 season Swansea had the dubious distinction of being the worst supported team in Division Two.

In many ways, it is surprising that a town like Swansea had allowed its premier soccer club to find itself in such sorry straits. The town was much better placed than the mining valleys of the east and, indeed, ports like Cardiff and Newport, to withstand the economic blizzard. The introduction of protective tariffs had helped the steel industry to prosper and the anthracite coal industry had entered a period of expansion. The setting up at Llandarcy of the first major crude oil refinery in the United Kingdom had been a major boost to employment, and from 1920 the town could boast its own university which, from its inception, specialized in metallurgy and engineering. The town confidently projected itself as the 'Industrialist's Haunt' and the 'Holiday Seeker's Haunt', and editorial columns in the *South Wales Evening Post* in the early 1930s regularly described Swansea as 'the bright spot in the South Wales Coalfield'. There was every reason to be 'of good heart and cheer'.

But the burgeoning middle classes in Swansea were neither interested in the privations of working people or the declining fortunes of 'Soccerites' at the Vetch. Insulated from the socio-economic ravages of the times, they lived in salubrious communities, bought goods in fine shops, strolled along the palm-lined promenade in their Sunday best, and dreamed of the day when Swansea would eclipse Cardiff as the premier city in Wales. For them, the opening of the Guildhall, built according to a design by Sir Percy Watkins, in 1934 was one in a series of municipal developments which would bring Swansea richly deserved fame and self-esteem. Well-to-do people in the Uplands area, who wafted through life on a cloud of privilege and affluence, were reckoned to be 'frightful snobs'. Among them was the Conservative grandee Michael Heseltine, who confessed that his upbringing in these leafy suburbs was marked by 'a very considerable degree of comfort'. Likewise, the literati of the town turned a determined blind eye to the hardships of working people. The Kardomah Café circle, headed by Dylan Thomas, Alfred Janes and Vernon Watkins, might have been a lively focus for writers, poets and artists, but it stood aloof from the underprivileged and the unemployed. The artist Mervyn Levy blithely admitted that the misery of the depression 'passed me by'. Nor did the travails of the town's soccer club arouse a flicker of interest among these worthies, and many years went by before university dons came to believe that watching and commenting on professional soccer at the Vetch was a sign of intellectual vitality as well as social engagement.

Although the social composition of crowds at the Vetch included lower middle-class people and a growing number of women – some of whom, sitting comfortably in the stand, were pelted with snowballs by the swinish multitude before the Swansea versus Stoke fixture in 1929 – the ethos of the game was heavily masculine and working class. Richard Holt has shown how soccer in these years became 'a potent source of masculine cohesion' and most people would have agreed with the sentiments of Trevor Ford, soon to become the most fiery, bone-bruising centre forward in the club's history: 'Football is not a woman's game; it's not a pastime for milksops or cissies. It's a man's game.' The overwhelming majority of loyal fans were drawn from working-class communities in the town and in the Swansea Valley. Committed supporters of the Labour movement, they figured among those who bore the brunt of the slump. Swansea might not have been an unemployment 'black spot' like Dowlais, Bryn-mawr and

Blaenau, but its dole queues were stretching. Unemployment levels shot up from 23 per cent in 1927 to 39 per cent in 1931. For these unfortunate people, every penny counted, and it was not surprising that many of them spent what little spare money they had on cheaper but more comfortable counter-attractions. From 1932 onwards the newly built Plaza and Rialto cinemas offered filmgoers a taste of Hollywood in luxurious surroundings for as little as sixpence, half the admission fee to a football match. How could the wet and windy Vetch Field compete with such irresistible dream palaces?

The club thus depended heavily on the loyal support of several thousands of cloth-capped stalwarts who continued to turn up at the turnstiles, come rain or shine, in these trying days. From its headquarters in the High Street, the Supporters Club worked tirelessly. Prize draws, lotteries, whist drives and social evenings were arranged in and around the town to raise funds to improve facilities at the Vetch or help to pay off the soccer club's mounting overdraft. Better use was made of the Vetch during the close season. On 23 June 1934 Urdd Gobaith Cymru (the Welsh League of Youth) came to town to hold its annual version of the Olympics. Ten thousand children took part and large crowds at the Vetch were treated to 'a thrilling spectacle of mass displays by virile, happy and healthy youth' in warm sunshine. A fortnight later a slogging match between bantamweights Len Beynon and Mog Mason was the highlight of a boxing tournament at which Tommy Farr, cruiserweight champion of Wales, made a guest appearance. But much more financial support was required as financial meltdown loomed. 'The Swans must be saved' was the headline in the editorial column of the *South Wales Evening Post* on 15 June 1935 as the newspaper, together with public-spirited tradesmen in the town, launched a 'Ten Thousand Shillings Fund' in order to give the 'bob-bank' supporters the opportunity to donate a shilling per head to the club. But although the initial response, sometimes from unexpected quarters, from well-wishers calling themselves 'Calon Lân', 'Y Deryn Pur' and 'A Referee's Widow' was encouraging, the sum of £1,171 13s collected by May 1936 fell far short of what was required. Had the well-to-do bourgeoisie also dipped into their pockets, the story might have been different.

Nonetheless, it was abundantly clear that the hard core of supporters were determined to keep the ship afloat. In spite of its quirky discomforts and reputation for low and heavy skies, the Vetch Field itself had become a rallying-point for the fans. Geographers refer to love of place as topophilia and what is striking about this period is the extent to which loyal supporters viewed the ground as a warm community base on match days. In Bradshaw's era, stylish and entertaining games had made life worth living, but even in the dark 1930s, when supporters turned up more in hope than expectation of success, there was a strong sense of fellowship. Some of those who were unable to afford the admission price perched precariously on surrounding rooftops to glimpse their heroes from afar. Elizabeth Simmons, a widow living in Madoc Street beside the ground, ingeniously arranged for a 30-foot makeshift stand, supported by scaffolding, to be built in her garden in order to allow penurious supporters an uninterrupted view of play at a discount price. Even those who stayed at home were surely aware of the club's plight on and off the field. Running commentaries and reports on the radio fanned interest among armchair supporters, and 'doing the pools' became a weekly ritual. Extensive coverage of matches and club meetings in the local press kept readers abreast of developments, and cartoons, some of which were splendidly wicked, highlighted the feats of players and poked fun at the management.

Yet, there was no finer sight than a heavily attended cup match at the Vetch when more than 25,000 noisy supporters packed like sardines into the stands and popular banks. Waving flags, ringing bells and beating drums, sporting leeks, rosettes and streamers, they spontaneously burst into song in order to inspire the home team. Solemn Welsh hymns were still sung sonorously, but they were increasingly accompanied by 'I'm forever blowing bubbles' and a variety of other music-hall songs. Once the game was under way, they would roar themselves hoarse. The noise on the North Bank was often deafening. 'All shouting, that's all it is. They shout for any little thing', noted one cynical rugby diehard who had strayed into the wrong game and discovered that working-class people had a voice. Cases of mob violence were wholly absent, but there were always bellyachers who made nuisances of themselves. In the early 1920s, one particularly peevish half-wit, whose piercing voice was 'reminiscent of a rusty saw', used to ridicule the players loudly and urge the directors to 'sack the lot'. But those who let off steam by using vulgar expletives were often brought before their betters. When an unemployed man from Limeslade was summonsed for using obscene language during a match between Swansea and Tottenham Hotspur in 1931, he defended himself vigorously in court: 'It's only natural for a man, especially one who has been to France, to slip out things. I am very excitable.'

Such excitability often occurred when referees made inexplicable decisions. Nothing disfigures a football match more than the conduct of an incompetent referee, and at a small ground like the Vetch, where the crowd, players and officials were in close proximity, referees were judged to be fair game. Thunderous roars would echo through the stadium as the home crowd remonstrated with, or threw orange peel at, palpably unfit or officious referees. Tempers frayed on the pitch, for instance, whenever W. E. Russell of Swindon was officiating. A bossy-boots by nature, Russell treated the players like errant schoolboys and, once the game was in motion, he made it a habit never to venture beyond the centre circle. Sometimes passions reached boiling point. Following the West Wales Senior Cup Final between Swansea and Llanelli in May 1923, hundreds of furious spectators scrambled on to the pitch to vilify the referee, who eventually left the ground 'under the cover of darkness disguised as a police officer'. Examples abound of referees stopping games and appealing to crowds to calm down. During the 6–3 rout of Stoke in January 1926, the pompous referee delayed play for three minutes to address a section of the crowd who were booing him incessantly. For the most part, however, supporters were good-natured and reasonably well-behaved. The veritable army of 8,000 supporters who travelled to Millwall to support their favourites in February 1926 impressed local Cockneys – both policemen and home fans – with their wonderful good humour and sportsmanship.

Nor was a sense of irony absent from the popular banks. Drenched by torrential rain during the second round cup tie against Aston Villa at the Vetch on 31 January 1925, thousands of local supporters sang 'It ain't gonna rain no more' as the club's mascot, probably the earliest version of Cyril the Swan, performed a series of 'graceful gyrations' in ever-deepening pools of water along the touchline. And when Portsmouth scored what turned out to be the winning goal in the cup clash in 1934, the crowd heartily sang 'O God, our help in ages past'. Even when the team was battling against relegation, the spirit of the loyal, swaying, noisy bands of supporters on the North Bank remained undimmed. The club had good reason, then and now, to be grateful to them. As the clouds of war gathered in 1939, the board, the players and the fans steeled themselves nervously for the next chapter in the club's history.

Sketches in the *Cambria Daily Leader* of some of the action in Swansea's first game, against Cardiff City, on 7 September 1912
(courtesy of the National Library of Wales)

Swansea Town AFC in its first season, 1912–13, complete with mascot and dog (in Billy Ball's arms). The captain Jock Hamilton is flanked by chairman J. W. Thorpe and manager Walter Whittaker
(courtesy of the *South Wales Evening Post*)

The Vetch Field: Swansea's theatre of dreams from 1912 to 2005
(courtesy of Swansea City AFC)

Peerless Ivor: the statue of Ivor Allchurch, located outside the Liberty Stadium, was unveiled in 2005
(courtesy of Swansea City AFC)

Swansea's first international players: Billy Hole and Ivor Jones
(courtesy of the *South Wales Evening Post*)

Goalscorer extraordinary: Jack Fowler
(courtesy of Gwyn Rees)

Joe Bradshaw, Swansea's most successful manager in the inter-war years
(courtesy of the National Library of Wales)

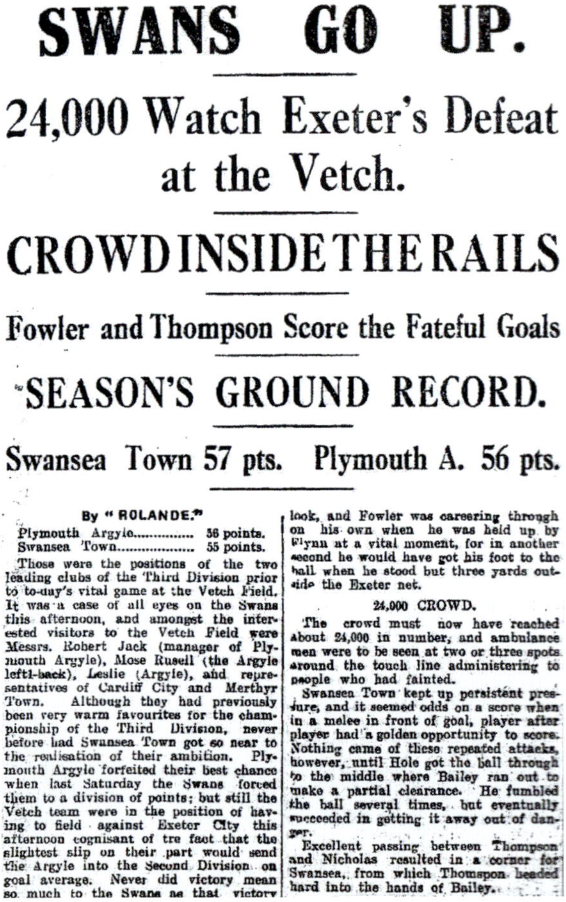

SWANS GO UP.

24,000 Watch Exeter's Defeat at the Vetch.

CROWD INSIDE THE RAILS

Fowler and Thompson Score the Fateful Goals

SEASON'S GROUND RECORD.

Swansea Town 57 pts. Plymouth A. 56 pts.

By "ROLANDE."

Plymouth Argyle.............. 56 points.
Swansea Town.................. 55 points.

Those were the positions of the two leading clubs of the Third Division prior to to-day's vital game at the Vetch Field. It was a case of all eyes on the Swans this afternoon, and amongst the interested visitors to the Vetch Field were Messrs. Robert Jack (manager of Plymouth Argyle), Mose Rusell (the Argyle leftl-back), Leslie (Argyle), and representatives of Cardiff City and Merthyr Town. Although they had previously been very warm favourites for the championship of the Third Division, never before had Swansea Town got so near to the realisation of their ambition. Plymouth Argyle forfeited their best chance when last Saturday the Swans forced them to a division of points; but still the Vetch team were in the position of having to field against Exeter City this afternoon cognisant of tre fact that the slightest slip on their part would send the Argyle into the Second Division on goal average. Never did victory mean so much to the Swans as that victory

look, and Fowler was careering through on his own when he was held up by Flynn at a vital moment, for in another second he would have got his foot to the ball when he stood but three yards outside the Exeter net.

24,000 CROWD.

The crowd must now have reached about 24,000 in number, and ambulance men were to be seen at two or three spots around the touch line administering to people who had fainted.

Swansea Town kept up persistent pressure, and it seemed odds on a score when in a melee in front of goal, player after player had a golden opportunity to score. Nothing came of these repeated attacks, however, until Hole got the ball through to the middle where Bailey ran out to make a partial clearance. He fumbled the ball several times, but eventually succeeded in getting it away out of danger.

Excellent passing between Thompson and Nicholas resulted in a corner for Swansea, from which Thomspon headed hard into the hands of Bailey.

'Rolande' reports on the vital promotion game against Exeter City, 2 May 1925
(courtesy of the *South Wales Evening Post*)

The legendary Joe Sykes, who wore the Swansea shirt 312 times and served the club loyally in a variety of roles until 1974
(courtesy of Gwyn Rees)

Part of the cloth-capped Jack Army in 1920
(courtesy of the *South Wales Evening Post*)

During the 1924–5 season the following squad helped Swansea to win the Third Division Championship, the Southern League and the Welsh League.

Back row: W. Wishart, Billy Whitehead, Wilf Lewis, Billy Hole, Lachlan McPherson, Ernie Edwards (trainer), Joe Collins, Bert Bellamy, Ernie Morley, George Hart (groundsman); third row: Joe Bradshaw (manager), Vic Rouse, Forbes, Hutchinson, Trench, E. R. Robson, Jock Denoon, Willie Davies, C. H. J. Handley, Abe Morris, S. B. Williams (secretary); second row: T. M. Martin (director), D. J. Bassett (director), Trevor Evans (director), Joe Sykes (captain), Owen Evans (chairman), Jack Fowler, T. M. White (director), B. W. Jones (director), J. B. Owen (director); front row: George Thomas, Sam Langford, Billy Corkingdale, Harry Deacon, Wilfie Milne, Jimmy Evans, Len Thompson, Brinley Humphries
(courtesy of the *South Wales Evening Post*)

Cyril Pearce in action against Bury, 7 May 1932. Pearce holds the club record (35 goals) for league goals scored in a single season
(courtesy of the *South Wales Evening Post*)

'Fiery' Trevor Ford, towering above supporters on the North Bank, in action against Southampton on 3 October 1946
(courtesy of the *South Wales Evening Post*)

Cliff Jones, captain of the Swansea Schoolboys team which won the English Schools Shield in May 1950
(courtesy of the *South Wales Evening Post*)

Champions of the Third Division South League in 1948–9

Back row: Sam McCrory, Edgar Newell, Terry Elwell, Danny Canning, Jack Parry, Stan Richards, Jim Feeney, Rory Keane; seated: Billy McCandless (manager), Billy Lucas, Roy Paul, Frankie Burns, Reg Weston (captain), Jack O'Driscoll, Frankie Scrine, Joe Payne, Frank Barson (trainer)
(courtesy of the *South Wales Evening Post*)

The demand for tickets when Swansea played Newcastle United in the fifth round of the FA Cup on 23 February 1952 overwhelmed the directors, the manager, the administrative staff and the postman
(courtesy of the *South Wales Evening Post*)

Two of the most popular brothers in Welsh football, Mel and John Charles, meet up as respective captains of Swansea Town and Leeds United in 1956
(courtesy of the *Yorkshire Post*)

The Golden Boy: Ivor Allchurch
(courtesy of the *South Wales Evening Post*)

Welsh caps for two sets of Swansea brothers: John and Mel Charles, Len and Ivor Allchurch
(courtesy of the Football Association of Wales)

Homegrown 'Swansea babes' dominated the line-up when Swansea demolished Ipswich Town 6–1 at the Vetch on 4 December 1954.
Back row: Arthur Willis, Tom Kiley, Johnny King, Ronnie Burgess, Dai Thomas, Mel Charles; seated: Len Allchurch, Harry Griffiths, Ivor Allchurch, Terry Medwin, Cliff Jones
(courtesy of the *South Wales Evening Post*)

Trevor Morris, manager of Swansea Town 1958–65
(courtesy of the Football Association of Wales)

Goalkeeper Noel Dwyer being congratulated by a jubilant Swansea fan following the famous 2–1 FA Cup victory at Anfield on 29 February 1964
(courtesy of the *South Wales Evening Post*)

The Swansea Town squad for the FA Cup semi-final tie against Preston North End on 12 March 1964.

Back row: Walter Robbins (trainer), Roy Evans, Peter Davies, Noel Dwyer, Brian Hughes, Herbie Williams, Brian Purcell, Trevor Morris (manager); seated: Brayley Reynolds, Barrie Jones, Keith Todd, Mike Johnson, Derek Draper, Eddie Thomas, Brian Evans, Jimmy McLaughlin

(courtesy of the *South Wales Evening Post*)

Jimmy McLaughlin scores Swansea's goal in the 1–2 defeat against Preston North End in the FA Cup semi-final on 12 March 1964

(courtesy of the *South Wales Evening Post*)

On 7 March 1968 parts of the grandstand and the dressing rooms at the Vetch were destroyed by fire
(courtesy of the *South Wales Evening Post*)

'The Faithful Few': some of the smallest 'gates' in the history of the club were recorded in the 1972–5 period
(courtesy of the *South Wales Evening Post*)

John Benjamin Toshack, manager of Swansea City 1978–83, 1983–4
(courtesy of the *South Wales Evening Post*)

Swansea's match programme for the visit of Tottenham Hotspur in the second round of the Football League Cup, 29 August 1978
(courtesy of Gwyn Rees)

Swansea's 'three musketeers' (Alan Curtis, Jeremy Charles and Robbie James) celebrate the 3–1 promotion victory at Preston North End on 2 May 1981
(courtesy of the *South Wales Evening Post*)

Swansea through and through: Alan Curtis
(courtesy of the *South Wales Evening Post*)

The Swansea City squad for the 1981–2 season

Back row: David Giles, Dave Rushbury, Dudley Lewis, Dave Stewart, Dai Davies, Ante Rajković, Leighton James; middle row: Phil Boersma (assistant manager), John Mahoney, Brian Attley, Neil Robinson, Chris Marustik, Džemal Hažiabdić, Tommy Craig, Doug Livermore (coach); seated: Jeremy Charles, Nigel Stevenson, Alan Curtis, John Toshack (manager), Wyndham Evans, Robbie James, Bob Latchford

(courtesy of the *South Wales Evening Post*)

Club dies as High Court judge winds it up

SWANS–IT'S THE END

Directors meet

SWANS directors Dave Savage, Peter Howard, Harry Hyde, Mel Nurse and Bobby Jones in crisis talks at Vetch Field this afternoon.

By Bob Bryant

SWANSEA CITY FOOTBALL Club's fight for survival finally ended today in the High Court in London when the club was wound up.

It is the first Football League club to fold in mid-season since Accrington Stanley 25 years ago. And this afternoon a liquidator was visiting the club to take over its affairs immediately.

Despite the news Swansea's directors were not prepared to go down without a fight. The board was in emergency session seeking advice on whether it would be possible to appeal against the judge's decision. Possibly overturn it.

At this morning's 35-minute hearing, both the Inland Revenue and the Vetch Field REsidents' Association opposed any further application by the club for an adjournment into the New Year.

The judge, Mr. Justice Harman, listened impassively as the court was told how the club had made repeated appearances but failed to meet any of its obligations or promises.

Looking on in the public gallery stone-faced was club vice-chairman Mr. Doug Sharpe, who had been working up until the last minute in an attempt to find financial aid.

Counsel for the club intimated there was a possibility of £500,000 being injected into the Vetch via America, but the promises fell on deaf ears.

Summing-up, Mr. Justic Harman lashed into the club, saying their case has been "all promises, promises, promises".

He accused them of illegally using money destined for the Inland Revenue and refused a passionate plea that the club was part of the life of Swansea — a piece of social history.

"Perhaps I was unwise to allow a further five days after hearing the case on Monday," said Mr. Harman.

"But money has been deducted from wages and should have been held by the club to be paid to the Inland Revenue, not to be disposed of or misappropriated on who knows what by the company.

"This company has very bad debts, but its promises of future funds are very vague and extreme. I see no grounds to seek any further indulgence of this court. This is a bad case and I also refuse the club leave to appeal."

This now means that from this morning the club has ceased trading and will not be allowed to fulfil any further League fixtures. No date has been set for a liquidator to be appointed.

A shocked Mr. Sharpe and club solicitor Mr. Robin Kirby

● To back page.

Walsall match off — League

THE High Court decision means that Swansea have effectively played their last competitive match.

Swansea were due to face Walsall at Vetch Field tomorrow in a Third Division fixture while the reserves were due at West Ham for a Football Combination game.

"We have clarified the legal position and have been told that Swansea City have ceased to trade. On that basis they are clearly unable to fulfill their fixture commitment tomorrow," confirmed Football League press officer Andy Williamson.

He added, "By not playing tomorrow Swansea would lose their membership of the League by default.

"The only way Swansea could play Walsall would be if a rescue act was concluded today. There is no way we want to nail down the coffin lid before every avenue has been explored, but it looks hopeless."

Although it is believed that Walsall have let it be known that tomorrow's game is off, director Mr. Harry Hyde said this afternoon: "We are investigating urgently every possibility of playing the game. As far as I am concerned the game is not finally off."

SWANSEA CITY FOOTBALL CLUB
CANON LEAGUE DIVISION III
SWANSEA CITY v WALSALL
SATURDAY, DECEMBER 21st

THE advertisement in last night's Post for the match

The spine-chilling headline in the *South Wales Evening Post* on 20 December 1985

(courtesy of the *South Wales Evening Post*)

The resurrection of the club: Doug Sharpe (seventh from the right) celebrates the success of the rescue package in London
(courtesy of the *South Wales Evening Post*)

Terry Yorath, with Doug Sharpe and Tommy Hutchison in the background, celebrates promotion to Division Three outside the Guildhall on 29 May 1988
(courtesy of the *South Wales Evening Post*)

Swansea's first visit to Wembley: winners of the Autoglass Trophy against Huddersfield Town on 24 April 1994
(courtesy of the *South Wales Evening Post*)

Swansea City's best-loved goalkeeper Roger Freestone clutches the Autoglass Trophy at Wembley
(courtesy of the *South Wales Evening Post*).

3

The Swansea Babes

SWANSEA AND ITS surrounding districts have been blessed with some enchanting Welsh-language place names, among them Cwmbwrla, Cwm-du, Fforest-fach, Gendros, Llansamlet and Plas-marl, the meaning of which has been known to tax the knowledge and ingenuity of scholars. But to soccer lovers, these place names, together with anglicized districts closer to the town centre like Townhill and the Sandfields, bear a very special resonance. For it was these communities that gave birth, broadly during the period between 1923 and 1937, to an extraordinary crop of young players who collectively stood comparison with any in Britain. Those who are interested in counterfactual history or, to put it in layman's terms, the 'What if?' parlour game, will often have wondered what the fortunes of the club might have been had not major stars like John Charles, Ray Daniel, Trevor Ford and Jack Kelsey either slipped through the net or been lured away by dastardly scouts from beyond Offa's Dyke; had Roy Paul not disgraced himself by embarking on an ill-starred adventure to Bogotá and then been hastily transferred to Manchester City; and had outstandingly gifted local players like Ivor Allchurch, Mel Charles, Cliff Jones and Terry Medwin resisted the temptation to join bigger clubs. Had this galaxy of talent remained intact, it is not inconceivable that Swansea by the mid- or late 1950s would have found itself in the upper echelons of Division One and with a reputation as high as that of the Busby Babes.

Who would not salivate at the prospect of supporting the

following team: Jack Kelsey, Harry Griffiths, Ray Daniel, Mel Nurse, Dai Thomas, Terry Medwin, Mel Charles, Ivor Allchurch, Cliff Jones, John Charles and Trevor Ford? Such a line-up would have graced any stadium in the world. All were Swansea-born (Dai Thomas lay within hailing distance at Abercregan), all were Welsh internationals, and six of them (John and Mel Charles, Ford, Jones, Kelsey and Nurse) published autobiographies, which must be a record for such a relatively small town. Never before or since in the history of the club has such a flowering of creative, home-grown talent occurred and, as Cliff Jones, perhaps the nicest and certainly the fastest footballer born in the town, argued, Swansea could boast 'a roll of honour of which any town could justly be proud'.

John Charles liked to claim that there was something about being born in Swansea which injected into the bloodstream a deep love of soccer. To his credit, Haydn Green, the newly-appointed manager of Swansea on the eve of the Second World War, not only realized that there was a wealth of footballing talent in working-class communities in and around the town but that a broad strategy of identifying, harnessing and encouraging that potential was required. Green was an intelligent and civilized man. Formerly manager of Lincoln City, Hull City and Guildford City, he was an experienced handler of young players and well able to sense the mood of the times. He immediately made it a priority to invest in, and persevere with, bright young local prospects. Convinced that Swansea could become a football nursery of great repute, he expressed his desire to 'give a fair deal to all local products and to develop Swansea's own players to the greatest extent possible'. Investing in youth was an admirably sound policy and the board of directors, astutely chaired by Abe Freedman from 1938 to 1952, was confident that time would justify the club's readiness to pin its faith on local talent. Creating a highly attractive, young footballing side would also give the town a distinctive identity.

This was an especially propitious time for bringing on

working-class youngsters. Working-class housing estates had sprung up in the old industrial districts in the north of the borough and also in the Sandfields area close to the Vetch and in the sprawling Townhill community high above the town centre. In such communities, poor families enjoyed few social advantages and in wartime their lot was made all the harder by the shortage of food, clothes, beer, tobacco and fuel. During such periods of adversity, working-class families supported one another and made great sacrifices on behalf of their children. They prided themselves on their roots and unhesitatingly supported the Labour movement. John and Mel Charles were the sons of a steel erector, Ivor and Len Allchurch's father was a furnaceman, Trevor Ford was the son of a van driver who later became under-manager of a cinema, while Terry Medwin was born in Swansea prison where his father was a warder. Although none of this generation of players was a fluent Welsh-speaker, vestiges of the old language and its associations remained within families. Even during his long sojourn in Leeds, Turin and Rome, John Charles never lost his Welsh lilt and, without exception, this crop of youngsters, even those who did eventually leave, remained Swansea boys through and through.

Since a career in soccer offered a range of socio-economic opportunities, fathers encouraged their football-mad sons to dedicate themselves to improving their skills on streets, parks and derelict sites. Trevor Ford's father was a hard taskmaster who spent hours in Paradise Park teaching him to pass, dribble and shoot with both feet. John Charles honed his skills by playing with a rolled-up ball of rags or a pig's bladder, while his brother Mel was described at the tender age of six as 'a terror with a tennis ball at his feet'. Under the watchful eye of his father Ivor, Cliff Jones mastered basic skills by practising with a tennis ball on a sandy patch on the site of a bombed house in Beach Street. During informal, but heavily competitive, 20-a-side games in local parks, these youngsters swiftly realized that every first touch was vital and that every shot on goal needed to be accurate. So engrossed were they in kicking footballs, tin cans and tennis balls in parks and side-streets that parents would often have to search for them as dusk fell. For both parents and sons, the greatest ambition was to wear the all-white Swansea strip and, with a bit of luck, a Wales shirt in due course.

One critically important conveyer belt of future stars was the Swansea Schools Football Association. On 13 May 1939, before a raucous crowd of 20,000 at the Vetch, Swansea Schoolboys captured the English Trophy for the first time by beating Chesterfield 2–1. The victory was widely seen as a harbinger of future glories and so it proved. Between 1945 and 1955 the Swansea Schoolboys won the Welsh Trophy on seven occasions and the English Trophy three times. The key figure was Dai Beynon, a sports teacher who, as trainer and coach of successive Swansea Schoolboys teams, made a colossal contribution to youth football in the region. Like the Jesuits, Beynon believed in inculcating the young early. To him, soccer was a character-forming sport and he strongly believed that his role was as much about cultivating values and attitudes off the field as fostering skills on it. He treated youngsters as mature and responsible young men and was also rather good at persuading untrusting parents that their son could become the greatest player in the world. It was at least partly thanks to him that the Swansea Town nursery became so fecund. Beynon had many superstitions, including wearing his 'lucky suit' at big games, but he was not averse to weeding out those who lacked discipline and loyalty. The most dedicated local youngsters worshipped him and readily acknowledged their debt to him for instilling in them an unquenchable fighting spirit. With the assistance of his colleagues, Dai Beynon made the Swansea Schools Football Association a natural recruiting ground for Swansea Town AFC.

Ironically, the declaration of war against Germany on 3 September 1939 brought new opportunities for budding soccer players. The Football League suspended the 1939–40 season and replaced it with a regional competition. Military call-ups and postings tended to play havoc with team selections and, in order to fill the gaps, promising colts were taken on the ground staff and given the chance to shine in friendlies and junior football. For two seasons, however, the Vetch was converted into an anti-aircraft fortress and home games were played on the rugby pitch at St Helen's. Scratch teams, playing competitive fixtures on an ad hoc basis and sometimes including distinguished 'guest stars', at least kept the game alive and helped fledgling players to develop. Miraculously, the Vetch survived the war unscathed, which suggests that Luftwaffe pilots were either soccer lovers or poor marksmen. The former was probably the case because the rest of the town was attacked from the air on as many as 45 occasions.

The most devastating of these occurred on 19–21 February 1941 when the town was targeted by Kampgruppe 100, an elite unit of German aircraft dispatched by the Luftwaffe High Command to drop high explosive and incendiary bombs which killed 230 people and reduced central Swansea, including many of its fine Victorian and Edwardian buildings, to rubble. The so-called 'Three Nights Blitz' etched itself on the public mind. From as far away as Pembrokeshire, the Welsh poet and pacifist Waldo Williams could see 'Swansea in flames' ('Abertawe'n fflam'), while Dylan Thomas referred to the 'flat white wastes where all the shops had been'. Families were deeply traumatized by the wail of sirens, the parachute flares, and the human and material destruction wrought by the aerial bombardment. Several future soccer stars were swiftly evacuated. For a short period, John and Mel Charles were shipped out to the rural fastnesses of Nantgaredig in Carmarthenshire, where their grounding in soccer was strong enough for them to resist the attractions of the oval ball. Cliff Jones was evacuated to Merthyr where his family roots lay, and there were many young players like Trevor Ford and Roy

Paul who suffered the misfortune of having their careers in the Football League interrupted by the need to dispose of Adolf Hitler and his armed forces as swiftly as possible.

There was a curious air of unreality about wartime football and it proved extremely hard to keep the club's flag flying and its administrative procedures in good working order, especially after the retirement in 1947 of S. B. Williams, its long-serving and meticulous secretary. But the scouting system and familiarity with signing-on and transfer regulations thereafter were clearly far from foolproof even before his departure. How else could several gifted youngsters have slipped through the net? As early as 1936 Jack Roberts, one of five Welsh internationals raised at Alice Street, Cwmbwrla, joined Bolton before his 18th birthday, while Glyn Davies, who hailed from the same street and was a former captain of Swansea Schoolboys, left for Derby County at the age of 17. Even bigger fish somehow got away, largely because they had only signed amateur forms for Swansea. Among them was Ray Daniel, a self-confident, ball-playing centre half from Plas-marl who developed the extraordinary skill of dropping a half-crown coin on his left foot, flicking it to his right, then his thigh and shoulder before dropping it into his top pocket. Daniel signed for Arsenal in 1946 and went on to win 21 Welsh caps. By the time of his return to Swansea in 1958, his best days were behind him. Another even greater player who never pulled on a Swansea jersey was Jack Kelsey, arguably Wales's finest goalkeeper of all time. Born in Llansamlet, on the strength of his agile performances in goal for Winch Wen he was whisked away to Highbury at the age of 20 before Swansea had properly gauged his potential.

But the most grievous loss – the result of a catastrophic administrative oversight – was the abrupt departure of Cwmbwrla-born John Charles, the most prodigiously gifted of all the Swansea youngsters in the 1940s. At the invitation of Haydn Green, Charles had left Manselton Senior School at the age of 14 to join the ground staff at the Vetch. Although his preternatural gifts were plain to see even at that early stage, for a couple of years he played in the Welsh League and was given menial chores such as sweeping the terraces and cleaning boots. He soon tired of this and when Jack Pickard, a part-time scout for Leeds United whose name will always be loathed by Swansea supporters, got wind of the fact that this young colossus had only been registered as an amateur on Welsh League forms, he spirited him away to Leeds in September 1948. At a stroke, Swansea had lost the services of a player who would not only become the greatest footballer in Britain in his day but also, following his record-breaking transfer to mighty Juventus in 1957, win the respect and affection of fans all over the world as the 'Gentle Giant'. Charles's departure was deeply felt subsequently and, to rub salt in the wound, he just happened to excel whenever Leeds played against Swansea. What a splendid ambassador he could have been for the town had things been handled differently.

Long before the war ended, Haydn Green had realized that the vagaries of the military campaign and the demands of national service would inevitably undermine his aim of fielding a swift, young team in the post-war years. The seedbed of local youngsters would need more time and stability to mature. That is not to say that when Swansea joined the transitional league in 1945–6 which comprised First and Second Division clubs from the Midlands and the south of England it could not boast young Welsh stars. Two of them, stormy petrels in both cases, were outstanding. Trevor Ford may have had the handsome good looks of a film star, but on the field he was known as 'Terrible Trevor'. Having served in the Royal Artillery during the war and won plaudits as an ultra-physical centre forward, he returned to the Vetch determined to make up for lost time. To describe him as combative would be to underestimate the man. He kept goalkeepers in a state of permanent trepidation and liked nothing better than using his brute strength to bundle them into their own net. Goalkeepers were not mollycoddled by referees as they are in our day and Ford took full advantage. A fiery, swashbuckling leader of the attack, he never knew the meaning of fear. He believed that soccer was 'a tough, rough, catch-'em-young and hit-'em-hard game' and viewed every stadium as an arena for matadors. He asked and gave no quarter, took knocks without complaint, and revelled in the jeers and hoots of opposing fans.

During the 'Victory League' season of 1945–6, when relieved supporters poured into the Vetch in their thousands, Ford's rapier thrusts and sharp shooting brought him a record 40 goals. Many of them were memorable. As one local reporter observed: 'Whenever Ford gets a goal, it is one to talk about.' Off the field, 'Fiery Ford' was a contrarian by nature. Rather like Billy Meredith, he was seen as a rebel and a firebrand because he stood up for the rights of players. Following his transfer to Aston Villa in 1947 and thereafter to Sunderland in 1950, he became in the eyes of authority the bad boy of the football world by exposing the hypocrisy of under-the-counter payments and by championing the cause of poorly paid professional footballers. But in the eyes of the Swansea fans, the handsome lad from Townhill was the first authentic working-class local hero to wear their club's shirt. Haydn Green had hoped to build his young team around this free-scoring marauder and, unsurprisingly, the goals dried up following his departure.

Just as fearsome and inspiring was the wing half Roy Paul. Born in the Rhondda, he became one of Swansea's adopted sons. War intervened before he could make his debut as a professional footballer, but he continued to ply his considerable craft as a player during the hostilities. In 1943 he joined the Marines, where he made a name for himself as a 'pocket Hercules' on football pitches. On his return he became the kind of player who could lift a team by his powerful headlong style of play and never-say-die attitude. Although Paul was not universally liked in the dressing room, he was a natural leader, and of his skill and spirit there was no doubt. He led players on to the field as if they were there to do battle, and the redoubtable post-war Swansea half-back line of Paul, Weston and Burns lived long in the popular memory. None of these three stalwarts had any patience with 'airy-fairy feather-puff-footballers' and every contest was viewed as a red-blooded battle. Their style might not have been consonant with 'the Swansea way', but it delighted gnarled onlookers who liked to see players getting stuck in. Their robust, no-prisoners approach gave plenty of protection to the young Pontardawe-born goalkeeper Jack Parry, who compensated for his lack of height by his agility and bravery, and also allowed more space for the inside forward Frankie Squires, a former Dan-y-graig and Swansea Schoolboy player whose creative skills often had fans purring with approval. Squires also brought the best out of Ernie Jones, a remarkably swift and tricky right winger from the Alice Street stable.

But since other youngsters who were playing in the Combination League and the Welsh League were still too raw to be effective at a higher level, Haydn Green decided to buff up his squad with gritty, rough-hewn players from across the Irish Sea. This dramatic shift of direction, which at least helped to Celticize the club, raised some eyebrows, but the likes of Norman Lockhart, Sam McCrory, Jack O'Driscoll and Jim Feeney proved to be strong characters as well as decent players who won caps for Northern Ireland. Yet, although the club acquired the reputation of being the best team between the penalty areas in the division, defensive lapses (often triggered by the lamentable condition of the Vetch), Ford's departure, and fragile confidence led to an alarming slump. Time and again, local newspapers ran headlines such as 'Swans fall away after a grand opening', and although the team roused itself and displayed admirable fighting spirit in the closing matches of the season, the battle to avoid the drop was lost. The adverse financial consequences meant that the board was forced to sell Ernie Jones to Spurs for £7,000 in May 1947 and Frankie Squires to Plymouth for £7,500 in October. Since he felt that his team-building plans were now placed in jeopardy, Haydn Green, being a man of honour, decided to step aside. One of the most undervalued managers in the history of the club, Green left his successor with an impressive squad of players and every prospect of a swift return to Division Two.

That successor was the legendary William (Billy) McCandless, a squat, inscrutable Ulsterman with a reputation for making silk purses out of sows' ears. He had already worked miracles by leading both Cardiff City and Newport County to promotion from Division Three (South) and, on his arrival at the Vetch in November 1947, he vowed to achieve his own personal hat-trick as quickly as possible. Whereas Green had been affable, McCandless was fearsome. From the outset, he governed with a strong hand. His scowling presence, invariably vividly displayed in team photographs, intimidated young players, and even some veterans, having witnessed his bouts of aggressive ill temper in the dressing room, dreaded having to go to his office. This gruff, rough-hewn autocrat undoubtedly had an aura about him. Nobody dared criticize him. He had no time for shirkers and his ruthless streak soon manifested itself. As he glowered on the sidelines and barked orders during games, he commanded absolute obedience and respect.

His backroom lieutenants also exuded authority and were ideal foils for each other. Both Frank Barson, the trainer, and the old stalwart Joe Sykes, his assistant, had been appointed by Green in July 1947. Like McCandless, Barson had no patience with softies or whingers. A former blacksmith who had made his reputation as an 'Iron Man' with Manchester United and England, he instituted a rigorous training routine based on physical endurance. Lung-bursting laps, short sprints and body exercises left little time for ball work, except for the occasional kickabout on the beach. As his own players became strangers to a football during the week, on match days Barson insisted that opponents should not have the luxury of dwelling on it either. Even in his retirement, it appears that Barson was a fearsome tackler. 'Don't push out a tentative toe like a man testing the Serpentine on a cold and frosty morning', he instructed Roy Paul (who was no shrinking violet by any standards). 'Put your weight into the tackle. Make it bite.' Barson was convinced that giving and taking hard knocks was an integral part of the game, and if one of his players happened to limp after a collision or tackle during training or league games he would loudly urge him to 'run it off, son'.

It was left to Joe Sykes to help untutored youngsters to learn their trade as footballers. While Barson ranted and raved, Sykes would put his arm around his young charges, point out their weaknesses and set them achievable goals. Shrewd and personable, he was an unrivalled spotter of talent. He had already identified two gems. In 1944 he had watched with mounting pleasure a golden-haired youngster from Plas-marl called Ivor Allchurch dominating a practice game at Cwm Level. He loved him at first sight, not least because of his exquisite first touch. Allchurch was just 14. Sykes also identified the extraordinary potential of John Charles – 'He's got the lot – strength, heading ability, ball control, timing and body balance' – and no one at the club was more distraught than this native of Sheffield when his priceless recruit was spirited away to Yorkshire. Sykes used to spend hours grooming young players and teaching them the technical essentials of the game. Universally – and respectfully – known by the youngsters as 'Mr Sykes', he exerted a powerful and enduring influence on their development. While McCandless barked and Barson cussed, Sykes would quietly encourage the players to value the use of 'carpet passes' and work together as a cohesive unit. This unlikely trio ensured that a new spirit began to course through the club.

During this period of transition, McCandless relied largely on proven players of talent and experience whom his predecessor had recruited. But he also dipped into the bargain basement of the transfer market and ventured across the Irish Sea where his reputation as a former Irish international enabled him to sign players with a strong desire to succeed. Even so, the half-back line of Paul, Weston and Burns remained the linchpin of the team. Experienced and dependable, they were men after McCandless's heart. Roy Paul's crunching tackles and fierce will to win caught the imagination of the fans, while the Londoner Reg Weston, who made 229 league appearances for the club, was a commanding pivot. The third, Frankie Burns, a left half as tough as tungsten, put the fear of God into referees as well as opposing forwards. McCandless had the nucleus of a fine side, but in his first season at the helm a lack of goals and a poor away record meant that hopes of promotion were premature. Yet, to finish in fifth place was no small achievement. With youthful assets waiting in the wings, the auguries were extremely good.

Three signings made a world of difference to the 1948–9 promotion team. In March, Newport-born Billy Lucas, an experienced orchestrator in midfield and a Welsh international, arrived from Swindon for a record fee of £11,000. Appointed captain, Lucas made over 200 league appearances over five seasons and brought both intelligence and inventiveness to the side. Of the Irish incomers, Sam McCrory, bought from Linfield, made the greatest impression by scoring 19 goals in his first season. But even his sparkling displays as a marksman were eclipsed by the proven goal-scorer Stan Richards, who was transferred from Cardiff. Jeremiahs warned McCandless that Richards's well-publicized knee problems were bound to recur, but the irrepressible striker chalked up 35 goals in 62 appearances. Throughout the team, individuals performed with impressive maturity, with the doggedness of Jim Feeney at full back, the inspirational Paul and the terrier-like Burns in midfield, and the creative link-up play of Lucas, catching the eye. In contrast to the 'big boot' tactics employed by most teams in the division, Swansea played neat and constructive football.

The upsurge of energy on the pitch was matched on the terraces. The Vetch pulsated with noise and fervour as the fans, who had for so long yearned for the chance to dance with joy, hug each other and invade the pitch, thronged to the rickety old stadium with a spring in their step. The average home attendance of 22,372 in the 1948–9 season was an all-time record, and the players rewarded their followers by winning every single game at home except one (a draw against lowly Southend United in April) and by scoring 60 goals at home and 87 overall. The climax came on 18 April 1949 when splendid goals by Frankie Scrine and Stan Richards in a 2–1 victory over Newport County virtually assured the club of its first promotion since 1926. Even McCandless was seen to smile, and a euphoric Abe Freedman claimed that Swansea was now poised to go on to storm the citadels of Division One in due course. Having won the championship by a decisive margin of seven points, the club was warmly, even effusively, congratulated by the editor of the *South Wales Evening Post* for its 'vicariously-shaped experience of a dogged uphill fight, recovery and victory'. There was optimistic, and unrealistic, talk of increasing the ground capacity to 60,000 and, with the benefit of hindsight, we can appreciate how wise leaders of the borough council were in insisting that improvements could only come about if the stadium was transferred to a location some three miles from the town centre.

Having achieved his ambition, Billy McCandless now set his mind on blooding some of his young apprentices. The era of the 'Swansea Babes' had arrived and, one by one, they joined the first-team pool in the early 1950s. Some followers must have questioned the wisdom of introducing them at a time when the club was rocked by a financial scandal of global proportions. Most players at that time reluctantly accepted their lot over matters such as the maximum wage and freedom of movement, but two in particular – Trevor Ford and Roy Paul – railed against what they believed to be 'football slavery'. Ford rattled a few dustbins in the complacent corridors of the Football League after leaving the Vetch, but Paul was on the Swansea staff in the close season in 1950 when he scandalized the board by flying to Bogotá in Colombia in the fond belief that a pot of gold awaited him. English stars like George Mountford and Neil Franklin, outraged by the maximum wage system, had already defected to this alleged El Dorado, but for Paul the expedition turned out to be an unmitigated disaster. No one was more surprised to hear of his defection than his unsuspecting wife, who had been led to believe that her beloved spouse was in Blackpool. Paul soon returned home in dudgeon and disgrace. Seething with rage at his disloyalty, McCandless made his feelings known to the board and Paul was duly transferred to Manchester City for £18,000. Fortunately for the club, Paul's colleagues deplored his shenanigans and the up-and-coming players were much more interested in improving their skills and making the most of their opportunity of representing their town.

The accidents of demography and the vagaries of national service meant of course that the new crop of youngsters did not mature or capture a place in the first team at the same time. Nor did they all reach the same heights. But there is no question that four of them – Ivor Allchurch (who made his debut in December 1949), Terry Medwin (January 1952), Cliff Jones (October 1952) and Mel Charles (December 1952) – were truly outstanding, and the club constantly found itself fending off bids for their services from big clubs. The greatest of these players was Ivor Allchurch who, during his glittering days with Swansea from his debut on Boxing Day 1949 until his transfer to Newcastle United in October 1958, made 330 league appearances and scored 124 goals, almost all of which seemed to have been spectacular drives from outside the penalty box. In his admirable book *The Perfect Ten*, a work whose only defect is the inexcusable omission of Allchurch in favour of pipsqueaks like Pelé and Maradona, the journalist Richard Williams shrewdly analysed the role of the midfield choreographer. 'Nothing in the game', he wrote, 'presents quite as inspiring and satisfying a sight as that of a great No. 10 giving the fullest rein to his abilities as he directs the course of a match.' Those who were privileged to see Ivor Allchurch in his pomp over the best part of ten years at the Vetch will readily acknowledge that no other player lodged himself so firmly in the collective memory as this wonderful playmaker.

As we have seen, Joe Sykes could recognize a born footballer and he knew at once that Ivor was 'a gem of rare quality'. Tall, blond and suntanned, from an early age he was superlatively gifted with a football at his feet. He was the archetypal working-class hero at the Vetch and the nearest thing to 'Roy of the Rovers' that local fans would ever see in the flesh. A disarmingly humble, even bashful, man, he came to life on the pitch, where his flawless technique enabled him to perform the basic skills smoothly and swiftly. He caressed heavy leather footballs with a soft, almost loving, touch. Perfectly balanced, he could turn on a sixpence, and his clever close control, thrilling feints and body swerves made him a masterly dribbler. His phenomenal acceleration and long raking stride took him away from despairing markers and his two-footedness enabled him to make long or short passes which brought wingers into the game or created openings for strikers. His shooting power and accuracy were legendary and he scored countless goals with thunderous rising drives into the top corner of the net. He was simply incapable of scoring a run-of-the-mill goal. Lurching defenders often scythed him down in full flight, but he took each knock uncomplainingly and was never booked or sent off. Never has Swansea had a finer exponent of the beautiful game or a finer ambassador for the club.

Even at the start of his career, his glorious form stirred the spirit. When Swansea hosted mighty Arsenal in the fourth round of the FA Cup on 28 January 1950, not even the likes of Barnes, Compton, Goring, Logie and Mercer managed to catch the imagination as young Allchurch did. Tom Whittaker, the Arsenal manager, was greatly taken with him and praised his slide-rule passes and deceptive dribbling skills. The team came to depend on him for inspiration and he developed a remarkable ability to influence the outcome of games almost single-handedly. Some of his skills were simply astonishing. While playing at Bury on one occasion, he waltzed around five flailing defenders in an 'amazing piece of soccer jugglery'. Local newspapers regularly sported headlines such as 'Outstanding skill of Allchurch' and 'Allchurch goals win Cup match', and reporters soon exhausted their fund of superlatives. First chosen to play for Wales in 1951, he went on to win 68 caps and score 23 wonderful goals, most of them shots from outside the penalty area. His goal against Hungary in the 1958 World Cup, a piledriver from 25 yards, was reckoned to be the finest in the tournament and Santiago Bernabéu, president of Real Madrid, dubbed him 'the greatest inside-forward in the world'. Arrigo Sacchi, the distinguished Italian coach, used to maintain that the true footballer was 'born in the brain' rather than the womb. Ivor Allchurch may not have been the most confident or fluent communicator off the field, but in terms of footballing intelligence he was a genius. Swansea has never found anyone to replace him and probably never will.

For several years Allchurch was fortunate to be flanked by two outstanding international wingers, both of whom hailed from the Sandfields area. The son of a former Southampton footballer, Terry Medwin was one of those players for whom all fellow professionals had the greatest respect. He learned his trade properly. Having captained Swansea Schoolboys, he benefited from the wise guidance of Joe Sykes, who ensured that his technique was so sound that he was able to shine consistently during 147 league appearances for Swansea. Adoring female supporters were convinced that this handsome, fair-haired winger could easily masquerade as a Hollywood film star. Yet, Medwin was a level-headed, undemonstrative player who was sufficiently versatile to play on either wing or at centre forward. Superbly balanced, quick on the turn, and light of foot, he created scores of opportunities for his colleagues with his precise crosses and penetrating corners. Unlike whippet-like wingers who relied exclusively on pace, Medwin's approach work was more measured and his selection and application of crosses and passes brought greater dividends. He was a player's player. Although he disliked playing centre forward, whenever he was called on to do so he led the line intelligently by dropping deep in the manner of Hidegkuti or Revie, and close to goal he was swift and decisive, as his goal tally of 57 shows. Terry Medwin was a model professional and his colleagues at Swansea and later at Spurs held him in the highest regard.

Medwin's colleague on the left flank was also raised within shouting distance of the Vetch. Cliff Jones, born and bred at 8 Beach Street in the Sandfields, became the most dangerous winger in British football. Although, from his days as captain of Swansea Schoolboys, Jones had all-round skill in abundance, his main asset was his blistering pace. Soccer was in his blood. He was part of a remarkable football dynasty from Merthyr Tydfil which began with his grandfather William David Jones (known as 'Big Daddy'), who raised five outstandingly gifted footballing sons, including Ivor Jones (Cliff's father) and Bryn Jones, whose silky skills took him to Wolves and then, for a record fee of £14,000, to Arsenal. Cliff was Ivor's youngest son and his initial ambition was to emulate his skilful father by playing in midfield. When he made his first-team debut against Bury on 18 October 1952, he played at inside right. But his astute mentor Joe Sykes soon persuaded him that a place on the wing would give fuller rein to his exceptional speed. So it proved. Leaden-footed defenders had no answer to his sheer pace and thrust, and whenever he set off on his darting, twisting runs he threw defenders off balance and created countless openings for his fellow attackers. No one in his day, except Francisco Gento of Real Madrid, had such an explosive turn of speed. Even though he was small and slight, he was exceptionally brave. He not only scored many splendid goals with either foot but also jumped high to challenge successfully for crosses in the penalty area. With pardonable exaggeration, the journalist David Miller once claimed that Cliff Jones 'could leap to heights unknown to Nureyev with utter fearlessness and self-disregard'. But the prevailing memory among supporters of this modest, match-winning winger was his breathtaking speed. There was nothing more exciting at the Vetch in the 1950s than the sight of Cliff Jones running straight and fast at defenders. In full flow, he was untouchable.

The fourth was Mel Charles, the younger brother of peerless John. Even though his autobiography was entitled *In the Shadow of a Giant*, Mel Charles never displayed any semblance of envy over the fame and fortune of his brother. He was no mean player in his own right. At 6' 1" and 14 st, he was big of stature and of heart. Although his debut, at the tender age of 17, against Sheffield United at Bramall Lane ended in a 1–7 drubbing, he remained undaunted. He never lacked confidence in his own versatile abilities and the Swansea management were never quite sure where to play him. Although he was not entirely happy in that position, he was voted the best centre half in the 1958 World Cup tournament. But he was also a sturdy and free-scoring centre forward who scored four goals for Wales against Northern Ireland in 1962. He always insisted, however, that his favourite position was wing half, where his adventurous streak matched his reputation for mischief off the field. Willing to work from penalty box to penalty box, he foraged tirelessly, challenging for every ball in the air and on the ground, and posing a constant threat with his powerful shooting. His ratio of goals – 66 in 233 league appearances for Swansea – was impressive and this lion-hearted Cwmbwrla boy fully deserved each of his 31 Welsh caps.

Then there was a group of players who, though not as prodigally gifted as the above, were very fine professional footballers. In goal was Johnny King, a native of Blaenllechau in the Rhondda, who proved during 370 league appearances between 1950 and 1964 – a long time for a goalkeeper – to be a highly reliable, sturdy shot-stopper who kept his concentration at key moments and was strong enough to withstand the toughest of challenges as well as risk injury by hurling himself at the feet of attackers. No player had a more happy-go-lucky approach to the game than Harry Griffiths, a talismanic figure whose place in the folklore of the club and his home town is assured. His sense of fun and cheeky-chappie smile endeared him to everyone, and his daily cheerfulness was matched by his indomitable commitment on the field and to the club in general. An invaluable utility player, with a huge appetite for the game, Griffiths wore the Swansea shirt 421 times in league matches and, whether playing at right wing, inside forward or full back, he always took his trade seriously. So, too, did Dai Thomas, a former coal miner from Abercregan, near Port Talbot, who played each game at full back as if it were his last. Combining skill, muscle and stamina, he was known as 'a 90-minute player'. Darwel ('Davo') Williams was a robust wing half. At centre half, Tom Kiley, who was raised in the Greenhill, St Joseph's district, and who was a little older than his colleagues, was not only commandingly tall but also a composed and reliable presence at the heart of the defence. His successor, Mel Nurse, was as hard as nails. A solid, uncompromising defender, known for his bone-shaking tackles, Nurse was more robust than Kiley but also more hot-headed. But of his lifelong affection for the club there is no doubt, and the title of his memoirs – *Mr Swansea* – was entirely appropriate, given his loyal service as a player and later as a board member and businessman. Among the forwards, Des Palmer was a strong, mobile and alert goal-scorer. Not quite the top-class striker he aspired to be, he nevertheless scored goals aplenty, especially in the 1956–7 season, and won three caps.

By a curious biological accident, at one stage there were four sets of brothers on the club's books, and had John Charles refused to head north there might have been five. One set was Tamworth born. The Beech brothers were left-sided players: Gilbert was a solid, undemonstrative left back, while Cyril was so fleet of foot that he was nicknamed 'Tulyar' after the startlingly swift racehorse. Unlike his brother Cliff, who regularly left gasping full backs for dead, Bryn Jones was more like his father: an intelligent, well-balanced player, he threaded neat passes from midfield and, when given time and space, dictated patterns of play. Colin and Alan Hole were talented sons of the legendary right winger Billy, while Len Allchurch, a stocky but swift winger, refused to live in the shadow of his inspirational brother and produced flashes of brilliance which brought him goals as well as a host of admirers. These players, who were often called on to fill a variety of roles, some of them unfamiliar, kept the team ticking over and could be relied on to give of their best at all times.

As a spectator sport, soccer had no rival in Swansea during the 1950s, and the strong working-class roots of the game intensified its popularity. As natives of the town, this particular crop of beguilingly fresh-faced and gifted youngsters were acutely aware that the team was a reflection, even a symbol, of the community of working people that supported it. To be a Swansea man through and through was a badge of pride for them and whenever players considered asking for a transfer they always agonized long and hard over the wisdom of tearing up their roots and letting down their keenest admirers and friends. Most of them were home birds by nature and were instinctively hostile to siren calls from English clubs. Mel Charles never forgot the 'strong family feel' which bound club and community together and in this affectionate account, exclusively written for this book, Cliff Jones shows how players and supporters were tied together by bonds of class, schooling and community:

> The Sandfields was a totally working-class area, very close-knit and where everybody seemed to know one another. The proverbial key hung on a piece of string inside the letter-box of each front door. Within a radius of around a hundred yards of my home we had Camden's the barbers, Bryn Wilkie's the cobblers, Dolly Furzland's the greengrocers, Thomas the Welsh shop and the local butchers where we got our home-made faggots and peas every Thursday. In addition, opposite our house was Joe's ice cream parlour, the best ice cream in south Wales. When the war ended, Joe supplied our street with free ice cream on celebration day. There were two pubs, the Brooklyn's and the Westbourne, St Paul's church, Billy Hole's newsagents, Barclays Bank, Swansea General Hospital,

> and Messer's fish and chip shop which my grandfather owned and where he cooked the best fish and chips in Swansea. My mother would leave the house around ten every morning to buy food and, after stopping to talk to all the neighbours and shopkeepers, would rush back at about 12.30 to cook lunch. We also had Dai Salmon, a copper on the beat who knew everybody in the Sandfields, especially the villains. You can't get more of a community than that.

Ivor Allchurch came close to joining Wolves in 1952 and thereafter was plagued by managers desperate to sign him. But he was an intensely loyal player and when further rumours spread of his impending departure, working-class townspeople were deeply touched when their hero not only chose to stay but also publicly declared, 'I am one of you'. Such loyalty struck a deep chord on the terraces. Unlike modern stars, these were not brash, selfish, attention-seeking players, and none of them was driven by overweening ambition and greed. Off the field there was a strong sense of camaraderie. While they were not spotless models of probity – Mel Charles could be Jack the Lad, Harry Griffiths was always up to mischief, and smoking and drinking after a game was part and parcel of the footballing culture of the times – the Swansea Babes would never have dreamt of bringing the club they loved into disrepute.

Players were household names in the town. Star-struck young fans often found themselves sitting alongside one of their idols during bus rides to the ground or into town. Those who lived in the shadow of the Vetch used to walk to the ground (Cliff Jones often jogged there as part of his pre-match warm-up), greeting well-wishers on their way and signing autographs. Mel Charles once caused a stir by turning up on a rag-and-bone cart and indulging in some light-hearted banter with the fans. Having borne the heavy burdens of wartime and post-war shortages and restrictions, supporters yearned for promotion battles and glory games, for the chance to dance with joy and invade the pitch. They felt in their bones that a new era was emerging. Handsome new buildings were replacing the bomb-gutted town centre and, as one newspaper editor rapturously wrote, 'with this brand-newness is coming a sense of exhilaration'. Investing in skilful local youths was part of this great upsurge of energy and anticipation. The Vetch became a cauldron of noise on match days and fans, many of whom occupied the North Bank which had been levelled across the top and its front part lowered below the level of the pitch, were intimately involved in the action and fully expected their players to respond by playing in 'the Swansea way'. In his day, Trevor Ford had found them 'darned contrary and difficult to please' and in the 1950s Tom Kiley also described them as 'demanding'. But they deserved to have their say. Minimum admission charges increased from 1s 3d in 1946 to 1s 9d in 1952 and to 2s 6d in 1960, and, as the crowds still came in their droves, they watched games intently and continued to set exacting standards. In many ways, they were blessed with more entertainment, thrills and spills, glorious goals and abject defensive errors than in any other period in the history of the club.

The great mystery is how Swansea Town AFC, with its wealth of young stars and fervent supporters, underachieved so spectacularly during the 1950s. Golden opportunities to gain promotion were spurned and, as the prospects of success dwindled, the club's most skilful players turned to pastures new in England, and attendances began to fall alarmingly. The facts speak for themselves. Between 1952 and 1959 Swansea never achieved higher than tenth place in the league at the end of a season, and on two agonizing occasions it was haunted by the spectre of relegation until the eleventh hour. The club's record in the FA Cup was lamentable, and only on one occasion – on 19 May 1950, when Frankie Scrine scored a hat-trick against Wrexham – did it win the Welsh Cup during the 1950s. Each season seemed to end either on a note of anticlimax or in nail-biting apprehension. By the end of the decade, the principal stars had been transferred to bigger clubs for substantial fees.

All the hopes of the board, the players and the supporters had crumbled into dust.

Everything had augured so well during the early 1950s. A golden era was surely at hand. The club had unearthed a rich vein of talented players whose 'great spirit and youthful enthusiasm' delighted expectant crowds and boosted the self-image of the town. When Swansea played Fulham at the Vetch on 22 November 1952, ten of the players were Welsh and seven of them were Swansea born. Those who visited the old ground sensed an air of optimism as glorious attacking play led to an abundance of goals. There was something innocent and carefree about the youngsters, and their sense of adventure was shared by the spectators. On good days at home, the team ran more experienced opponents off their feet, and even when they conceded three goals the players were always confident of scoring four or even more.

Therein lay Swansea's Achilles heel. Entertaining attacking play was not matched by the defensive skills, concentration and determination required of a team bidding for promotion. Points were dropped prodigally because of defensive frailties and time and again supporters would groan as Swansea yielded goals against lesser lights. Some statistics are telling. In the 1954–5 season Swansea scored 86 goals, but also conceded 83 goals. But for the heroic King in goal, the goals-against tally would have exceeded a hundred. Whenever Swansea came up against powerful and better-resourced clubs like Blackburn, Birmingham, Leeds and Liverpool or any hard-bitten teams that relied on 'kick-and-rush' or 'up-and-under' tactics, they were often found wanting. Some unfathomable collapses and a tendency to crack under pressure on big occasions strongly suggest that some players lacked physical and mental toughness, and that the balance between experience and youth was awry. Lacklustre, and often abysmal, performances away from home cost the club dearly and contrasted sharply with many exhilarating displays at home.

Although many still hark back nostalgically to the days of

Billy McCandless and refer admiringly to his extraordinary presence, he had little to crow about in the early 1950s. He made fundamental errors in the transfer market. Apart from the free-scoring Ron Turnbull, whom he recruited for £7,500 from Manchester City in January 1951, he was content to buy run-of-the-mill journeymen. Moreover, to have allowed Billy Lucas, his experienced midfield general, to leave for Newport County at a critical time in December 1954 was an act of criminal negligence. Somehow McCandless appeared to have lost the will to succeed. He was no longer able to motivate his charges, several of whom were convinced that he preferred to spend more time with his beloved pigeons than with them. Dark rumours of his fondness for whisky spread around the club. Mel Nurse, perhaps uncharitably, claimed that he was 'as pissed as a parrot' most of the time, and on match days he would usually poke his head round the dressing room door, whisky glass in hand, to implore the players to go for 'death or glory'. Many critics were increasingly concerned about his antiquated management style. The tubby Irishman clearly had no wish to emulate 'tracksuit managers' like Matt Busby and Stan Cullis, and he never used a blackboard in his pre-match briefings. He belonged to the old school of managers who stubbornly refused to learn new tricks.

Many players also believed that Frank Barson's training routines were not conducive to 'the Swansea way'. Tom Kiley was shocked to be told by Barson that he was 'not dirty enough' and that his main duty was to 'get it [the ball] down field' as quickly as possible. Cliff Jones was convinced that McCandless failed to harness the unprecedented talent at his disposal because of his over-reliance on Barson and his reluctance to encourage players to think for themselves on the training ground and during matches. There were sighs of relief when ill health forced Barson to resign in February 1954 and when the more progressive Joe Sykes took his place and began introducing intensive ball work and breeding confidence rather than fear. Sykes had always been able to establish a rapport with players and make them want to play for him. Meanwhile, McCandless's relationship with the board became increasingly uneasy. He was admonished on several occasions for neglecting his coaching duties and for sloppy preparation and tactical naivety. His unexpected death aged 61, on 18 July 1955, shortly before the players returned to prepare for the new season, ironically ushered in the club's best opportunity of winning promotion.

That this opportunity was spurned was due largely to the myopia of the board. Until the mid-1950s the directors, for the most part, had acted responsibly and judiciously. Time and again supporters were informed by the chairman Phillip Holden that no rash and speculative expenditure would be incurred and that nothing would deflect them from their aim of developing home-grown talent. But occasions arose when loosening the purse strings in order to buy experienced players, especially defenders, to exert a steadying influence, would surely have brought dividends. This was especially the case when Ron Burgess, a former pit-boy from the Rhondda who had made a name for himself as an excellent all-round player with Spurs and who had won 32 caps for Wales, was appointed player-manager. Burgess had joined the club earlier as player-coach in August 1954 and, even though he was a yard slower than before, he had won the hearts of the home crowd by his perpetual piston-like running style, fierce tackling and passing ability. Wisely, he co-opted Joe Sykes and Ivor Allchurch on to a selection panel and introduced the 'push and run' style so successfully employed by Arthur Rowe at White Hart Lane. This more flowing style of football dovetailed neatly with 'the Swansea way'.

Basing their play on swift, accurate inter-passing and energetic support, the team began to blossom in the 1955–6 season. After 16 games Swansea sat proudly at the top of Division Two and, as Burgess's tactics made a growing impact, many supporters fervently believed that the team was at last bound for promotion to Division One. But then, calamitously,

Tom Kiley, the club's dependable pivot and a father figure to so many of the younger players, seriously injured his knee during training in mid-November. The situation called for urgent action, but instead of signing a powerful and reliable centre half to fill the gaping hole left by Kiley, the board dillied and dallied in the hope that the inexperienced Mumbles-born Jim Pressdee or even the old warhorse Burgess could fill the role. Meanwhile, news of the state of Kiley's kneecap became as important to Swansea fans as Jenkins's ear and Nelson's eye had been to sailors in Georgian times. In the event, however, there was to be no early return for Kiley and as a result the team slipped out of the promotion race. Tenth place at the end of the season plainly showed that the board had badly misjudged the situation. How hard Ron Burgess had pressed the directors to provide him with a proven replacement is impossible to tell, but Bill Nicholson, a shrewd judge of men, claimed that he was 'too nice a person to order people about'. The truth is that both players and supporters had every right to feel let down at the end of another fruitless season.

In other ways, too, the board did the club a disservice. One can only imagine what spectacular results the team might have achieved and sustained had the Vetch been in better playing condition. Too many unimportant non-league games were allowed to be played on what was already a poor surface. The virtually grassless pitch would often become a sea of mud on which it was well-nigh impossible to play constructive football. 'Mudlarks' was a popular depiction of the Vetch in local newspaper cartoons as torrential rain turned games into a lottery in mid-winter. Penny-pinching also lay at the root of Swansea's wretched away record. Making long and exhausting journeys to away fixtures on the morning of a game was counter-productive and it was not the least bit surprising that weary players did themselves less than justice on the road. Nor did the club invest properly in the administrative structure. Panic broke out whenever Swansea was matched with a major club in the FA Cup. For instance, when a home draw with

Newcastle United came out of the hat for the fifth round of the Cup in February 1952, over 40,000 applications for tickets were received. One loyal fan appended the following verse to his bid:

> I follow you in sunshine,
> I follow you in rain;
> If I get no — ticket,
> I won't follow you again.

The club's inadequate clerical staff were thrown into disarray by this unexpected flood of applications and, having failed to get a quart into a pint jug, it was just as well that a goal by Mitchell sent the Geordies home happy, thereby avoiding a similar administrative nightmare for Swansea in the sixth round. Visitors to the Vetch could not but notice the down-at-heel atmosphere of the ground when it was empty. When Percy M. Young, a distinguished musicologist who was also besotted with what he called 'this whacking good game' known as soccer, called at the 'subterranean' offices of the club, he was reminded of the first bars of Grieg's 'In the Hall of the Mountain King'.

Lack of sustained success on the field disheartened members of the board and there are grounds for believing that the club lacked a clear sense of purpose at a time when Cardiff had achieved promotion to Division One in 1952, had become the capital of Wales by 1955, and had developed a disconcerting conceit about its national and cultural status. As Cardiff City placed itself on a pedestal, Swansea Town crept under the table. Picking up vibes from their comments and body language, Percy M. Young certainly gained the impression that directorial ambitions at the Vetch were low: 'Swansea by reason of its being neither outrageously large nor yet inconveniently small will, perhaps, remain – strictly in a football sense – in the Second Division.' Perhaps the players, too, had accepted the view that the board was ready to yield supremacy to the

Bluebirds and had reconciled itself to being a good middle-of-table side in Division Two. Not until the advent of John Toshack was this complacent defeatism laid to rest.

Although Phillip Holden insisted that there was no intention of allowing young local stars to leave, once Tom Kiley's injury ushered in a run of poor results the 'no buy, no sell' policy was abandoned and the haemorrhage began. Terry Medwin, who had scored 20 goals during the 1955–6 season, was immediately allowed to join Spurs for £18,000, and from then on the die was cast. Cliff Jones became Britain's most expensive footballer by joining Spurs, Ivor Allchurch left for Newcastle and Mel Charles signed for Arsenal. By 1959 Swansea's 'famous four' were plying their glittering wares with big city clubs and a wave of sadness, tinged with heartfelt gratitude for the memories they had left behind, swept over the Vetch. A decade which had radiated such glowing promise at its inception had petered out miserably.

4

'Swansea Town are Falling Down'

UNTIL FAIRLY RECENTLY goalkeepers came in all shapes and sizes. Noel Dwyer, Swansea's Dublin-born net-minder (as they were often quaintly called) in the early 1960s, was a plump figure who always gave the impression of never liking to be too far away from a plate of food and a pint of beer. Held in great affection by the Vetch faithful for his extraordinary agility as well as his idiosyncrasies, Dwyer's heroic performances during the 1963–4 FA Cup campaign were largely responsible for the club's biggest moment since 1926, its appearance in the semi-final of the competition on 12 March 1964. Never before had Swansea played before 68,000 people, around half of whom were wildly enthusiastic, hymn-singing supporters from south-west Wales. The venue was Villa Park, at best a dowdy, uninviting relic of the Victorian age, and whose virtually grassless pitch was a disgrace. To make matters worse, soul-chilling rain, the heaviest for months in Birmingham, fell incessantly throughout the game and played a decisive part in the result.

At around 4.25 p.m., 15 minutes from the end and with the scores level at a goal apiece, Dwyer made a fatal error by straying too far from his goal-line. He may have been seeking a better view of the proceedings as the billowing rain increasingly hampered his vision. Possibly, too, he was escaping from the distracting, babbling pet leprechaun he kept in the net behind him. A more plausible explanation, however, is that he was urging his hard-pressed defenders to push up as their opponents, Preston North End, pressed hard for the winning goal. Suddenly and totally unexpectedly, Tony Singleton, Preston's lanky centre half, latched on to a clearance and hoisted a speculative punt from around the halfway line. Caught on the wind, the ball soared over the frantically back-pedalling Dwyer and dipped into the net. This fluke, alas, proved to be the winning goal.

Swansea had begun the game well, responding energetically to the fervour of their supporters as strains of 'Hen Wlad fy Nhadau' and 'Calon Lân' arose from every corner of the rain-sodden stands and terraces. The team pressed early for the ball and their clever approach play drove their opponents deep into their own half. Increasingly, however, the clogging mud and harsh tackles of their more physical opponents disrupted Swansea's passing, poise and rhythm. But they took the lead a minute before half-time with a superbly executed goal. Full back Roy Evans lofted the ball into the Preston goalmouth, Derek Draper touched it on, and Jimmy McLaughlin swivelled expertly before driving the ball powerfully with his trusty left foot past goalkeeper Kelly. The Swansea supporters cheered and sang lustily throughout the interval.

The second half was a different story. The lashing rain had turned a mud-heap into a quagmire. Albert Barham of the *Guardian* described it as a pitch 'whisked to a brown batter by the flailing feet and skidding bodies'. It was scarcely possible to recognize the players and the conditions undoubtedly worked to Preston's advantage. Their rugged physical approach, and willingness to hustle and bustle untiringly, enabled them to gain the upper hand in the churning mud. As Preston raised their game, the tank-like rushes of their brawny centre forward Alex Dawson became increasingly influential. When he barged into the Swansea captain Mike Johnson and fell theatrically in the penalty box, the referee J. E. Carr of Sheffield (which, as maps show, is located much nearer to Preston than to

Swansea), though trailing far behind play, decided to even things up by awarding Preston a penalty. Howls of anger arose from Swansea's vociferous fans and, with a wry grin, Dawson thumped home the equalizer. Having hotly disputed the award, the Swansea players fretted and fumed as their opponents resorted to crude aggression. The game degenerated into a tale of frayed tempers, petty fouls and wasted opportunities. Floundering in the mud, Swansea surrendered the initiative and by the closing stages they could hardly drag their exhausted bodies through the morass. 'What a dull, destructive success' was the verdict of the *Times* reporter on Preston's unlovely performance, while the Swansea players and supporters were left to reflect disconsolately on the disputed penalty and the fortuitous goal which had robbed them of the chance of reaching the final of the FA Cup for the first time in their history. The team had played their hearts out and perhaps justice was done when West Ham United beat Preston 3–2 in the final.

Those who know next to nothing about Welsh football will probably remember that weekend as the time when Elizabeth Taylor, an insatiable collector of husbands, married Richard Burton, but genuine Swansea fans will always recall the defeat at the hands of the legendary 'Invincibles' with a deep sense of injustice. Swansea's moment of glory had been snatched away and the despair ushered in a period of decline which stretched over ten seasons. Indeed, at the end of the 1974–5 season, the club suffered the terrible indignity of having to seek re-election to the Football League. How that spiral of decline came about is the theme of this chapter.

As Wales prepared to do battle in the World Cup in Sweden in June 1958, Swansea supporters were distinctly underwhelmed when news filtered through of the appointment of Trevor Morris as the new manager of the club. Born in Gors-las, Carmarthenshire, Morris's playing experience as a wing half in the pre-war years had been limited to a short spell with Ipswich and then with Cardiff City, where he broke his leg and eventually hung up his boots prematurely. He served in the RAF Bomber Command, flying more than 40 missions and winning the Distinguished Flying Cross. In 1946 he returned to Ninian Park as assistant-secretary of the club and eight years later he was promoted to the post of secretary-manager. In many ways, it was a strange appointment for Swansea to make. Indeed, several Swansea players believed that the board had taken leave of its senses by appointing a 38-year-old Welshman whose managerial record was far from impressive. The Bluebirds, having finished 20th and 17th in his first two years in charge, were relegated to Division Two in his third season, and had ended the 1957–8 season hovering perilously close to the relegation zone. The supporters were also suspicious of him. Not only had he come from Cardiff City, but he was also reckoned to be more of an accountant than a genuine football man. With his balding pate, three-piece suit, bow tie and trilby, Morris could easily have been mistaken for a bank manager. Clearly the directors at Swansea, deeply concerned about their mounting debts, saw Morris as the ideal man to place the club on a secure financial footing. He had a good head for figures and knew how to wheel and deal in the transfer market.

Trevor Morris had a certain presence about him. A confident, well-spoken man, he was more interested in airing his own views than listening to others or heeding advice. His dry wit and cute one-liners beguiled local reporters and he was never short of a sharp barb or a quotable quip whenever a microphone was thrust under his nose. When Swansea visited Anfield to play mighty Liverpool during the successful FA Cup run in 1964, the former bomber pilot invited local reporters into the dressing room and regaled them with his martial verve: 'Look at my team, white shirts, white shorts, white legs – and all of them shaking. Boys. Just boys. But they'll come back from that pitch as men – if they come back at all.' But the Swansea players, especially those whom he had inherited, doubted his football knowledge and despised his autocratic ways. Tom Kiley, a veteran in the ranks, disliked his abrasive manner and his unfortunate tendency to treat them like schoolboys. Only grudgingly did they submit to his authority. It was common knowledge that Morris was there to balance the books and, by implication, to sell the club's stars for the best possible price. A deeply uneasy Ron Burgess, who had been demoted to assistant-manager, tendered his resignation within a month and by mid-December another stalwart, Joe Sykes, had relinquished his post as trainer-coach.

It was under Morris's watch that the local hero, Ivor Allchurch, now approaching 30, was allowed to join Newcastle United, thereby fulfilling his long-delayed ambition of playing league football at the highest level. His departure in October 1958 deepened the sense of insecurity among the players and the fans were most certainly not amused. Next to leave was Mel Charles, who was transferred to Arsenal on 31 March 1959 after a prolonged transfer tug-of-war during which the burly wing half became convinced that Morris treated players as commodities rather than human beings. Mel Nurse was no more complimentary about him, especially after Morris ordered him in October 1962 to travel to London to accept and sign an offer from Middlesbrough. 'Mel', he barked, 'you're going to Middlesbrough. Get your boots and go, otherwise you won't play football again.' Oblivious of his rights, Nurse meekly obeyed. Morris often ruthlessly rode roughshod over the players and he became known in the dressing room as 'a selling manager'.

Morris's tactical knowledge was often called into question during his tenure, as was his appreciation of the traditional style of football played at the club. He mystified the squad by playing Ray Daniel at centre forward at the start of the 1959–60 season, and when he experimented with what he called 'the Barcelona system' against Scunthorpe in mid-March 1960 he demeaned himself by claiming that any successful manager needed 'a strong flair for showmanship'. The system was swiftly discarded as the team conceded 84 goals over the season. Other instances of crassness exposed his tactical deficiencies and mishandling of players.

For example, during the FA Cup run in 1964, the quicksilver winger Brian Evans, who had made a major contribution by outstripping defenders and sending a stream of inviting crosses into the box, was dropped for the semi-final against Preston in favour of the less gifted, though plucky, forward Keith Todd. When questioned beforehand about the wisdom of his decision, Morris tempted fate in his reply: 'By 4.40 on Saturday afternoon I could be a genius or an idiot.'

The board, however, believed that Morris could do no wrong, and it must be said that, given the parlous financial state of the club and the rising costs of wages, transport and administration, let alone changing socio-cultural tastes, he made a fair fist of fulfilling his brief of reducing the financial deficit, selling stars, signing decent 'old pros', and nurturing local youngsters. On his appointment, the club's five-figure overdraft was daunting, but Morris's astuteness in the transfer market brought the club into profit within two years. Losing key players did little for morale, but it placated creditors and the taxman. And whenever the fiscal prospects were gloomy, Morris unhesitatingly shipped out players. Out of the blue, Len Allchurch was transferred to Sheffield United for £14,000 in March 1961 and, much later, the rising star, flaxen-haired winger Barrie Jones was sold to Plymouth Argyle for a whopping £45,000. Oblivious to the moans and groans of the supporters, Morris kept his eye firmly on the financial bottom-line.

Nor was he unsuccessful in bringing in experienced players. His record in this field was not unblemished but, by canny wheeling and dealing, as well as stubborn negotiation, he contrived to attract some decent footballers to the Vetch. When Ivor Allchurch left for Newcastle, Reg Davies, a skilful Welsh international schemer, arrived as part of the exchange deal. Though no Allchurch, Davies's spry football brain, sleight of foot and scoring prowess served the club well. Roy Saunders, a combative and crafty wing half from Liverpool, knew every trick in the book and had the Scouser's unshakeable belief in his own ability as well as the knack of holding his nerve at crucial moments. Llanelli-born wing half Peter Davies arrived from Arsenal as part of the transfer deal of £42,750 which took Mel Charles to Highbury. Colin Webster, a hot-headed but free-scoring centre forward came from Manchester United at a bargain fee of £6,000. Although Webster often blotted his copybook by committing egregious fouls and contesting referees' decisions, his ratio of scoring a goal in every three games for the Swans proved invaluable. Two other recruits found the net frequently. Eddie Thomas scored 21 goals in two seasons and Brayley Reynolds, signed from Cardiff, was seldom found wanting in key games. Derry-born winger Jimmy McLaughlin's natural flair, competitive skills and powerful shooting made him Morris's most expensive and long-lasting recruit, though some would argue with justification that Brian Evans, the swiftest of wingers, who was signed from Abergavenny Town for a mere £650 in the summer of 1963, was the best bargain of them all. A born showman, Noel Dwyer – a bargain buy from West Ham – proved to be as good a goalkeeper as any in Europe on his day. Less convincing were the performances of wingers Graham Williams and Ken Morgans, signed from Everton and Manchester United respectively. The former, nicknamed 'Flicka', was just as likely to exasperate as to excite fans with his elaborate tricks, and his finishing was erratic. The latter understandably never overcame the trauma of Munich and was a shadow of the player who had shown so much promise among the illustrious 'Busby Babes'.

Morris also set great store by nurturing young local players. He prided himself on being a shrewd talent-spotter and knew that this could prove to be a money-making enterprise in itself. Mike Johnson, initially an understudy to Mel Nurse, blossomed into a commanding pivot, while Roy Evans, a cultured full back, was swift and determined on the overlap. There was great sadness at the club when Evans and his colleague Brian Purcell, a robust centre half, were killed in a car accident during their playing days with Hereford United in 1969. Clydach-born Keith Todd compensated for his lack of size by showing zest and commitment in attack and by scoring hat-tricks with remarkable regularity. But the only real star to emerge in the wake of the incomparable Ivor was Herbie Williams. Herbie – as he was universally known – was the unlikeliest of soccer idols. Tall, gangling and unprepossessing, he had protruding teeth (when he wore his dentures) and had been blessed with poor eyesight (he later wore contact lenses). Yet this former dockworker was a naturally gifted and versatile player who, during a career spanning 17 years, made over 500 league appearances, scored 102 goals, and played at wing half, centre half, inside forward and centre forward. Cool and imperturbable, he had an elegant left foot, an uncanny ability to find space and deliver pinpoint passes, and a gift for scoring dazzling goals. It was almost always a pleasure to see him play and the local reporter Bill Paton never tired of praising his 'classical touches of genius'.

Broadly speaking, therefore, the achievements of Trevor Morris were twofold. First of all, he commendably assembled a largely Welsh-born squad in which local youngsters were afforded the opportunity to better themselves. When Swansea beat Fulham 2–1 at Craven Cottage on 3 January 1959, every single player had been born in Wales and eight of them were internationals. Six of the team that beat Leeds 2–1 on 21 October 1961 were products of Swansea Schools football. Grooming local talent and sprinkling the side with hard-working professionals paid dividends initially. During the 1960–1 season the team embarked on a run of 16 league games without defeat, which enabled the club to finish seventh, its highest position since 1926. Buoyed by this achievement, at the end of the season goals by Brayley Reynolds, Barrie Jones and Reg Davies in the 3–1 defeat of Bangor brought the Welsh Cup to the Vetch for the fourth time in the club's history. This opened doors to Europe and to bruising encounters against SC Motor Jena of East Germany in the European Cup Winners' Cup, a short-lived odyssey marked by vexations over dates, venues and visas, as well as a 15-hour journey by air, rail and road. Having been ordered by UEFA to play both legs on the Continent and drawn the first leg at Linz in Austria, the leg-weary Swans lost 1–5 in the second leg, played two days later at Jena. Yet they still summoned sufficient energy to delight their generally truculent hosts by singing 'Calon Lân' and 'Cwm Rhondda' at the ensuing banquet.

Secondly, by instilling into his largely home-produced team a taste for teamwork and a fighting spirit, Morris spearheaded an outstandingly successful FA Cup run during the 1963–4 season, a run which rheumy-eyed supporters still recall with great fondness. In early January 1964 lowly Barrow were brushed aside in the third round. Three weeks later, over 24,000 noisy supporters packed into the Vetch and were rewarded with four spectacular goals as Sheffield United (sporting Len Allchurch in their team) of the First Division were demolished 4–0 in the fourth round. Trevor Morris described it as 'the best result since I have been with the club' and, as the fans sang 'The Swans go marching on', the distant towers of Wembley became visible once more in their imagination. Stoke City were the next giants to fall. Although the evergreen Stanley Matthews opened the scoring on a liberally watered pitch, the youthful Swans, playing in a new strip, did not disappoint the 6,000 travelling supporters whose vociferous cheers rang loudly around the Potteries. Two extraordinary opportunist goals by that persistent gadfly Keith Todd earned Swansea a richly deserved replay. Even though Stoke recalled Peter Dobing and Dennis Viollet to their team, the visitors were overwhelmed by the sheer pace and verve of the rampant Swans. A crowd of 29,000 witnessed goals by Todd and McLaughlin which sealed the victory. The drab, mediocre performances in the league were forgotten as Swansea prepared to defy the predictions of bumptious sports correspondents in England by embarking on what became known as 'The Siege of Anfield'.

Trevor Morris convinced himself that winning the quarter-final tie against Liverpool was not impossible. Exuding an air of confidence as well as mischief, he sought to outwit his canny adversary Bill Shankly in pre-match quips and worldly wisdom. On entering Beatlesville, he declared: 'It will be a change for Liverpool to hear some good Welsh singing instead of listening to the Beatles!' A chartered plane, several special trains, dozens of buses and many more cars ferried around 10,000 supporters to Anfield to serenade their favourites. Facing a star-studded side which included Callaghan, Hunt, St John and Yeats was an intimidating prospect, and Liverpool would shortly go on to win the Championship of Division One. Never one to play down his team's chances, Bill Shankly reckoned that they would win 'by a mile' and nobody outside Wales seriously believed that Liverpool could lose the tie in front of their own supporters. But once more the Swans raised their game. Johnson marshalled the defence splendidly and some robust harrying and tackling in midfield disrupted Liverpool's rhythm. Barrie Jones and Brian Evans tormented their opposing full backs with their swift and sinuous running, and as Swansea swarmed forward the Merseysiders were forced to defend resolutely. In the 38th minute Jimmy McLaughlin scored with a sumptuous strike and four minutes later, to the disbelief of the home crowd, Eddie Thomas swept home a cross by McLaughlin.

Storming forward through the mud towards the Kop, Liverpool dominated the second half. But although Peter Thompson reduced the arrears after 63 minutes, thereafter they could find no way through the Swansea back-line. The hero of the hour was Noel Dwyer, who seemed determined to show that it is goalkeepers who win matches. On this particular Saturday he was phenomenal. His judgement in coming for crosses was impeccable and his shot-stopping was remarkable. One reporter claimed that 'it was like tossing herrings to a sea lion'. At least six of his saves were world-class and, as the former Swansea player Dai Nicholas commented: 'Never in my life have I seen anything like it.' Unsettled by Dwyer's sheer brilliance, a hapless Ronnie Moran skied a penalty kick into the stand with nine minutes remaining. Swansea clung on to record a memorable victory, prompting scenes of great jubilation among their travelling supporters and stay-at-homes glued to the radio. And when the post-match euphoria had died down, everyone's abiding memory was of Dwyer's extraordinary performance.

As we have seen, the semi-final proved to be a bridge too far for Swansea and it brought to an end the most exciting FA Cup odyssey in the history of the club. Trevor Morris was rightly proud of the achievement and no manager since then has brought Swansea closer to an FA Cup final at Wembley. But whereas Morris in Churchillian mode could inspire his charges to play above themselves in glamorous cup ties, he was unable to bring them anywhere near the point where they could challenge for promotion. During his last four seasons at the helm, the team finished 20th, 15th, 19th and 22nd. Perpetually troubled by relegation worries, the club eventually tumbled into Division Three in April 1965. Morris must bear a large part of the responsibility for that slump. Rightly or wrongly, he was regularly berated by fans for selling the team's brightest stars and for recruiting less able replacements. Crucially, at key moments he also failed to persuade the board to loosen their rein on the purse strings. Morale plummeted as free transfers were granted to loyal stalwarts like Harry Griffiths and Roy Saunders at the end of the 1963–4 season and the dressing room became a much quieter place. The club's lack of ambition was palpable and by February 1965 one correspondent described the team as 'the worst Swansea side for nearly 20 years'.

As the seasons had rolled by, Morris's tactical naivety and lack of coaching skills were increasingly exposed. He confessed that he would never be seen dead in a tracksuit and his chief coach Walter Robbins – a dead ringer for Errol Flynn – was a disciplinarian in the Frank Barson mould. Training routines were boringly repetitive to veterans and juniors alike. Clearly, too, the quality of the players coming through the youth ranks and settling into the first team was not high enough to enable them to cope with the challenges of League Two football.

Unforgivably, some outstanding talent was lost because of flaws in the scouting system. Old lessons had not been learned. How was Barrie Hole, the youngest son of Billy Hole and a former star with Swansea Schoolboys, allowed to sign for Cardiff City in September 1959? Even the ageing Jack Pickard moved more nimbly than the Swansea scouts and he confirmed his reputation as the most hated man in Swansea by enticing goalkeeper Gary Sprake of Winch Wen away to Leeds United, where he made 506 appearances and won 37 caps. Several youngsters underachieved, notably Derek Draper, a Greenhill boy whose initials and skills earned him the nickname 'Didi' and a first-team place in the 1962–3 season, but who never reached great heights as a player. It might have been expected that some of Morris's youngsters would have gone on to win many more international caps than proved to be the case. True, the competition was stiff in those days, but the fact remains that Roy Evans and Mike Johnson won only one cap each, and even the multi-gifted Herbie Williams only played for Wales on three occasions.

Trevor Morris also had the reputation of favouring journeymen rather than players with flair. His judgement was called into question in October 1964 when he signed the lumbering centre forward George Kirby from Coventry City for £13,000 at a time when the talented young Italian Giorgio Chinaglia was clamouring for an extended run in the first team. Ever the martinet, Morris saw him as a troublemaker bent on clubbing, drinking and thieving his way through life. Walter Robbins famously told him that he would end up selling ice cream in his native Italy. Chinaglia's father was so incensed by Morris's brusqueries that he threatened him with a meat cleaver. The manager's reluctance to take a chance with the likes of Chinaglia was closely associated with his calamitous decision to withdraw from the Combination League. This piece of financial expedience might have reduced costs, but it consigned up-and-coming youngsters either to being brutally clogged by cynical defenders in the Welsh League or becoming used to coasting to victory against vastly inferior opposition. As a result, many of Morris's protégés were ill-prepared for the gruelling grind of life in Division Two.

Attendances also dipped appreciably during Morris's period in charge. On his appointment the average seasonal gate was 14,162, but when relegation became a reality in 1964–5 it had fallen to 10,467. This malaise, however, was common to most clubs. Soccer was no longer the only, or even the prime, attraction on Saturdays. Former supporters preferred to pursue other family-based leisure activities or to loll in front of a television. The proliferation of motor cars and better public transport meant that people were more mobile, more choosy and less willing to endure the inconveniences of a dump like the Vetch. Even when newly installed floodlights were officially opened before a friendly match against Hibernian on 10 October 1960, many of those who turned up were more interested in whether the lights would last the game than in the result. In the event, the teams shared eight goals and the lights shone brightly and kindly throughout. As usual, fair-weather fans returned on big-match occasions, often trebling the average gate, but general disapproval of the board and the manager was plain to see. During the 1962–3 season, derisive slow hand-clapping regularly broke out on the terraces and at a meeting of the shareholders in December 1962 Tom Griffiths, a former schoolmaster, launched a blistering attack on the board: 'The only thing that can save the club from degradation is a wind of change to sweep away the board of management, and replace it with young, virile men whose outlook on life is more progressive.' The voice of dissent could not be silenced and a pressure group, led by a local businessman Denzil Davies, a solicitor Malcolm Struel and former player Tom Kiley, forcibly expressed their lack of confidence in the board and reminded them of the unhappy fate of Accrington Stanley.

In the end, the directors refused to budge, but once the club was relegated on 24 April 1965, following a spell of 15 years in Division Two, they decided that it was time to part company with the manager. So ended the seven-year stint of one of the most flamboyant and outspoken managers in the history of the club. That impish rascal Giorgio Chinaglia reckoned that Morris was 'a public relations man' rather than a thinker about the game. He may well have been right. Nevertheless, things were about to take a turn for the worse.

'How will the Swans fare in the Third Division?' was the question posed by the *South Wales Evening Post* on the eve of the 1965–6 season. Much would depend on the financial state of the club and its ability to attract new funds at a time when Swansea itself was experiencing a modernization programme. The non-ferrous, steel and tinplate works in the region were swiftly being replaced by manufacturing works located in the Fforest-fach Industrial Estate or the Ford Motor Company at Jersey Marine, and there were new service jobs available at the Land Registry or the Driver Vehicle Licensing Centre at Clase. Local boosters depicted Swansea as 'the developing town of diverse industries'. Local pride may therefore have prompted the board to appoint its first Swansea-born manager. Glyn Davies was a product of the Alice Street factory of footballing stars in Cwmbwrla and a former player. Still only 33, he arrived in July 1965 fresh from a short but productive apprenticeship as player-manager of Yeovil Town. Buoyed by the inspiring presence of Ivor Allchurch, who had been signed for £8,000 from Cardiff City, Davies promised a return to the days when Swansea played open, stylish football. Lifelong cynics wondered whether this would prove to be the case. After all, Davies had burned on a short fuse as a player and had gained a reputation as a merciless tackler rather than a skilful tactician. Moreover, his assistant Tommy Casey, an Irish international, had the abrasive style of a fitness fanatic.

In the event, Swansea made a disastrous start to the season. A series of shambolic displays led to some of the worst results in living memory. Those who witnessed the 1–6 thrashing at the hands of bottom-of-the-table Workington Town were filled with a deep sense of foreboding. Given the chance to salvage their dignity in the return fixture at Workington, the players meekly succumbed to a 0–7 defeat. Davies shuffled his side so often that he became known as 'Mr Maverick'. By mid-October the team had lost seven consecutive away games, scored two goals and conceded 26. But both Davies and Casey were hard taskmasters and, although relegation worries persisted until the final weeks of the season, sheer fitness and a readiness to fight for every ball helped the team to survive. Nevertheless, a pugnacious spirit was not enough to keep the supporters happy. Hand-to-mouth tactics and erratic performances meant that the team conceded a massive 96 goals over the season. The only consolation was victory over Chester in the Welsh Cup final following a play-off at Sealand Road, but an aggregate 1–5 defeat to Slavia Sofia of Bulgaria in the Cup Winners' Cup early in the following season was a graphic reminder that Swansea were unfit to grace the stadiums of Europe.

Much of the damage of course had been done during the latter years of Trevor Morris's stewardship and Glyn Davies was forced to work within such tight financial parameters that he simply could not afford to buy top-class players. His best recruit was probably Vic Gomersall from Manchester City. A muscular full back with thighs like railway sleepers, Gomersall liked galloping forward and his wholehearted commitment was in sharp contrast to the attitude of some of the gauche and rebellious younger players at the club. By the mid-1960s the habits and lifestyles of youngsters were changing. While Swansea could not boast the same dizzy array of attractions as London, it was impossible for its teenagers to ignore the cultural effects of the new spirit of permissiveness and toleration. The so-called 'youth culture' embraced rock and pop music, heavy drinking, drugs and casual promiscuity. As a result, many young apprentices at the Vetch were more self-indulgent and restive than their forebears had been, less likely to respect authority, and more reluctant to spend long hours practising their skills.

The most red-blooded scallywag was Giorgio Chinaglia.

Trevor Morris had not handled the unruly teenager well and the heavy-handed response of Davies to the Italian hell-raiser made matters worse. According to the apprentice goalkeeper John Black, Davies's man-management skills were 'nil', but even a saint could not have turned a blind eye to the serious breaches of discipline committed by Chinaglia. Eventually, he was given a free transfer. In future years it amused him to recall Davies's parting shot: 'You'll never make it in professional soccer.' Three years later Chinaglia joined Lazio for £140,000, went on to represent Italy in the 1974 World Cup and eventually to play for New York Cosmos in the company of Pelé and Beckenbauer. The staggering irony is that no player in the entire history of Swansea City Football Club made as much money as the young tearaway from Tuscany.

Even though Glyn Davies had a full summer to prepare his team for the 1966–7 season, it soon became clear that he was unable to get the best out of his admittedly limited (Allchurch excepted) players. His tactics, too, were either bewildering or lamentable. Since the club was carrying a bank overdraft of £30,000 and was still laden with debts, there was no prospect of strengthening a team which evidently lacked confidence. Early elimination from the Football League Cup and the European Cup Winners' Cup, as well as a disastrous sequence of league results, forced the board to sack Davies and Casey on 28 October 1966. Lack of funds had meant that the Cwmbwrla man had been obliged to keep faith either with players who had seen better days or callow youths who were incapable of playing consistently well. The old maestro Joe Sykes was thus called in to work his magic once more, but by Christmas the club was languishing just above Workington Town at the foot of the table. Inexplicably, the board failed to make an immediate appointment and the chairman, Phillip Holden, was lambasted for lack of due diligence. One correspondent described the directors as 'fossils, barnacle-encrusted hulks incapable of real drive and initiative'. Few outside the boardroom disagreed.

Eventually the directors bestirred themselves and by

mid-February a safer pair of hands was in post. Former player Billy Lucas was now 45 and had 14 years' experience under his belt as manager of Newport County. It is hard to understand why he accepted a post which held out such little prospect of success. Mulish directors were unwilling to admit to the board more progressive candidates with funds at the ready. There was no money to buy good players and supporters were deserting the cause in alarming numbers. But, unlike his fiery predecessor, once in post Lucas seldom lost his cool, even though he knew in his heart that there was little hope of avoiding relegation. He brought to the dressing room a sense of honesty and commitment. He was well liked by the players and, even though he recognized their weaknesses, he never spoke ill of them. He gained the genuine respect of the fans, some of whom fondly remembered his sterling service as a player under McCandless. But although he instilled a fighting spirit into the team, with the old fox Ivor Allchurch and a bulldozing young centre forward from Abercynon called John Roberts leading by example, it was not enough to stave off the inevitable. The damage had been done long before Lucas arrived and, humiliatingly, by the end of the season Swansea Town had been relegated to Division Four. The directors, having lost any semblance of credibility, doggedly refused offers of help from members of the pressure group led by Malcolm Struel and there was a genuine fear that a further slide, perhaps to oblivion, would follow.

With Harry Griffiths back at his side as coach, chief scout and loyal lieutenant, Lucas stiffened the resolve of senior players and also blooded local youngsters. Among the latter were Geoff Thomas, a gifted midfielder from Hafod who was the kind of player that might have become a genuine star had he been playing in a successful side; Carl Slee, a robust defender from the Sandfields area; Willie Screen, a tiny midfielder from Winch Wen who, in modern parlance, worked his socks off in every game; Clive Slattery, a fast and tricky winger from St Thomas; and David Gwyther, a powerful striker from

Pen-clawdd. Significantly, however, none of these went on to win full international honours. They were useful players, but no more than that, and on many occasions they found it hard to cope with the rigours of highly competitive games in the lowest division of the Football League.

But such was the gloom that pervaded the Vetch that to be drawn at home against Arsenal in the fifth round of the FA Cup came like manna from heaven. Greybeards recalled the club's success against the Gunners in 1926 and six of that team were invited to lunch when the game was held on 17 February 1968. Fearing the worst, the Swansea-born comedian Harry Secombe offered to play in goal on the perfectly reasonable grounds that his ample frame would fill every available space between the goalposts. Ironically, the goalposts themselves came under attack overnight. It being rag week, dimwits who passed for students at the university sawed through both goalposts at the east end of the ground. Unfazed, the groundsman Syd Tucker hurriedly bandaged them together to the satisfaction of the referee and the record crowd of 32,796 that had packed into the old ground long before the first whistle. Swansea played with great tenacity, but a header by Bobby Gould in the 56th minute secured victory for the Londoners. A week later, only some 5,000 supporters turned up to watch the team beat Notts County at the Vetch. Within a year, in the corresponding fixture the crowd had dwindled to a meagre 1,984.

At times Billy Lucas must have felt that the Gods had resolved never to smile on Swansea Town again. During the early hours of 7 March 1968 the east section of the centre stand was razed to the ground by fire. Flames leaping as high as 20 metres forced the emergency services to evacuate nearby homes, and the damage to the club's premises – the dressing rooms, the boot room, the physiotherapy room and the offices – was estimated at £40,000. For the remainder of the season, teams changed in the headquarters of the nearby Territorial Army building before emerging on to the field, in traditional strip rather than camouflage, from a tunnel located under the old enclosure.

There was also a tear-laden finale to the season. The board disgraced itself by offering Ivor Allchurch, who had scored 21 league and cup goals over the season, a one-year contract on a reduced salary. Even at 38, Allchurch had outshone his teammates in most games and, without him, the club would not have finished in 15th place. The directors' crassness caused a sensation, though Allchurch rejected their offer with good grace and duly turned up in fine fettle for a testimonial match held in his honour on 25 May. Leeds United, still celebrating after winning the Football League Cup, brought their stars to the Vetch to pay their own homage. Eyes misted over among the best part of 20,000 people, who witnessed for the last time the Golden Boy's peerless skills on his home-town pitch. Some three weeks later, another poignant note was struck when long-standing servant Joe Sykes retired at the age of 71. Ivor and Joe had exemplified all that was noble and good both on and off the football field, and true Swansea supporters mourned their departure so deeply that it felt like a twin bereavement.

Working on a shoestring budget, Billy Lucas found it hard to rally his troops during the 1968–9 season. Some of them, sensing that the future was bleak, sought pastures new. Brian Hughes, one of the club's most dependable defenders, joined Atlanta Chiefs – a far cry from the Vetch – in January. By March, Lucas himself no longer had the stomach for the task and left in order to pursue his business interests. Once again the club had reached a critical crossroads in its history. Then, as summer approached, two decisive events brought hopes of a revival. Disaffection with the way in which the club was being run had become widespread. Sensing the public mood, Malcolm Struel, who had long argued that the club's supine directors were unfit for purpose, assembled a robust business consortium that called loudly for root-and-branch reform. The increasingly infirm chairman, Phillip Holden, who had found it difficult to cope with the financial consequences of the abolition of the maximum wage for players, poor results and falling gate receipts, relinquished control to the consortium which duly promised to bring fresh energy as well as much-needed funds into the club.

The second turning point was the fulfilment of a long-standing ambition of leading townspeople: that the town be granted parity with Cardiff by becoming a city. When the announcement was made in December 1969, it was generally greeted with great interest and excitement. Some diehards among the fans were understandably reluctant to jettison the traditional nomenclature, but the strong sense of local identity as well as a burning desire to compete with Cardiff persuaded them of the value of supporting the newly christened Swansea City. Dislike of the Bluebirds had intensified during the 1960s, partly as a result of the absurd behaviour of the Ninian Park directors before a Welsh Cup quarter-final on 2 February 1960. Because the Welsh FA had refused to re-schedule the date, in a fit of pique Cardiff fielded a reserve team at the Vetch and their directors refused an invitation to join their counterparts in the boardroom. During a bad-tempered game, in which players tore into challenges, boots and elbows flew, and fights broke out, three players were sent off and Cardiff were subsequently fined 350 guineas for failing to select their strongest side. In subsequent derbies, scuffles broke out on the terraces and, as Swansea's plight in the league worsened, Jacks did not take kindly to hearing the chant 'Swansea Town are Falling Down'.

The first priority of the reconstituted board was to inject new funds into the coffers and appoint a new manager. The carrot dangled before prospective applicants was a startlingly large annual salary of £5,000. By this stage, recent experience had convinced the directors that there was nothing to be gained from appointing another former Swansea player. In their view, the priority was a tracksuited manager, preferably a high-profile candidate from England, and on 7 August 1969 Roy Bentley, a former England international centre forward with a reputation for goal-scoring derring-do with Chelsea, was installed at the Vetch. That he had once scored a hat-trick against Wales in 1954 was not held against him. Nor was the fact that, as manager of Reading since 1963, he had failed to fulfil his well-publicized aim of lifting them out of Division Three.

An avowed disciplinarian, Bentley was shocked by the air of listlessness and gloom at the Vetch, and the players soon discovered that this son of a bare-fist fighter was not a man to trifle with. He immediately instituted afternoon as well as morning training sessions, and regularly played a full part in practice matches. Once the season was under way, he read the riot act to goalkeeper Anthony (Tony) Horace Millington, a Welsh international who had just joined from Peterborough and who would become a great favourite at the Vetch, not least because he was living proof that all goalkeepers inhabit a different planet from the rest of humankind. Millington used to converse animatedly with the crowd behind the goal, swap sweets with them, and celebrate a Swansea goal by hanging from the crossbar or by performing handstands. Bentley marked him out as 'one of the game's natural clowns' and ordered him to knuckle down, lose two stones in weight and rediscover his form in the reserves. The dressing down had the desired effect and cases of sloppy indiscipline by the goalkeeper and his colleagues swiftly disappeared.

Probably the kindest thing to say about the team which Bentley assembled in his first season is that it was unspectacularly effective. His stratagem was straightforward enough: once the ball was lost, forwards were expected to funnel back and defend stoutly. It was not 'the Swansea way', but at least Bentley ensured that the team was fit and ready to run tirelessly. The blend of youth and experience worked well. Although Len Allchurch, now in his second spell at the club, was no longer to be seen in headlong flight down the wing, he still had an eye for the telling pass. As always, Mel Nurse, who had rejoined the club from Swindon, was an unyielding obstacle in defence, while bread-and-butter players like Geoff

Thomas toiled away fruitfully. David Gwyther ploughed his energy-sapping way through muddy pitches and Brian Evans still made brave sorties down the left flank. At the very least, Bentley hoped that endeavour and teamwork would mask some of the technical deficiencies in the side. Results certainly improved, the crowds began to return (the average home attendance in 1969–70 was 8,386) and Bentley repaid the board's faith in him by securing promotion in his first season.

But life once more in Division Three provided a stiffer test. Despite the inspired goalkeeping of Millington – Bill Paton reckoned that 'any adjective seems superfluous to describe some of his saves' – as well as the guile and experience of Barrie Hole, newly signed from Aston Villa for a record £20,000 fee, and the seemingly ageless skills of Herbie Williams, the team failed to finish higher than 11th in 1971 and 14th in 1972. The retirement of the younger Allchurch and Nurse were grievous blows and the record fee of £26,000 paid to Coventry City for the international winger Ronnie Rees failed to bring dividends. At the last home game against Chesterfield on 22 April 1972, a miserable crowd of 2,887 watched in silence as Swansea lost 1–3 and another season of mediocrity petered out. Over two seasons, Bentley had muddled along, confusing his players with his selections and blooding too many ill-prepared youngsters. No one could detect any signs of tactical coherence and, as the players were encouraged to try 'up-and-under' tactics, they lost faith in the manager. Bemused by this turn in his fortunes, Bentley was dismissed in mid-October 1972, by which time Malcolm Struel had replaced David Goldstone as chairman.

Having accused his predecessors in the 1960s of wilful ineptitude, by some extraordinary oversight Struel made what turned out to be a catastrophic appointment. In recruiting the handsome Ulsterman Harry Gregg, the former Manchester United goalkeeper who had survived the trauma of the Munich air crash, Struel believed that he was appointing a heroic figure who would command the respect of the players and the admiration of the fans. But goalkeepers seldom make good managers and over the next three years Swansea found itself saddled with a Rambo-like figure whose outlook on the game was as far removed as possible from the club's traditional style of play. Relegation was already looming when Gregg was appointed on 8 November and, desperate for points, he instructed his team to treat their opponents to a physical battering. He insisted that this was no time for neat passing football or for namby-pambies wearing kid-gloves and fancy pants. Fearful that the game was losing its 'manliness', he warned his players against the kind of silky skills practised 'by a bunch of fairies' on the Continent. As a result and probably for the first time in its history, the club was accused of resorting to 'rough-house tactics'. At Walsall in February 1973 the referee awarded 43 free kicks against Swansea, and a month later six players were booked against Blackburn. Despite, or perhaps because of, the x-rated tackles and the use of every unsavoury trick in the book, relegation duly came to pass.

Thereafter it became difficult for supporters to fathom the decision-making of the manager. On the one hand, he was eager to give youth its head. Alan Curtis, the Rhondda-born nephew of Roy Paul, was given an extended run in which he demonstrated excellent dribbling skills, speed of thought and goal-scoring prowess. Swansea-born Robbie James (or Robert, as he was then called) made his debut at 15 and impressed with his delicate touches, subtle passing and thunderous shooting. Gregg admired Willie Screen's wholehearted endeavour and he signed Pat Lally, a skilful, bearded Londoner who liked to orchestrate play. Goalkeepers brought in on loan made a favourable impression. Jimmy Rimmer, borrowed from Manchester United, was a revelation, and Dai Davies, a youngster from Ammanford, returned from Everton to learn more about the art of goalkeeping under Gregg than at any other point in his career. These were promising assets. Paradoxically, however, Gregg also decided that the rest of his players should kick their way out of Division Four. A boxing devotee, he had always been good with his fists. Young apprentices quivered in his presence and old hands needed to be nimble to avoid flying teacups at half-time. To add to the air of fear and trembling, Gregg signed two snarling rottweilers in defenders Micky Evans and Paul Bevan, whose technical bankruptcy was matched by their ability to perpetrate some of the crudest fouls ever seen on the Vetch. The bang-thud-bang treatment brought out the worst in Wyndham Evans, a Llanelli-born defender who, under Gregg, surpassed even his own exacting standards as a late tackler. Doubtless he would have argued that he was simply obeying the instructions of his bellowing manager and, to his credit, over the years Evans became one of the most versatile, loyal and best-loved members of the playing staff. Indeed, he played in all four divisions for the Swans.

As Gregg psyched up his players by urging them to get their retaliation in first, many games degenerated into brawls. The Christmas spirit was wholly absent at Gillingham in December 1973 when Paul Bevan was sent off, Wyndham Evans was booked and Gregg cautioned. During an ill-tempered affair at Darlington in August 1974 the youngster Steve Thomas, having evidently learned something from his manager, was sent off for punching an opponent. Cynics sometimes wondered why Gregg neglected to arm his players with swords or machine guns. Appalled by this disgraceful lack of discipline, the Swansea supporters squirmed with embarrassment, especially when opponents exacted retribution on innocent youngsters like Curtis and James. Most remarkable of all, Malcolm Struel was mystified that a club which he believed had a catchment area of 600,000 (surely an exaggerated figure) could only command gates of under 3,000. The answer was plain to see. Fans were so shocked by the transformation in style and behaviour at the Vetch that they no longer bothered to turn up. Under Gregg's watch, the club registered the lowest home attendance in its entire history – 1,301 against Northampton Town on 18 September 1973. The swiftly emptying terraces were also becoming unsafe. The hail of abuse and obscene chants emanating from the North Bank were unwelcome developments, and the only comfort was that the swathe of empty spaces on the terraces meant that the authorities were easily able to identify so-called 'skinheads and such-like yobs' and remove them from the ground.

Abysmal performances in the league were hard to bear, but losing to minnows in cup competitions was unforgivable. Under Gregg, it became a habit. A first-round FA Cup defeat at the hands of tiny Margate in 1972 was followed two years later by another humiliation in the same round, this time after a replay at Kettering, during which tempers boiled over on and off the field. Rather than shaking hands at the end, Gregg and Ron Atkinson, the Kettering manager, laid into each other behind locked doors. Nor was the Welsh Cup immune from such unexpected setbacks. In 1973 non-league Stourbridge came to the Vetch in the fourth round and dispatched the hosts with aplomb. The fact that Stourbridge was not even in Wales made the pill even harder to swallow.

The sense of relief was palpable when Harry Gregg, who had tarnished the club's reputation so badly, took up the managerial reins at Crewe in January 1975. Another Harry – the old stalwart Harry Griffiths – was belatedly drafted in as caretaker manager. Had the board appointed him five or even ten years earlier, they might well have saved themselves a considerable amount of money and a good deal of heartache. Griffiths immediately put a smile on the players' faces and curbed the appalling disciplinary record of the club. But the colossal damage wrought by Gregg meant that the club finished in the bottom four. Swansea City had reached the nadir of its fortunes and Griffiths, with the club secretary Gordon Daniels, was forced to spend the summer persuading clubs in the Football League to endorse Swansea's bid for re-election. It was a deeply humiliating ordeal but, fortunately, the club was reprieved. Storm clouds over the future of the club were also lifted when Malcolm Struel negotiated a highly favourable deal with Swansea City Council by which the club transferred the freehold of the Vetch to the Council in return for a sum of £50,000 and an additional grant of £150,000 to remove the club's massive overdraft. The football club had survived, it had a pitch to play on, and a manager who was described by his protégé Alan Curtis as a man who had 'a huge heart and an immense love for his home-town club'. Things could only get better.

5

Tosh

John Benjamin Toshack has a *curriculum vitae* which other players and managers can only fantasize about. He made his debut for Cardiff City at 16, scored 100 goals for them, and won three Welsh Cup medals. In November 1970 Bill Shankly, manager of Liverpool, signed him for £110,000 and over eight seasons he scored 96 goals, won three First Division championship medals, two UEFA cup medals, an FA Cup medal, and a European Cup medal. He won 40 Welsh caps and scored 13 goals. In 1978 he joined Swansea City as player-manager and over four seasons wrought such a transformation that the club found itself battling against the giants of the First Division. Under his leadership the club also won three consecutive Welsh Cup finals. When he left in 1983 he became a citizen of the world, managing clubs in five different countries. With great distinction he filled the managerial hot seat at Sporting Lisbon, Real Sociedad (three times), Real Madrid (twice), Deportivo de La Coruña, Beşiktaş, Saint-Étienne, Catania and Real Murcia. He also managed Wales twice, briefly in 1994 and more extensively from 2004 to 2010. At the time of writing he is the manager of FYR Macedonia. By any standards, this constitutes a glittering career. For our purposes, however, his most sensational achievement was to preside over the rejuvenation of Swansea City, guiding it from a moribund Division Four into the highest stratum of the Football League in just four magical seasons. To this day, Toshack remains the most stunningly successful manager in the history of the club.

As his mentor, the legendary Bill Shankly, put it: 'What John Toshack has achieved at Swansea is a miracle. No man in the game will ever match it again.'

The appointment of Toshack as player-manager in late February 1978 took everyone by surprise. It came about following a serendipitous chain of events. Troubled by a long-term thigh injury, Toshack was eager to return to his former club in some coaching capacity, but Cardiff showed little interest. In contrast, when Malcom Struel saw the opportunity to win over the Anfield icon he immediately impressed Toshack with his drive and ambition. Liverpool waived the transfer fee and by St David's Day Toshack was at his desk. He was just 28. The appointment shocked many supporters. Without managerial or coaching experience, did he have the necessary skills and vision to lift Swansea out of the bottom division? Would hard-core Jacks, steeped as they were in the poetry of Dylan Thomas, warm to the doggerel published in the new manager's anthology of poems *Gosh it's Tosh* (1976), a collection which lived up to its title? Moreover, what did a Canton-born man know of Swansea's traditions and values? Most of all, why was the club embarking on a foolhardy gamble at a time when the current manager Harry Griffiths was steadily building an attractive and successful team?

Following the ignominy of having to apply for re-election to the Football League in 1975, James Henry (Harry) Griffiths had brought dignity and respect back to the club. With his red mane, long sideburns and toothy grin, he was a familiar and much-loved figure in the city. Supporters appreciated his devotion to his home-town club and his burning desire to see it prosper. The players adored him. Full of energy, warmth and enthusiasm, he had excellent motivational powers and, as a natural mimic and joker, he lightened the mood in the dressing room following the unpleasantness of the Gregg era. Behind the jokey manner, however, lurked a touch of steel. He needed it, since he was expected to work within the tightest of budgets and one of the lowest salary scales in the Football League. With only 15 full-time professionals at his disposal, his freedom of manoeuvre was severely restricted. But there was something of the romantic in Harry Griffiths and, at a time when most clubs still sported a 'Nobby', a 'Chopper' or a 'Bite yer Legs', he was determined to restore Swansea's reputation for adventurous, free-flowing football. Under his stewardship, supporters turned up in growing numbers at the Vetch to witness exhilarating forward play and some thrilling goals.

In building a team, Griffiths placed his faith in the young and they, in turn, gave him unqualified respect and trust. Three attacking musketeers became his principal assets. The richly creative skills of Alan Curtis (who lodged at Griffiths's home) blossomed swiftly. Curtis was light on his feet, had a quick eye, a gloriously varied passing range and the ability to score stunning goals. The strong, forceful style of Robbie James was also a powerful asset. Surging forward from midfield, he had a lethal shot in both feet and good aerial ability. These two forged an excellent understanding with Jeremy Charles, Mel's son, whose gifts as a striker included a decent first touch and soaring headers at the far post. In defence, too, the young Port Tennant centre half Nigel Stevenson, universally known as 'Speedy', was blooded and, like the others, would go on to win Welsh caps.

To support these thrillingly talented youths, Griffiths relied on veterans like Wyndham Evans and Dave Bruton. He also put new heart into the club by signing steely, experienced players like George Smith, a blond Geordie who came on a free transfer from Cardiff in May 1975. Appointed captain, he donned the mantle of the midfield general and, by precept and example, brought leadership and drive to the team. Eddie May, a streetwise stopper from Wrexham, stiffened a leaky defence, Les Chappell, a gritty midfielder from Doncaster, brought greater thrust to the engine room, and Mickey Conway, the trickiest of wingers, arrived from Brighton at a bargain price of £2,000. Slowly but surely, Griffiths fashioned a team which was well worth watching. The financial situation began to improve and the general feel-good factor was reflected when a mid-June rock concert in 1976 starred The Who, whose smash hits entranced a sun-kissed, gyrating crowd of 25,000 fans at the Vetch. Although an abysmal away record during the 1975–6 season had mystified supporters and angered the board of directors, there was every reason to believe that the exciting alliance of youth and experience would pay rich dividends very shortly.

Ever the optimist, Griffiths placed his faith in attack and during the 1976–7 season the Swansea faithful were treated to some of the most adventurous, high goal-scoring games in the entire history of the club. Until Christmas, however, the prospects were gloomy. A stuttering start, a slump in form, poor away results, and defeat at the hands of non-league Minehead in the FA Cup, boded ill, but by the end of the calendar year the club was still only five points behind leaders Bradford City. During the scramble for promotion in the latter half of the season, there were spectacular goals aplenty, heroic comebacks (including four goals in a 14-minute purple patch to secure a 4–4 draw at home to Stockport on 22 March) and countless defensive errors. Some of the remarkable goals scored by Curtis, Charles and James had the crowds purring with pleasure. In the end, however, brittle defending and the smallness of the injury-ravaged squad cost the club dearly. In the penultimate match against rivals Watford at the Vetch, a silent crowd of over 10,000 witnessed the worst defensive display under Griffiths's stewardship. The 1–4 defeat had serious consequences for the manager. Several directors lost faith in his methods and there was a growing feeling that his coaching skills and tactical knowledge, as well as those of his assistant Roy Saunders, were deficient. In several respects, it could be argued that Griffiths had worked wonders on such a tiny budget. His team had scored 92 goals – the highest total of any club in the Football League – and the gifted threesome (Curtis, Charles and James) had bagged 51 of them.

One point short of promotion and an average seasonal

attendance of 5,315 was arguably an extremely respectable achievement. But the chastening experience of watching goalkeeper Stephen Potter retrieving the 84 league goals conceded from his own net was deeply unsettling, not least for chairman Malcolm Struel. Not even the joyous news that the club had made a profit of £12,221 – its first for 13 years – over the season was enough to mollify Struel and his fellow directors. Following a run of poor results in the early part of the 1977–8 season Harry Griffiths – to great public outrage – agreed to stand down on 28 October. Disgruntled supporters vented their anger loudly. One irate 'Regular Small Bank Supporter' enquired of the chairman: 'Why the panic, Mr Struel? Is your memory that bad that you cannot remember the success of Harry Griffiths and Roy Saunders who, in their short managerial career together, turned a team of "cloggers" into a team the city was proud of, not only by scoring goals but also by fair play.'

Characteristically, Griffiths agreed to continue in a caretaker role until Struel appointed the 'young, tracksuited manager' he was hoping to recruit. Knowing that their manager had always served the club with undeviating loyalty and had earned their affection as few managers could, the players responded by raising their game. A month after being relieved of his duties, Griffiths was reinstated, though it soon became clear in the New Year that the board had by no means abandoned its search for a successor. The names of several possible candidates were bandied about, but Colin Addison refused to be prised from Newport County and Eddie McCreadie, the former Chelsea manager, preferred the challenge of guiding the fortunes of Memphis Rogues in Tennessee. Once the opportunity arose, Malcolm Struel wasted no time in beginning negotiations with the tall Cardiffian who had become a hero to the Anfield Kop and had played such a significant role in the all-conquering Liverpool team that had dominated European football from 1973 onwards. John Toshack had learned his trade under Bill Shankly and Bob Paisley, two of the shrewdest managers of the day, and Struel was convinced that if Swansea was to punch its weight as a football city it needed a dynamic and intelligent leader at the helm. He believed that Toshack could take the club a long way and promised him the substantial financial support which he had denied his predecessor. It was time for a fresh start, though Toshack, anxious to win over sceptical supporters and also to benefit from the wisdom of an old friend, insisted that Harry Griffiths should serve as his assistant, an offer which the latter gladly accepted.

During the latter stages of the season an air of anticipation enveloped the Vetch. The youngest manager in the club's history was in charge, ticket sales were rocketing, and fresh energy was coursing through the squad of players. Toshack immediately embarked on a policy of all-out attack. He believed that promotion was not out of the question and called on his players to defend resolutely, pass the ball swiftly and creatively, and create a sense of excitement by scoring an abundance of goals. In a very short space of time, he brought a sense of purpose and self-belief to the club. A proud and ambitious young man, he had a statement to make and the players duly responded in his first match in charge. Before an expectant crowd of 15,000, Swansea earned a hard-fought 3–3 draw against top-of-the-table Watford at the Vetch. With 15 games to play, the dream of promotion was still alive.

A maximum return of six points from three fixtures over Easter catapulted the team into fourth place. On 1 April the Swans, thanks to hat-tricks by Curtis and Robbie James, made fools of Hartlepool to the tune of 8–0, the biggest league win since Bradford City were trounced 8–1 in February 1936. Showing greater discipline and making fewer unforced errors than before, the team brushed aside Southport and rivals Brentford. Defeat at Northampton increased the pressure and, with two home matches remaining, victories in each were required to gain promotion. Calamitously, however, on the morning of the penultimate match against Scunthorpe on 25 April, Harry Griffiths suddenly collapsed while treating

Les Chappell in the physiotherapy room and died as a result of the heart attack on his way to Singleton Hospital. He was just 47. As a distraught Toshack put it: 'If ever a man died for a football club then that man was Harry Griffiths.' The tearful young turks in the team, who had grown to love him as a father, were spurred on to defeat Scunthorpe 3–1 before an anguished crowd of 12,228 spectators for whom Griffiths had been the authentic 'Mr Swansea'. Only Halifax now stood between the club and promotion from the basement league. On Saturday, 29 April, an expectant crowd of 16,130 assembled at the Vetch to cheer the side to victory over Halifax. The new gaffer did not disappoint them, scoring a 68th-minute goal with a Beckham-style free kick which swerved past the defensive wall. Then, with four minutes left, Alan Curtis sealed the victory. Harry Griffiths could rest easily in his grave in the knowledge that he had laid the groundwork for John Toshack's successful bid for promotion.

Toshack set his sights high. He exuded the air of a man with much loftier ambitions than the average fan at the Vetch. He viewed his early success as simply a springboard to greater things and over the following three seasons the meteoric rise of Swansea City continued. He saw no reason why the club could not be a force in Europe as well as in the upper echelons of the First Division. One of Bill Shankly's one-liners – 'If you're second, you're nothing' – had etched itself on his mind and he was determined to rid the club of the sense of inferiority and unworthiness which had dogged its progress for so long. He had no illusions about the difficulties he faced and he knew that he was bound to make enemies along the way, but he genuinely believed that glorious triumphs lay ahead.

Before turning to the excitements of the promotion bids which took Swansea into the top flight almost in fairy-tale fashion, something must be said about the factors which transformed the fortunes of the club. First of all, appointing Toshack was undoubtedly a master stroke. Malcolm Struel clearly believed that Swansea needed a charismatic young leader in charge, but even he could not have predicted how successfully Toshack would blossom in his first post as manager. The mood at the Vetch changed almost overnight. 'Everyone in Swansea is talking soccer', claimed the *South Wales Evening Post*. For such a young man, Toshack carried immense authority. Mike Smith, the Wales team manager, had already marked him out as a thoughtful student of the game and as one with tactical awareness far beyond his years. Although he had left school with only two 'O' level certificates, he was deeply intelligent and astute. At Liverpool he was respected rather than loved by his colleagues, largely because he was something of a lone wolf. The babble and banter of the dressing room did not appeal to him and he was very much his own man. Members of the fabled boot room at Anfield, however, recognized his keen football brain and Toshack benefited greatly from their collective wisdom. As a result, he grew up with good habits which stood him in good stead on his return to south Wales.

There was a proud and stubborn streak in John Toshack. Like many self-absorbed men, he was hypersensitive to criticism and had an inflated view of his own abilities. He was determined to do things his own way and ensure that no one stepped on his toes or refused to do what was asked of him. His predecessor had been too close to the players and Toshack did not make the same mistake. He laid down hard disciplinary rules and acted ruthlessly whenever players consistently underperformed or became troublemakers. Even the most experienced players sometimes felt the rough edge of his tongue and he was never reluctant to criticize them in public, a trait which led to several private spats. There were several blazing rows with errant strikers when Toshack sarcastically reminded them that 'the posts don't move'. He surprised the boo-boys on the North Bank by vigorously defending the performance of goalkeeper Dai Davies, who was prone to make inexplicable blunders, and he was no stranger to dust-ups with the Football Association of Wales and the local press. In the match programme on 15 September 1979 Toshack maintained that the *South Wales*

Evening Post consistently misquoted him, was indifferent to the progress of the club, and was not to be trusted, charges which the editor robustly refuted. Both parties refused to yield an inch and some time passed before relations were repaired. Toshack had learned from Bill Shankly never to concede defeat or let it become a habit. No manager of Swansea City was less likely to suffer fools gladly.

Sometimes he misread situations and inadvertently annoyed both the board and supporters, The first league game involving Swansea after the death of Bill Shankly on 29 September 1981 was at Anfield. Toshack, who had been one of the pall-bearers at the funeral, lined up alongside his players before the minute's silence and paid his own personal tribute by peeling off his black tracksuit top to reveal a red Liverpool number 10 jersey. Following the predictably ill-tempered game, Toshack was sharply criticized by many supporters for what they believed to be his misplaced loyalty to Liverpool at the expense of his employers and loyal fans. While Toshack's gesture was probably misguided, no great harm was done and most fair-minded people acknowledged the manager's special relationship with Shankly and that something in him had also died when the great man passed away.

Perhaps the strongest of Toshack's assets was his tactical awareness. He had not only gained a sound footballing education at Anfield but had also become receptive to innovations from abroad. By using different styles of play and adjusting his tactics according to the strengths of the opposition, he kept his players mentally alert. There was nothing one-dimensional about his teams and, as he introduced better training methods and worked on different shapes on the pitch, the tactical appreciation of his players improved appreciably. Tommy Smith, not unexpectedly perhaps, believed that Toshack used to overanalyse, but most players benefited from having a thinker in charge. He employed *catenaccio* whenever he felt the need to have a spare man at the back, and even selected himself as a sweeper on occasions. Towards the end of the

1978–9 season he flummoxed the Blackpool management by playing on the left side of midfield. He revelled in pitting his wits against rival managers like Terry Venables. When Swansea played star-studded Crystal Palace on three occasions in a third-round FA Cup tie in January 1980 Toshack outwitted Venables by adopting a different tactical formation in each game and, after an enthralling trilogy, won the day. Set plays were honed to perfection and were often designed to maximize the aerial prowess of Toshack himself and Alan Waddle. Most of all, however, Toshack's teams played with attacking flair. Full backs were urged to overlap and to join clusters of attacking forwards who played the creative and adventurous kind of football that had always been part of 'the Swansea way'.

Toshack's professional approach, his handling of team selection, appreciation of tactics and eye for detail were critical to the club's success. So, too, was his habit of acting dramatically and decisively at key moments. For instance, on a nerve-racking Friday night, 11 May 1979, before 22,341 supporters – the best gate at the Vetch since 1971 – Swansea needed to beat Chesterfield to reach Division Two. With the score at one apiece and some 20 minutes left, Toshack came off the substitutes' bench to join the attack. With just five minutes remaining, a scene from *Roy of the Rovers* unfolded. Danny Bartley curled a free kick into the penalty box where an unmarked Toshack rose majestically to head the ball powerfully into the billowing net. Few memories have given the thousands of exuberant supporters who were present more pleasure than seeing the Chesterfield goalkeeper clawing at thin air as Toshack came to the side's rescue. On many other occasions the Swansea faithful had cause to celebrate the generalship of the manager both on and off the field. In a curious way, by using his strength in the air Toshack seemed to convey his determination to help the club reach for the sky.

Having been assured by the board of directors that funds were available to strengthen the squad and embark on ground improvements, Toshack established a more robust and effective support structure at the club. The long-serving secretary Gordon Daniels was given the administrative assistance he deserved. Terry Medwin was appointed assistant manager, Phil Boersma first-team coach, Les Chappell reserve- and youth-team coach, and David Williams physiotherapist. Such an impressive cadre indicated strongly that Toshack and the board were preparing for life in the First Division. Although the club still relied heavily on bank loans and overdraft facilities, success on the field attracted larger crowds and, in a bid to secure new revenue streams, the commercial department began to market the club more aggressively. From Toshack's appointment season-ticket sales soared in the run-up to his full first season in charge. Within a year, non-gate income had reached £240,000, an unheard-of sum at the Vetch, and these welcome developments enabled the manager to splash out on new players and also turn parts of the dowdy old stadium into a more comfortable theatre of dreams. The release of scores of pigeons and multicoloured balloons marked the opening of the new East Stand on 10 January 1981, a stand which afforded a great many new seats but which also served to accentuate the maladroit, if not bizarre, configuration of the ground.

But the main key to his success was the investment in the playing staff. When Arsène Wenger was once invited to give his views on what made a great manager, he replied, 'Great players'. Toshack knew that the squad he had inherited from Harry Griffiths boasted some outstanding locally groomed players who, with proper tuition, would blossom at the highest level in the Football League. He used to refer to Curtis, Charles and Robbie James as his 'jewels' and he also knew that Wyndham Evans's commitment would stir the blood. The young beanpole Nigel Stevenson was full of promise and the muscular Chris Marustik was one for the future either at full back or midfield. But Toshack was also aware that the city's footballing nursery could not produce a sufficient supply of fresh talent to fill all positions and that some members of the playing staff did not meet his exacting standards. Several players, among them

Mickey Conway, Pat Lally (beard and all) and Eddie May, were ushered out and, for the 1978–9 season, Toshack turned to his own former stamping ground for competitive veterans who could pass on their experience and cope with the rigour of life in Division Three. The first of the Scousers to arrive, via Leicester City, was Alan Waddle, Toshack's former understudy at Anfield and a deadly header of the ball. Then, in late summer and early autumn, came two Liverpool veterans whom Toshack believed would relish an Indian summer in balmy Swansea.

Tommy Smith – the 'Iron Man' – had made 632 first-team appearances for Liverpool and, at 33, had been plying his formidable trade as a defender with Los Angeles Aztecs. Offered the same basic wage as he had received at Anfield, Smith brought with him a mature football brain, organizational qualities and, most of all, a reputation for making sledgehammer tackles and falling foul of referees. No one who saw him play could ever imagine him wearing gloves, let alone a snood. The Swansea players soon discovered that he had a body hewn of granite and an abrasive playing style which intimidated his own players, let alone opponents. Wyndham Evans, the club's favourite hard man, was distressed when Smith accused him of being 'too nice'. Bill Shankly once claimed that Smith was capable of causing a riot in a cemetery, but no one ever imagined that he would call Wyndham a wimp. His get-your-retaliation-in-first was totally alien to 'the Swansea way', but Toshack needed a mentally strong character to patrol the space in front of the back four. On 29 August 1978 Swansea played host to Tottenham Hotspur in the second round of the Football League Cup. Having heard that Osvaldo Ardiles and Ricardo Villa, two World Cup stars from Argentina, were among his opponents, Smith stomped on to the field, glowered at the foreigners and made some disparaging remarks about mercenaries sullying England's green and pleasant football pitches. As the first whistle sounded, Smith charged into Ardiles and felled him with a bone-crunching tackle. The ball was not in the vicinity at the time and Smith had made his point. Thereafter Villa and Ardiles avoided the thunder-thighed Liverpudlian like the plague and, although the match was drawn, Swansea went on to thrash Spurs 3–1 in the second leg at White Hart Lane.

The second veteran – Ian Callaghan – was three years older than Smith, but twice as fit. He, too, had tasted glory in Europe and had spent the summer playing for Fort Lauderdale Strikers before joining Swansea in mid-September. He and Smith were allowed to live and train in Liverpool. Callaghan was a manager's dream. He epitomized all the clichés of the lazy reporter: he worked his socks off, covered every blade of grass on the pitch, and ran himself into the ground in every game. A model professional, he was the most reliable workhorse Toshack could have wished for. True, his passes were almost always sideways and John Mahoney had every reason to berate him for never playing one-twos. But 'Cally' had the stamina to harass opponents and could be relied upon to remain unruffled under pressure and to give his all in every single game. Although Smith and Callaghan were the first, and most celebrated, Liverpudlians to appear in John Toshack's team, over the seasons doors were opened to other talented crowd-pleasers from both Liverpool and Everton. Unfortunately, however, the three most high-profile additions were dogged by misfortune. Phil Boersma, the Liverpool-born midfielder who was signed from Luton for £35,000 and made his debut on 12 September 1978 lasted barely eight months before suffering a compound fracture of the right ankle which eventually ended his playing career. Many reckoned that Toshack had taken leave of his senses when he spent a small fortune – a club record fee of £350,000 – on Colin Irwin from Liverpool. An average defender, Irwin made only 48 league appearances before a snapped patella sustained during his second season curtailed his progress. More eye-catching was Ray Kennedy, an England international and Liverpool left-sided midfielder whose excellent control and vision meant that he always seemed to have time and space on the ball. For a fee of £160,000, he was given a four-year contract in 1982. Unbeknown to Kennedy,

Toshack and everyone else, however, symptoms of Parkinson's disease had already begun to manifest themselves and, as Kennedy became increasingly morose and ineffective, he lost his form and was bitterly criticized for lack of application and effort. In contrast, Max Thompson, a Liverpudlian bought for £20,000 from Blackpool for the 1981–2 season, proved to be full of buzzing energy and commitment, and no one who was at the Vetch to witness his net-busting volley against Arsenal will ever forget it.

But former Evertonians also ensured that Swansea during Toshack's tenure became 'a little bit of Liverpool once removed'. Gary Stanley and Neil Robinson were both vigorous marauding full backs who could also figure in midfield, but the most successful recruit was Birmingham-born Bob Latchford who came from Everton in the 1981 close season at a bargain price of £125,000. With twelve England caps to his name, Latchford was a powerful centre forward whose scoring power was legendary. His barrel chest and bulging thighs meant that he was difficult to knock off the ball. Prepared to throw himself at crosses where boots and heads flew, he could score from all angles. In 77 appearances for Swansea he scored 35 goals, a marvellous record which amply justified Toshack's faith in him. Prior to his arrival he had acquired a reputation for picking up injuries, but Toshack nursed him back to full glory. Although the 5–1 drubbing of Leeds at the Vetch in August 1981 will always be remembered for Alan Curtis's spectacular goal, it was Latchford who proved to be the scourge of Leeds by scoring a splendid hat-trick on his debut in an eleven-minute spell after half-time.

By giving a vote of confidence to former colleagues and other recruits on Merseyside, Toshack showed that he had the loftiest ambitions for Swansea. But he also gave due weight to the Welshness of the squad and was eager to bring back to Wales proven internationals who were capable of performing under pressure in the most hostile environments. As Swansea moved upwards through the divisions, Toshack's squad bubbled with gifted Welsh players who produced some magnificent football and scored goals of supreme quality. Bought for £70,000 from Aston Villa in late 1978, Leighton Phillips was an excellent reader of the game as a sweeper. John Mahoney, Toshack's cousin, was enticed from Middlesbrough for £100,000 in the 1979 close season. Muscular as well as skilful in midfield, Mahoney won the hearts of supporters with his never-say-die approach and disregard for physical danger. The startling pace and verve of David Giles, signed for £70,000 from Wrexham in November 1978, made such an impression on the cognoscenti that Crystal Palace offered £400,000 for him, an offer which Toshack unwisely refused, and four years passed before a past-his-best Giles left in a part-exchange deal for Ian Walsh, another Welsh international with an eye for goal. But the one who became an instant favourite was Loughor-born Leighton James who arrived from Burnley for a mere £100,000 in May 1980. This mercurial genius was a joy to watch. Whether deployed on the left or right wing, he brought pace, guile and penetration to attacks. Unfazed by burly full backs who tried to clatter him as he made his stooping, darting runs, he was capable of changing the course of a game with a flash of brilliance. He never lacked confidence and, with him in the team, games were never dull. He used to assure everyone prepared to listen that he was the best winger on the planet, and 90 minutes of Leighton at his glorious best was certainly a sight to behold.

If Toshack had a blind spot it was deciding on a sound and reliable goalkeeper. To some surprise, he transferred the capable Geoff Crudgington to Plymouth for £45,000 and replaced him with Glan Letheren from Chesterfield, whose nervous gaffes did not make for defensive solidity. Then, in February 1980, the athletic Glaswegian Dave Stewart was signed from West Bromwich Albion for £55,000 and immediately became a popular talisman with the North Bank supporters. But Toshack wanted an experienced international to cope with the rigours of Division One and persuaded Ammanford-born Dai Davies, then 33, to rejoin his old club from Wrexham in July 1981. Davies had 52 caps to his name and was no mean keeper. Unfortunately, his lapses were seized on and magnified by the pro-Stewart lobby at the Vetch. Even supporters of the feisty Welsh-speaker lived in fear that 'Dai the Drop' would live up to his name at a crucial moment. As far as is known, Davies is the only honorary member of the Gorsedd of the Bards to play in goal for Swansea, though the endearingly eccentric Millington would surely have been a strong candidate, had he been fluent in Welsh. Davies's autobiography, *Never Say Dai*, in which he pulled few punches, offers a revealing account of life at the Vetch during Toshack's heyday.

Others played their part in Swansea's quest for glory. Brian Attley, bought for £20,000 from Cardiff, in February 1979, showed stunning pace either at right back or in midfield. Composure was the hallmark of Tommy Craig, a streetwise Glaswegian who arrived from Aston Villa in 1979 and showed all and sundry how to let the ball do the work. Toshack's reputation for talent-spotting was also enhanced when he signed two brilliantly gifted Slavs whose tongue-twisting names provided the payroll with a touch of exoticism. Džemal (or 'Jimmy' to the Vetch faithful) Hadžiabdić, formerly of Velez Mostar in Yugoslavia, was a full back noted for his lung-bursting, overlapping runs. From Sarajevo came Ante Rajković, a commanding, ball-playing centre back who could be elegant or rugged as the situation demanded. Some of his sorties upfield made life difficult for Dai Davies, but he was a player of the highest class. This huge outlay on new players, somewhere in the region of £2.2 million, was unprecedented in the history of the club and it enabled the manager to guide it into previously uncharted waters. For supporters more used to seeing the team striving to save themselves from the quicksands of relegation, there was no likelihood that the proud Swansea squad assembled by Toshack would ever revert to being ugly ducklings.

How did these players fare? As we have seen, it was with

Harry Griffiths's team that Toshack had successfully climbed out of Division Four in 1978. By August, however, there was a fresh look to the side as Toshack unveiled an organized unit, rich in talent and experience, which made a promising start to the season. At various stages in the three-month run up to Christmas, Smith's grittiness, Callaghan's painstaking toil, Boersma's effervescent running, the aerial threat posed by Waddle (and Toshack himself when required), and the coolness of Phillips enabled Swansea to seize the initiative in the bid for further honours. Although patches of poor form and a serious stomach injury to Curtis hampered progress, the club was well placed in third spot by the New Year. Then came a mysterious slump during which the attitude and commitment of the players were questioned. Smith was loudly barracked by those who believed that his unlovely tackles were alien to the Swansea tradition and even Callaghan was publicly criticized for slowing down the game and inhibiting the free-flowing style favoured by Harry Griffiths. Toshack lashed his players for their 'disgraceful' lack of application and urged them to fight for scraps and be brave under duress. A more enterprising approach improved matters and the skill, craft and finishing power of Curtis, James and Charles and Waddle helped to sustain the momentum. By mid-March 1979 the club had re-entered the promotion race and by 21 April Swansea topped the table with four games to play. Against Blackpool, Toshack deployed a solid defensive formation which enabled his fleet-footed attackers to run at opponents and win the game 3–1. At home to Southend, Waddle gave a masterclass in the art of aerial power and his hat-trick kept his team ahead of the chasing pack. A disappointing 2–2 draw at Plymouth then prepared the way for the crucial promotion decider at home to Chesterfield in which Toshack's winning header produced an enthralling climax. Having scored 83 goals during the season, Swansea finished in third place. The celebrations, however, were muted when it was revealed that Alan Curtis had decided to fulfil his ambitions at the highest level. Swansea's favourite son joined Leeds United and even receipt of a club record transfer fee of £400,000 could not soften the blow.

Complacent diehards insisted that the club had returned to its rightful home in Division Two, but Toshack truly believed that there was enough ability, resilience and ambition in his squad to cope with playing demands at the highest level. Those who had survived the chastening experience of dipping their noses into the basement were determined to gorge at the Football League's high table. The international stars at the club could not wait to sample that cuisine and it was obvious to everyone that Toshack's appetite for success was far from sated. For a variety of reasons, however, the feast was postponed for a season. The loss of Curtis was a severe psychological blow, Boersma's injury was career-threatening, and Tommy Smith's contract was cancelled by mutual consent when it became evident that his troublesome knee could take no more. Opposing forwards breathed a sigh of relief at his retirement and no tears were shed on the North Bank. A nagging Achilles tendon complaint hampered Toshack's own playing career and, as pressures mounted, he had several altercations with local reporters. Newcomers, however, were integrated reasonably swiftly, with the subtlety of Craig complementing the aggressive ball-winning Mahoney in midfield, while the incisive running of Giles and thunderbolt shots by Robbie James kept the crowds cheering. Overall, the team played with considerable spirit, never more so than in defeating Cardiff City 2–1 – for the first time in 15 years – on New Year's Day before a joyful crowd of 21,400. But as the 1979–80 season unfolded it became clear that the club was taking stock and that the manager was preparing the way for a concerted bid for promotion in the coming season.

During the course of the 1980–1 season Bill Shankly became a regular visitor at Swansea's fixtures. He was impressed by the slick, intelligent passing on offer, but he also detected a greater measure of discipline and concentration: 'At Liverpool we built a side which was difficult to beat and could still be entertaining. Swansea are doing exactly the same.' The acquisition of Hadžiabdić and Leighton James brought greater width and pace to the team and with Stevenson and Phillips marshalling the heart of the defence there were fewer instances of Swansea buckling under sustained pressure. The return of Alan Curtis from Leeds for a mere £175,000 in mid-December was loudly acclaimed and, time and again, he proved to be the classiest player on view. Curiously, however, Alan Waddle was transferred to Newport County at the end of the year, shortly after Curtis's arrival. Waddle's control with both feet had never been perfect, but the sight of him rising high above a mass of shirts in the penalty box had become the stuff of legend. The supporters loved him for his never-say-die attitude and for his remarkable headed goals. One of them maintained that his 'massive hulk and honest endeavour' had made him indispensable, while even impartial observers noted that by rising to second place in Division Two by Boxing Day the club had reached its highest position for 25 years. Nor did they hesitate to attribute the alarming slump in the New Year to the departure of Waddle.

Even though his policy and selections came under intense scrutiny, Toshack held his nerve. A 0–5 drubbing against Middlesbrough in the FA Cup on 3 January was the heaviest home defeat since Boxing Day 1968. Seething inwardly, Toshack assured the press that 'a little disappointment sharpens the senses'. But a disastrous run of five defeats suggested that the season was about to unravel. Firm action was called for and, having appointed Mahoney his new captain, Toshack urged his players to show their battling qualities and sense of togetherness. Harsh words were exchanged in the dressing room and he drew encouragement from the stirring, defiant late rally which brought the team back into the promotion race by the end of March. Inspired by Mahoney's aggressive commitment and his demonic desire to win, Leighton James showed his mesmeric skills, Curtis and Robbie James were exhilarating in attack, and home-grown players like Dudley Lewis and Nigel Stevenson added youthful bite to the defence. Following an ill-tempered draw at home to Cardiff on Easter Monday, Swansea were in sixth place with four games to play. At this key stage, team spirit proved vital. Playing with zest and ambition, the team overwhelmed Bristol Rovers with a barrage of attacks and when manager-less rivals Chelsea arrived on 25 April the home side were simply irrepressible. The rampaging Swans scored three goals without reply, with the tiny Hadžiabdić scoring the most spectacular goal of the season. Following a nerve-jangling 2–2 draw against Luton at the Vetch, the stage was set for a grandstand finish to the season at Preston on 2 May.

There was everything to play for at Deepdale. Preston were battling to avoid relegation, while Swansea needed nothing less than a victory to climb into Division One for the first time in their history. Showing his steely side, Toshack left out his cousin Mahoney for attacking reasons and was fully vindicated when goals by Leighton James, Tommy Craig and Jeremy Charles paved the way for a convincing 3–1 victory. An armada of supporters – some 10,000 in all – had journeyed north to Deepdale. Some of them recalled the clogging mud, the dubious penalty and the freak goal by Preston which had thwarted Swansea's hopes of reaching Wembley in 1964. They created a wonderful cacophony of support in the stadium and were overcome with relief and joy at the final whistle. Fans cheered, sang and wept, and the celebrations went on long into the night. As one enthusiast put it: 'I just drank loads of beer and fell over.' Toshack had fulfilled his pledge: Swansea had reached the promised land and had become the premier soccer club in Wales. Shortly afterwards, Swansea beat Hereford 2–1 on aggregate to win the Welsh Cup for the first time in 15 years. This was Toshack's first piece of silverware at the Vetch. To round off a memorable season, thousands of supporters turned up to honour Wyndham Evans, the club's longest-serving player, in a benefit match against a Liverpool XI (which featured a certain scrum half called Gareth Edwards). An orgy of 13 goals figured in this not-too-serious thriller and Wyndham characteristically refused to shirk any tackles.

There was a delicious tingle of anticipation at the club as the players prepared for life in the First Division. Toshack took his squad to Sarajevo and Zagreb to play pre-season friendlies and new faces at the Vetch included goalkeeper Dai Davies and Bob Latchford. With Ante Rajković restored to full fitness, Toshack could boast a robust spine: 'Three six-footers right through the middle of the side'. Radiating confidence, he boldly declared: 'We are good enough to frighten some people to death.' His Shanklyan psychology rubbed off on the players as they met Leeds United's expensively assembled team in the opening fixture at the Vetch on 29 August 1981. Swansea had six Welshmen, three Englishmen and two Yugoslavs in the side and the game, played in glorious sunshine, was one of attack and counter-attack, swirling movement, goalmouth incident and stunning goals. 'Stylish Swans take Wing' was the headline in the *Guardian* and, after Dai Davies had made two vital saves, Jeremy Charles scored the club's first goal in top-flight football. A brilliant hat-trick by Latchford showed that there was no one better at turning half chances into goals, and then, to cap an extraordinary performance, 'Leeds reject' Alan Curtis silenced his critics with a goal as memorable as any scored at the Vetch. To the delight of the crowd of 23,489 he teased, twisted and tortured full back Trevor Cherry, unbalancing him with a feint before powering a rising 20-yard drive into the top right-hand corner of the net. Winning 5–1, Swansea played fine attacking football which made a mockery of those Jeremiahs who had expected them to crumble at the highest level.

Some snooty reporters, however, still believed that they would come unstuck against city slickers. Writing in the *Guardian*, Robert Armstrong reckoned that Swansea might be 'fit company for the likes of Middlesbrough and Coventry' but were certain to find themselves 'a little out of their depth in the big cities'. There is nothing more galling to Swansea Jacks than metropolitan condescension and, as it happened, the team went on to produce vintage performances against the most highly rated sides. Wherever they went, Swansea sought to wrestle control from startled opponents by playing with fire and verve. The upstarts from south-west Wales strung together some excellent results. For the only two survivors of the re-election campaign in 1975 – Curtis and Robbie James – the high excitement of the First Division was a revelation. Playing with delightful ease and grace, Curtis was at his magical best, while James's speciality – rasping 25-yard drives which fizzed inside the posts or billowed high in the top corners – astonished goalkeepers. By mid-October several illustrious scalps had been claimed. Breathtaking goals by Robbie James and Curtis helped to defeat Tottenham Hotspur 2–1 at the Vetch, while a wonderful goalkeeping display by Dai Davies earned a 2–2 draw at Anfield. The Vetch pulsed with excitement when a stinging half-volley by Leighton James and an absolute belter by Max Thompson sent Arsenal packing. A 2–1 victory at Stoke took Swansea to the top of the league on 17 October. This was truly a red-letter day that marked one of the most spectacular stories of progress in the history of British football. Within six seasons the club had climbed 90 rungs on the ladder to success.

By playing above themselves, the team managed to sustain the momentum up to Christmas. Ipswich, Birmingham and Aston Villa figured among their victims and, although there were setbacks and injuries to Charles and Rajković, by 21 December Swansea was still sitting on the topmost perch. Sod's Law then reared its head when, shortly after the manager was awarded an MBE in recognition of the meteoric rise of the club, a 0–4 defeat in the FA Cup was inflicted on a waterlogged Vetch by a ruthlessly effective Liverpool. A week later, a 0–2 result in Arctic conditions at Elland Road marked a seventh defeat in eleven away matches. To steady the ship Toshack bought Ray Kennedy from Liverpool and, despite injuries to

Charles and Latchford, the collective spirit was still good. A stylish 2–0 over star-studded Manchester United restored confidence and a hard-earned 2–0 victory at Anfield, courtesy of a 30-yard free kick driven by Leighton James past a nonplussed Grobbelaar and a late goal by Curtis, was one of the sweetest moments of the season for Toshack. The spirit of enterprise was rewarded with a 2–0 success at Highbury and a header by Ian Walsh at Molineux on 20 March took the club back to the top of the table. Toshack laconically observed: 'Let's just say we are pleased to have 91 teams below us.'

Mixed results followed. Home defeats to an excellent Ipswich and West Ham United were balanced by three victories, including a mesmerizing 2–0 defeat of Manchester City during the course of which Curtis was well-nigh untouchable. But with spring in the air Swansea showed unmistakable signs of fading firepower at the very stage when Liverpool were blazing ahead. By early May the team, virtually exhausted, had dropped out of the promotion race and eventually tired limbs and injuries meant that the club had to settle for sixth place, 18 points behind the champions Liverpool. Toshack had no cause to reproach himself. Indeed, his achievement had been extraordinary and has never been equalled. For devoted supporters, it was a fairy tale come true.

Swansea's odyssey in Europe during the 1981–2 season, however, proved disappointingly short-lived. The club lost 1–3 on aggregate to Lokomotiv Leipzig in the first round of the European Cup Winners' Cup, a result which made Toshack all the more determined to win the Welsh Cup once more. Thanks to two unstoppable goals by Latchford on 19 May, Swansea duly retained the Cup by beating Cardiff City 2–1 on aggregate in an enthralling match at the Vetch during which the captain Rajković was sent off in the 69th minute for a blatant professional foul. Mercifully his transgression did not prevent him from stepping forward, smiling broadly, to receive the trophy after the game. Overall, the season had been an enormous success. In spite of what one reporter described as 'his bouts of high anxiety',

Dai Davies had acquitted himself well in goal. Wyndham Evans had turned destructive endeavour into a form of art and the attacking instincts of Hadžiabdić had borne rich results. The unyielding presence of Rajković and the wholehearted effort of Mahoney had caught the eye, while the predatory instincts of Latchford had always commanded admiration. Leighton James's seamless changes of pace and elusive guile had tormented lumbering defences, some of Robbie James's strikes had been like bolts from a crossbow, Curtis had never failed to impress, and had Jeremy Charles not fallen victim to serious injuries his aerial prowess would have presented an even greater goal-scoring threat. Nothing could diminish the sense of achievement and joy felt at the Vetch. For Toshack it had been a personal triumph and he was deluged with richly deserved messages of congratulation.

How was this exceptionally successful phase in the club's progress reflected on the terraces? The board had fully expected that the team would play before sell-out crowds at the Vetch during this period, but only the plum fixtures attracted support of well over 20,000. The average home attendance in the glorious 1981–2 season was only 18,194. Set in an overall context, however, such gates were perfectly respectable and compared very favourably with the meagre average attendance of 2,866 in 1975–6. Social changes meant that people now had different leisure interests. According to the 1981 census, 60 per cent of households in Swansea had at least one car to carry families to new shopping centres and beauty spots at the weekend. Toshack's appointment broadly coincided with the imposition of the neo-liberal policies of Margaret Thatcher, which deindustrialized the south Wales valleys and caused mass unemployment. As a result, the working-class fan-base inevitably shrank and in a symbolic, if futile, gesture against the ravages of Thatcherism, a young Swansea man who had been on the dole for two years registered his protest by climbing into the Vetch at night in September 1981 to dig up parts of the penalty area. It was almost impossible for unemployed supporters to afford tickets for home matches. Social tensions simmered in and around the Vetch. Throughout 1981 the club became embroiled in a running battle with the city council and local residents over the amount of compensation to be paid to householders living under the shadow of the new two-tiered East Stand. Vociferous fans were resentful of the creature comforts afforded to the better-off supporters who, according to a correspondent from Ynysforgan, never cheered, sang or stamped their feet as they sat silently in their carpet slippers throughout games: 'We regulars beneath would not object to the odd flurry of dust, splinter or woodworm descending upon our proud First Division heads from time to time.' Others deplored the continuing presence of latrines which would have contravened health and safety regulations in early medieval Mongolia.

The hooligan problem also kept supporters at home. One form of hooliganism was the insulting ridicule and abuse heaped upon goalkeeper Dai Davies. Another was racial abuse and the chanting of obscenities. There were serious outbreaks of violence involving the throwing of bottles, glasses and stones. Some of the most disgraceful behaviour occurred in local derbies. In retaliation for the vile behaviour of Cardiff fans during the derby on Easter Monday 1981, more than a hundred Swansea supporters penetrated police barriers in Madoc Street and pelted houses and cars with bricks and stones, prompting Malcolm Struel to call for the reimposition of the birch. A year later, during the Welsh Cup final, rival fans hurled golf balls and metal washers at each other on the terraces and a policeman was stabbed in the head with a dart.

By the end of the 1981–2 season, however, such ugliness was forgotten as the club basked in its success on the field. In his memoirs, published in 1982, John Toshack justifiably claimed to be 'proud to have been associated with one of the great success stories of modern day football'. No one spoke of mounting debts and no one dreamt of the nightmares that lay ahead. There are not many opportunities for a historian of

Swansea City Football Club to end a chapter on a high note. This is one of them. In four dramatic seasons, John Benjamin Toshack and his star-studded squad had written themselves indelibly into the annals of the club.

6

Turmoil and Gloom

IN THE SUMMER of 1982 Swansea City basked in the achievement of finishing sixth in their first season in the top flight and looked forward to bringing further joy to the Vetch faithful. Just over 20 years later, however, by mid-September 2002 the team was languishing at the foot of the Football League and propping up the other 91 clubs for the first time in its history. Over these two fateful decades Swansea appears to have been in a permanent state of crisis. Between 1983 and 1986 it suffered the indignity of three relegations and steeply falling gates. As Stephen Knight put it in his amusing poem 'At the Foot of Division Four': 'Now we backin Division Phaw!' In truth, however, Swansea's plight was no joking matter. The colossal spending spree undertaken by Malcolm Struel and John Toshack had left a long-standing legacy of financial distress which very nearly brought about the demise of the club.

Swansea gained the headlines for all the wrong reasons. In December 1985 the debt-laden club was closed down by a High Court judge and, even after the chairman Doug Sharpe averted the threat of extinction by assembling a financial rescue package, Swansea continued to put the art of survival in the Football League to the test. There was no sense of strategic vision as the club embarked on a cycle of false starts, quick fixes and patch-up jobs. Nineteen different managers (some served twice and some were caretakers) boarded the managerial carousel at the Vetch. Some leapt off pretty sharply, some bumbled on without support or resources, and one infamous appointee was drummed out of town within a week. At times, to be brutally frank, the club was a total shambles and a laughing stock within the world of football. Having reached the potentially lucrative grand stage of Division One in 1981, two decades later the club was sold for a pound. As Sir Alex Ferguson once famously exclaimed: 'Football, bloody hell!'

Amid the turmoil and gloom, however, there were some glimmers of light. Terry Yorath guided the club up to Division Three in 1987–8 and in 1999–2000 John Hollins became the first manager to win a Championship title since Billy McCandless in 1948–9. Life was sweet at the Vetch, too, when Frank Burrows took his team to Wembley for the first time in the club's history and made off with the Autoglass Trophy in April 1994. Some players won the fans' hearts by giving their all in every game. Over 13 seasons goalkeeper Roger Freestone became the best-loved custodian in the history of the club by dint of his bravery, loyalty and, according to his biographers, 'a propensity for madness'. When the venerable Tommy Hutchison, an inspirational left-winger, dragged off his Swansea shirt for the last time in 1991, he was 43 years and 171 days old. Club legends Alan Curtis and Robbie James left the club for wealthier clubs but then, to hearty popular acclaim, returned for a last hurrah, while youthful successors like Andy Melville, Chris Coleman, Andrew Legg and Jason Bowen showed, if only briefly, that home-grown talent could still be tapped. But the general feeling was that Swansea City had such heavy debts and was run in such a chaotic manner that financial meltdown was the likeliest outcome.

That Swansea should find itself in such a financial pickle was all the more ironic given the fact that structural changes were transforming the game during this period. Had the club, by some miracle, managed to survive and then achieve some measure of stability in Division One, it might have been well placed to take advantage of the founding of the Premier League in 1992 and a share in the vast profits generated by Sky television as well as other lucrative commercial operations.

Football was prospering at the upper level. The 'haves', sustained by market forces, consumerism and greed, became infested with an assortment of fat cats and chancers, while the 'have nots' in the other divisions were left to work out their own salvation. Mean-spirited Thatcherism had turned the 'people's game' into a commodity. Money talked at precisely the time when Swansea had none to spend. Football was changing swiftly, but Swansea was not. It was left behind, a prisoner of its ballooning debts, its chaotic administration and its lack of democratic accountability. For all the fine promises and achievements of the 1978–82 period, the net effect was to consign the club to a battle for its life as a going concern both on and off the field.

During the Toshack era, the club clearly overstretched itself in its quest for glory and racked up unsustainable financial losses which threatened to bring it to ruin. Why was this allowed to happen? One explanation is that the board became besotted by the mania for successive promotions and thus fell victim to what economists call 'irrational exuberance'. They ignored or played down the perils because the rewards were so enormous. Even as Swansea climbed the divisions and spent money as if there was no tomorrow, the alarm had been raised by those with access to the balance sheets. But the club was hell-bent on making Toshack's dream a reality. Like Icarus in Greek mythology, it succumbed to hubris by flying too close to the sun and becoming a poignant example of failed ambition.

Not surprisingly, during 1982–3 the club suffered from 'second-seasonitis'. Since the Football League had imposed an embargo on further signings because the club had fallen behind on debts owed to Everton following the transfer of Latchford and Stanley, there were no fresh faces in the squad. Opponents now found ways of blunting Swansea's cutting edge and of hustling them out of their customary free-flowing rhythm. Injuries took their toll as Irwin, Mahoney and Curtis were laid off for long periods and in the case of the valiant Mahoney, the archetypal players' player, led to his premature retirement. Results on the field were poor. 'Soporific Swansea', wrote one reporter and regular ear-bashings from Toshack had little effect. By the end of the calendar year the club lay in 17th place, with just six victories and 23 points to its name. Progress in Europe had been short-lived. Having disposed of Sporting Braga 3–1 on aggregate and squeezed through 17–0 on aggregate against minnows Sliema Wanderers in the early rounds of the European Cup Winners' Cup, the Swans then crashed to defeat against an extremely classy Paris Saint-Germain, managed by Osvaldo Ardiles.

Unnerved by the new demands made on him and by the stodgy results, the hitherto seemingly infallible Toshack began to make serious errors of judgement. Cracks were opening up within the club. It was a mistake to make the morose Ray Kennedy club captain, not least because it deepened divisions within the dressing room between high-earning Merseysiders and the senior Welsh players. In his disquieting autobiography, Kennedy later claimed that the club was 'rotten to the core, in debt with underhand payments going on as well as wage top-ups', though his fractious relationship with Toshack probably coloured his view of affairs at the Vetch. The manager's own impatience as well as his foul temper led to clashes with the board and earned him a four-month touchline ban from the Football Association of Wales. In the new year his judgement was widely called into question when he panicked by placing several of his most experienced players on the transfer list and replacing them with untried youngsters like Darren Gale, Jimmy Loveridge and Colin Pascoe. For all their promise, such youthful home-grown products were barely out of school and were certainly not ready for a relegation dogfight in the top flight.

Moreover, when his assistant Terry Medwin resigned for health reasons, Toshack recalled the discredited Harry Gregg, presumably to toughen up the players. It was an extraordinary appointment which lasted for just two months. Worst of all, the manager himself no longer seemed able to inspire the players. With every defeat, his spirits drooped. As Dai Davies remarked: 'One could say his head had dropped so much that his chin was trailing the ground, and in complete contrast to what should happen the players had to gee him up!' He was also often abominably rude to various members of staff. Just about the only consolation was the sparkling goal-scoring form of Latchford. Over the season the burly striker notched up 34 goals, three of which helped the Swans to victory by 4–1 on aggregate against Wrexham in the Welsh Cup Final. But from early March onwards the club had never looked likely to save itself from relegation. A 1–2 defeat at Old Trafford on 7 May sealed its fate in the penultimate game of a bitterly disappointing and rancorous season during which the team had failed to register a single away victory. The slump in playing fortunes had begun.

Some clear thinking was now required, but once more there was no sign of a properly formulated plan of action. In a belated bid to control the club's runaway finances, ill-judged cost-cutting exercises were instituted which led to the departure of established Welsh favourites who still had much to offer. What sensible board of directors would have allowed Leighton James to leave for Sunderland on a free transfer? Likewise, the wretchedly low transfer fees which accrued when Robbie James left for Stoke for £130,000 and Alan Curtis joined Southampton for £85,000 were nowhere near the true market value of these proven internationals. But Swansea urgently needed money. The astronomical sums paid for, and to, underachieving Merseysiders had come back to haunt the club. The board and the manager had spent £2.2 million in bringing in players to the club, but recouped only £715,000 by selling players. The mathematics were seriously awry. It is one thing to dream of sporting glory, but quite another to achieve it by jeopardizing the future well-being of the club.

A swift exit at the hands of FC Magdeburg in the first round of the European Cup Winners' Cup did not bode well for life in Division Two. By this stage the departed stars included Dai Davies and Hadžiabdić, and after three successive defeats a panicky Toshack signed the 36-year-old Emlyn Hughes, another Anfield star who had seen many better days. In the event, 'Crazy Horse' only wore the Swansea shirt seven times and ended up on the losing side in all but one of them. Defensive shortcomings were cruelly exposed and the depressing run of away defeats continued. The chairman Malcolm Struel fell on his sword and was replaced by Doug Sharpe, a lifelong supporter who had made his fortune in property development and who, like his predecessor, was no stranger to controversy. On 29 October Toshack himself stood down, parting company with the club by 'mutual consent', only to return 53 days later in a vain bid to arrest the alarming slide. It was too late and, probably regretting his decision to return to the Vetch, he was duly sacked by Sharpe on 5 March. Former player Les Chappell began a second stint as caretaker manager and was at the helm on 24 April 1984 when defeat at Shrewsbury plunged the Swans into Division Three. Following consecutive relegations, the club was in danger of imploding.

On paper the new manager appeared to be a sensible choice. Colin Appleton was an experienced old hand who had served Leicester City and Hull City admirably. Quite what attracted him to Swansea is hard to say and someone must surely have warned him that his new club could boast an unfortunate run of 43 consecutive away matches without a single victory. Four defeats in the opening eleven days of the season gave prophets of doom ample ammunition and wherever the youthful Swans went they succumbed like lambs to the slaughter. Only the brilliance of Jimmy Rimmer in goal saved the team from shedding hatfuls of goals. A seriously leaky defence and a shot-shy forward line did not inspire confidence among the dwindling numbers of fans, and after the part-timers of Bognor Regis had sent the Swans crashing out of the FA Cup in the first round the beleaguered Appleton was sacked after 205 days in post. Short-termism ruled at the Vetch and when Tom Phillips, a former vice chairman, resigned from the board in mid-December he likened the running of the club to 'a Whitehall farce'.

Nine days before Christmas the seventh manager in 15 months was installed at the Vetch. At 51, John Bond was an experienced former West Ham player and a manager with a reputation for plain talking and a certain breezy charm. 'Call me Boss', he burbled on his arrival. He immediately appealed to the supporters to rally round the club, but hardly endeared himself to the players by threatening to lock up his defenders in Pentonville and by claiming that he had inherited 'the worst squad I have ever seen'. Nor did members of the board take kindly to being interrogated by him about their own playing experience and, presumably, their ability to sit in judgement on him if the worst came to the worst. But Bond knew the kind of players who were needed to help the squad to claw its way to safety. He signed gnarled old pros like Paul Price, a robust Wales international centre back, Ray McHale, a tough-tackling midfielder, and Derek Parlane, a strong and abrasive striker who had scored goals freely for Rangers and Scotland. A mini-revival followed, though by the time of the final game of the season – a home encounter with Bristol City – Bond's team needed a point to survive. A nail-biting 90 minutes was watched by a crowd of 10,709 and their loud vocal support worked in the home side's favour. The 0–0 draw proved sufficient to save Swansea from being relegated in three successive seasons.

Within days, however, Bond had blotted his copybook by announcing that ten players were to be given free transfers. Astoundingly, the list included the name of Dean Saunders, the young Swansea-born striker who had finished the season as joint top-scorer with Colin Pascoe. This calamitous misjudgement cost the club hundreds of thousands of pounds as the young star went on to win fame and fortune with Liverpool, Aston Villa, Nottingham Forest and Benfica, as well as win 75 caps for Wales. This gaffe cost Bond the respect of the supporters and no doubt some members of the board seized the opportunity, rather late in the day, to question his judgement.

Bond's second season in charge was dominated by matters off the field which threatened to bring the club to the brink of extinction. The club was still haemorrhaging money and no one seemed capable of providing a sense of purpose and direction. Storm clouds began to gather at the end of October 1985 as the Inland Revenue petitioned for a winding-up order in the High Court for an outstanding debt of £102,178. Other disgruntled creditors, including the Vetch Field Residents' Association, who had not received compensation following the building of the new stand, were also closing in. Local businessmen and supporters were urged to make sizeable donations and some leeway was granted when the High Court hearing, scheduled for 18 November, was postponed as the club frantically sought to discover a buyer. But Swansea was not exactly brimming with wealthy Arab businessmen or American tycoons, and successful local people were hardly likely to dip deeply into their pockets in aid of a club which had lost its grip on financial sanity over recent years. An eleventh-hour plea to Swansea City Council for a substantial loan was curtly rejected. Its members maintained that it was not their business to bale out a commercial organization which, through poor management, had accumulated such serious debts. Perhaps some of them still believed that the club would somehow muddle through and that the forthcoming hearing would take a sympathetic view of the club's predicament. If so, they were soon to be disabused.

A last-minute rescue package never materialized and the High Court hearing was held in a cold and wet London on 20 December. This was to become the club's very own 'Black Friday'. Unfortunately for the club, the case was heard by Mr Justice Harman, otherwise known in genteel circles as Sir Jeremiah (Le Roy) Harman. An old Etonian and a former Guards officer, he had been appointed Justice of the High Court, Chancery Division, in 1982. Harman was a hectoring bully who was known to his victims as 'Harman the Horrible'. Even the law profession described him as 'rude, discourteous, bullying, unpredictable and nasty'. Prone to make embarrassing sexist gaffes, he once exclaimed in court: 'I've always thought there were only three kinds of women: wives, whores and mistresses.' He had no interest at all in sport of any kind and once famously displayed his ignorance by publicly stating that he had no knowledge of anyone called Paul Gascoigne. Such a jaundiced figure was unlikely to view the predicament of Swansea City Football Club with any sympathy. So it proved. In summing up at the end of the 35-minute hearing, Harman gratuitously accused the board of 'stealing' money from the Inland Revenue and making false promises. To gasps of disbelief, he wound up the club. Swansea thus became the first club to fold in mid-season since Accrington Stanley went bust in 1962.

Once the news reached the Vetch, the doors were immediately closed and padlocked. Heartbroken fans huddled in groups outside the old ground, many of them angrily blaming the Council for its 'diabolical' dereliction of duty. One reporter described the atmosphere inside the Vetch as akin to being in a funeral parlour. Fighting back the tears, the players sat in stunned silence in the dressing rooms. John Bond, now out of a job, kicked in a few doors, though not the door of the cupboard where he kept his sharp suits. No one was more distraught than the groundsman Harold Woolacott, who had spent the best part of 30 years persuading grass to grow on the old cabbage patch. The match with Walsall scheduled for the following day was called off. Thirty-four players had their contracts taken over by the Football League and the club was placed in the hands of the official receiver. After 73 years Swansea City Football Club had perished; 1985 became the official *annus horribilis* of the club.

'We will need a miracle to save it', claimed Gordon Taylor, secretary of the Professional Footballers Association. But there were people in Swansea who were determined not to let Mr Justice Harman have the last laugh. Within hours of the verdict a 'Swans Aid' campaign had been launched by a consortium of five directors: Peter Howard, Harry Hyde, Bobby Jones, Mel Nurse and Dave Savage. This so-called 'Famous Five' managed to raise substantial pledges of financial support and further strenuous efforts were also made by a rival consortium led by Doug Sharpe and Malcolm Struel. The upshot was that the club was granted a three-week stay of execution on Christmas Eve by Mr Justice Scott. Jeffrey Payne, a chartered accountant at Swansea, was appointed special manager of the club under the supervision of the official receiver, while veteran Tommy Hutchison took charge of the playing staff. On 13 January Manchester United came to play a friendly match at the Vetch, an event which packed the ground and made a profit of over £45,000. Donations from concerts, whist drives and boot sales poured into the club. Buckets rattled noisily in the city centre, especially when collectors espied city councillors, and soon the club began to trade at a profit.

But old divisions hampered the fund-raising campaign. Rival consortia distrusted each other and could not agree upon one concerted rescue package. Fortunately, however, on 24 March 1986 Mr Justice Hoffmann was sufficiently convinced by the robustness of the campaign to grant the club unlimited breathing space to deal with its financial problems. Eventually, Doug Sharpe's financial package won almost unanimous support and he, together with his supporters and enemies, deserve great credit for their efforts in keeping the club afloat. On 20 July, to widespread joy and relief, Mr Justice Hoffmann lifted the winding-up order on the club. The club was alive once more. On the field, however, Hutchison and his players proved unable to work miracles. At the end of the 1985–6 season, even before the fate of the club had been settled, Swansea City had tumbled into Division Four where it had begun its upward journey eight years earlier.

Sadly, the reputation of the Swans was in tatters. While

many admired the way in which lovers of the club had rallied round in its hour of need, its financial predicament and the associated adverse publicity had tarnished its good name. Now that it had returned to the basement, it was even more unlikely that a sugar-daddy would appear from somewhere to revive its fortunes. Nor would it be easy to entice affordable quality players to ply their wares among the journeymen and cloggers of Division Four. Moreover, there was a strong possibility that home-grown youngsters would seek to improve themselves at better-resourced clubs outside Wales. Finally, large numbers of followers no longer darkened the Vetch. In just four seasons the average home attendance had fallen from 11,681 to 4,323.

In the circumstances, therefore, and especially in the light of Dylan Thomas's depiction of the city as the 'graveyard of ambition', it is astonishing that Swansea managed to recruit two high-calibre managers – Terry Yorath and Frank Burrows – to rebuild the team and produce attractive football. Securing the services of Yorath as player-manager in July 1986 was something of a coup by Doug Sharpe. Yorath did not need to earn respect. Having had an enviably competitive playing career with Leeds, Coventry and Tottenham, and won 59 caps with Wales, he was a big-hitter in the soccer world. As a player he called to mind his fellow Cardiffian Fred Keenor. Both were born leaders, coped manfully with physical pressure and tackled as if their lives depended on it. Yorath had not been overblessed with natural talent, but he was a battle-wise campaigner who knew the game inside out. His mentor Don Revie reckoned him to be the most astute reader of the game at Elland Road, as well as being the one most capable of surviving a roughhouse. At 36, he may not have had much left in the tank as a player, but he appeared to be the ideal manager to oversee the task of rejuvenating the club. Not everyone would have relished coming to a club which was still coping with the repercussions of 'Black Friday', but Yorath was no stranger to trauma. He had been manager of

Bradford City on 11 May 1985 when a wooden stand at Valley Parade caught fire and claimed the lives of 56 people. That harrowing experience was still etched on his face when he arrived at the Vetch.

Determined to put recent frustrations and embarrassments at the club behind him, Yorath brought a new sense of optimism to Swansea. He expected all-round industry and commitment from his players, and from the first game onwards the team played sharp, incisive football. He had some extremely talented local players in the squad. In Bridgend-born Mike Hughes he had an outstandingly brave and agile goalkeeper, while Dudley Lewis had matured into a tough and dependable centre back. Andy Melville, a Swansea-born trainee, had made his first-team debut at 16 and became such an impressive pivot that Yorath appointed him captain at the age of 20. He went on to win 61 international caps. Colin Pascoe, born in Bridgend but raised at Port Talbot, had survived the post-Toshack aftermath and developed into a stylish, creative midfielder with a sharp eye for goal. Bridgend was also the home town of Sean McCarthy, a bustling striker whose toothy smile lit up many photographs taken of the 14 league goals he scored during the 1986–7 season. Of the newcomers, the most striking was left back Terry Phelan, who joined from Leeds in the close season, established a fine rapport with the evergreen Hutchison, and showed during 45 lustrous league appearances that he was far too good for the basement league. Transferred for £100,000 to Wimbledon, Phelan was sold six years later to Manchester City for £2.5 million.

The trickiest problems facing Yorath were the smallness of his squad and the parsimony of the chairman. During the early months of 1987 Swansea were handily placed to push for promotion. But a run of injuries robbed the team of impetus and, at Molineux on 14 March, a palpably off-the-pace Yorath was forced to make a dramatic but unsuccessful first appearance on the pitch. Never again did he wear the Swansea colours. By April the Swans were on a downward spiral and when hopes of gaining a play-off place vanished the board paid the price for failing to invest in a larger squad. By this stage Yorath had become increasingly exasperated by the hands-on, interfering approach of his gruff chairman and also his penny-pinching ways. 'Sharpe by name and sharp by nature', was his verdict, and he took grave exception when the chairman once entered the dressing room and called the players 'a bunch of wankers' to their faces.

'We won't be splashing money around', cried Swansea's answer to Ebenezer Scrooge, and Yorath was forced to scour the lower leagues in search of bargains. Over the close season he spent £10,000 on Alan Knill, a frail-looking beanpole of a centre back who belied his critics by showing steely staying power over two seasons. He also shrewdly snapped up on a free transfer Alan Davies of Manchester United and Wales, a subtle, imaginative midfielder who was physically incapable of making an ugly pass, and Joe Allon, a prolific Gateshead-born centre forward who scored twelve valuable goals during the 1987–8 season. Fresh-faced optimism was also introduced by Chris Coleman, an unusually confident young defender from Townhill whose stylish left foot and calm presence served the club well for four seasons.

After a dreadful start to Yorath's second season in charge, the team began to stop leaking goals and to score more freely at the other end. Yorath successfully pleaded with his chairman to fund the return of Robbie James from Leicester City in January, but the subsequent loss of Pascoe to Sunderland for £70,000 was keenly felt. Nevertheless, by the skin of their teeth the team managed to reach the play-off positions. Two priceless goals by Sean McCarthy disposed of Rotherham 2–1 on aggregate in the semi-final. In the first leg of the final, played at home against Torquay on 25 May, Swansea triumphed 2–1, thanks to goals by McCarthy and Jimmy Love. Four days later a pulsating second leg was played on a mud-bath at Plainmoor. Having scored three times in the first half, Swansea just about survived a late surge and squeezed through to Division Three by 5–4 on aggregate. This memorable display rescued the season and also probably rescued the manager. In the light of the tiny budget at Yorath's disposal, it had been a remarkable achievement.

Yet, the relationship between Sharpe and Yorath continued to deteriorate. As the former's arms got shorter, his pockets became deeper. Starved of funds to strengthen the squad in Division Three, Yorath fretted and fumed, and nursed ambitions of becoming manager of Wales. Sharpe insisted on calling all the shots and by February 1989, even though the team was playing well, Yorath could brook no more interference. He returned to Bradford City, with six months of his contract still to run. This ushered in another familiar tale of managerial musical chairs. The ever-willing Tommy Hutchison held the fort for a month until Sharpe appointed a young manager who was far less likely than Yorath to challenge his decisions. A former Crystal Palace and Wales defender, Ian Evans was a rookie in the managerial world and the chairman's judgement was once more called into question when the team failed to win any of the last twelve league games. The only redeeming feature, following a decidedly shaky start, was success in the Welsh Cup. By thrashing non-league Kidderminster Harriers 5–0, another possibly lucrative passage into Europe was assured.

Predictably, Evans floundered and lasted little more than a year. A 5–6 defeat on aggregate against Panathinaikos in the first round of the European Cup Winners' Cup left the chairman furious, and his mood was even blacker when the Swans shipped eight goals without reply at Anfield in a third-round replay in the FA Cup. Woeful performances in the league eventually forced him to dispense with Evans's services in March 1990. To universal surprise, Sharpe then buried the hatchet by bringing Yorath back from Bradford. Even though Yorath probably sensed that it was a mistake to go back to the Vetch, there was unfinished business to complete. Eager to 'win over the unforgiving faithful' on the terraces, he swiftly raised spirits in the dressing room. But over the next twelve months he failed to conjure a run of decent results and by the time he was sacked on 21 March 1991 relegation was looming. At this critical moment, Doug Sharpe made arguably his best appointment. The in-coming manager, Frank Burrows, not only staved off the threat of relegation but also guided his charges to victory against Wrexham in the Welsh Cup Final.

Frank Burrows was no pushover. As a player he had brought physical presence and security to Swindon Town's central defence from the 1968–9 season onwards and helped them to win promotion and the League Cup. He became manager of Portsmouth and then Cardiff City, where he established a fine reputation as a shrewd tactician and a no-nonsense leader of men. With his Scottish brogue, bristling moustache and wild-eyed demeanour, Burrows would have made a wonderfully sinister villain in crime films. Except in team photographs and presumably in bed, he always wore a flat cloth cap. On the touchline he was a scary figure who sometimes unnerved his own players, let alone opponents, while in the dressing room his expletive-laden tirades were never-to-be-forgotten affairs. Often during the interval or after the final whistle he radiated menace as he hurled boots, cups and Vaseline jars in the general direction of those whose performances had fallen short of expectations. Yet, in spite of his volcanic temper, Burrows was deeply respected by the players and established a warm affinity with the fans. He was as straight as a die and passionately in love with football. He knew the lower leagues well and could recognize a decent player at a glance. Crucially, too, he was strong enough to cope with the machinations of the chairman.

Under Doug Sharpe, Swansea had revived its old reputation of being a selling club. No young player was allowed to settle for too long at the Vetch and Yorath had seethed impotently when Andy Melville was sold to Oxford United for £275,000 in July 1990. Doubtless Burrows's comments were unprintable when young Chris Coleman was allowed to join Crystal Palace for £375,000, but at least he now had some funds to allow him to wheel and deal in the transfer market. In fact, by 1993 he had managed to assemble a very good football team, arguably the most attractive since John Toshack's heyday.

In Roger Freestone, whose loan from Chelsea was turned by Burrows into a £45,000 transfer, he could boast an extraordinarily fine goalkeeper, perhaps the best outside the Premiership, and one who not only specialized in keeping clean sheets but also in saving penalties and converting penalties for his own side. Known as the 'Dodger', he was in many ways the club's life-force. Full backs Steve Jenkins and Des Lyttle were quick in the tackle and in support, while Mark 'Chopper' Harris and Keith 'Sky' Walker were a highly formidable pair of centre backs whose challenges sometimes made the blood run cold. 'You'll never beat Keith Walker' was a popular chant on the North Bank. Alan Davies's intelligent prompting and creative subtlety stood out in the hectic and sometimes witless flow of play in the lower divisions, and there was great sadness at the Vetch when he took his own life in February 1992. John Cornforth, bought for a snip from Sunderland, was a strong anchoring presence in midfield, while Dave Penney was a versatile midfielder capable of surprising goalkeepers with sharply hit shots. His game improved noticeably when Colin Pascoe brought creativity and flair on his return from the north-east.

Burrows also had a soft spot for fast wingers. One of the most popular was John Williams, a former postman who was signed for as little as £5,000 from Cradley Town in August 1991. During his three separate spells at the club fans readily testified that the sheer pace of the 'Flying Postman' was worth the price of admission alone. But local products were also impressive on the flanks. The dazzling speed and trickery of Jason Bowen was a revelation on the right wing and Andy Legg could not only torment defences with incisive left-foot crosses but also pepper them with throws so long that they won him a place in the *Guinness Book of World Records*.

The emblem of the Swansea City Supporters Trust, founded in 2001
(courtesy of Swansea City AFC)

Young supporters of the Supporters Trust in full cry against the discredited chairman Tony Petty
(courtesy of the *South Wales Evening Post*)

A priceless East Stand ticket for the critically important game against Hull City on 3 May 2003
(courtesy of Gwyn Rees)

Kenny Jackett, manager of Swansea City 2004–7
(courtesy of Swansea City AFC)

The Jack Army marks the end of an era: the final league game held at the Vetch, against Shrewsbury Town, on 30 April 2005
(courtesy of Dimitri Legakis / Athena Photography)

A new era dawns: the Liberty Stadium
(courtesy of Swansea City AFC)

'Magic Daps': Lee Trundle
(courtesy of Dimitri Legakis / Athena Photography)

Lee Trundle's scintillating goal against Carlisle United in the Football League Trophy final on 2 April 2006
(courtesy of Swansea City AFC)

Roberto Martínez, manager of Swansea City 2007–9
(courtesy of Dimitri Legakis / Athena Photography)

The 'Three Amigos': Ángel Rangel, Guillem Bauzá and Andrea Orlandi
(courtesy of Swansea City AFC)

Garry Monk raises the trophy as Swansea win promotion to the Championship on 3 May 2008
(courtesy of Dimitri Legakis / Athena Photography)

Paulo Sousa, manager of Swansea City 2009–10
(courtesy of Swansea City AFC)

Always the sweetest of victories: a 3–2 derby win at the Liberty Stadium against Cardiff City, 7 November 2009
(courtesy of Dimitri Legakis / Athena Photography)

The Swansea City squad for the 2010–11 season
Back: Shefki Kuqi, Joe Walsh, Darren Pratley, Alan Tate, David Cornell, Dorus de Vries, Jordi López, Albert Serrán, Andrea Orlandi, Ángel Rangel; middle: Kate Rees, Adrian Tucker, Chris Davies, Ryland Morgans, David Cotterill, Scott Donnelly, Daniel Alfei, Ashley Williams, Lee Lucas, Casey Thomas, Cedric van der Gun, Alan Curtis (coach), Chantelle Thomas, Richard Buchanan, Suzan Eames; front row: Scott Sinclair, Ashley Richards, Nathan Dyer, Joe Allen, Garry Monk (captain), Brendan Rodgers (manager), Colin Pascoe (assistant manager), Neil Taylor, Tom Butler, Mark Gower, Stephen Dobbie, Craig Beattie
(courtesy of Swansea City AFC)

True grit personified:
Alan Tate
(courtesy of Dimitri Legakis / Athena Photography)

Brendan Rodgers and Colin Pascoe celebrate victory in the play-off semi-final against Nottingham Forest, 16 May 2011
(courtesy of Swansea City AFC)

Playmaker supreme: Leon Britton celebrates his goal against Nottingham Forest in the second leg of the play-off semi-final on 16 May 2011
(courtesy of Dimitri Legakis / Athena Photography)

Part of the 40,000-strong Jack Army at Wembley for the play-off final against Reading, 30 May 2011
(courtesy of Swansea City AFC)

Hat-trick hero Scott Sinclair torments the Reading defenders during the play-off final at Wembley
(courtesy of Dimitri Legakis / Athena Photography)

Manager Brendan Rodgers proudly holds the play-off trophy at Wembley
(courtesy of Swansea City AFC)

The Wembley celebrations, led by a youthful Alan Curtis, begin
(courtesy of Dimitri Legakis / Athena Photography)

Michel Vorm: as adept with his feet as with his hands. Swansea City v Wigan Athletic, 20 August 2011
(courtesy of Swansea City AFC)

Club captain Garry Monk rises above Emmanuel Adebayor and Gareth Bale. Swansea City v Tottenham Hotspur, 31 December 2011
(courtesy of Dimitri Legakis / Athena Photography)

Ashley Williams challenges Wayne Rooney. Swansea City v Manchester United, 19 November 2011
(courtesy of Swansea City AFC)

Joe Allen: a home-grown star of the highest quality
(courtesy of Dimitri Legakis / Athena Photography)

Nathan Dyer at his wicked best in the first round of the Carling Cup. Swansea City v Barnet, 10 August 2010
(courtesy of Swansea City AFC)

Cyril the Swan, the club's mascot, on his best behaviour
(courtesy of Dimitri Legakis / Athena Photography)

Gwyn Rees, a lifelong fan, with his collection of memorabilia
(courtesy of Swansea City AFC)

Danny Graham celebrates his winning goal against Arsenal, 15 January 2012
(courtesy of Dimitri Legakis / Athena Photography)

The most highly acclaimed Premiership goal scored at the Liberty Stadium in the 2011–12 season: Luke Moore's header, on 11 March 2012, which toppled high-flying Manchester City
(courtesy of Swansea City AFC)

To great excitement, Michael Laudrup was unveiled as Swansea's new manager on 22 June 2012
(courtesy of Dimitri Legakis / Athena Photography)

Burrows also liked tall and mobile target men with a lean and hungry look. Into this category came Jimmy Gilligan, whom Yorath had signed in August 1990 and who scored a hatful of goals before a back injury forced him to retire. Then there was the abrasive, much-travelled Colin West, who was joint top goal-scorer in the 1992–3 season before he blotted his copybook by foolishly getting sent off after coming on as a substitute during a crucial play-off match against West Bromwich Albion. A furious Burrows sent him packing to Leyton Orient and pinned his faith on Andy McFarlane who, at 6' 3", was just as much a handful for defenders. Stephen Torpey, a beanpole whom Burrows signed from Bradford City for £80,000, repaid the club many times over by scoring 44 goals.

Burrows used the modest funds available to him wisely and managed to buy seasoned professionals who did not command inflated salaries. He also made sizeable profits in the transfer market. His £5,000-signing John Williams brought in a whopping £250,000 when he was transferred to Coventry. Des Lyttle, signed for just £12,500, left for Nottingham Forest after a season for a record fee of £375,000. Such transactions made good financial sense, but there was considerable disquiet when, presumably on Sharpe's bidding, both Andy Legg and Jason Bowen were allowed to leave. Their departure provided added proof that the club was not serious about gaining promotion, especially after failing by a whisker to defeat West Bromwich Albion in a play-off semi-final in May 1993.

Yet, in spite of the chairman's parsimony and unexpected setbacks in the league, Frank Burrows became the first manager in the club's history to lead out Swansea at Wembley. Following a long and arduous campaign, on 24 April 1994 Swansea City faced Huddersfield Town in the final of the Autoglass Trophy. Some disdainful reporters reckoned that this poor man's FA Cup final was a decidedly inferior competition, but the two managers – Frank Burrows and Neil Warnock – and their teams took it very seriously indeed. So did the respective sets of fans. The best part of 20,000 Welsh supporters, dressed in black and white, converged on the Twin Towers on a high tide of emotion. For the first time ever, the Jack Army was able to cheer on its favourites at Wembley and lay to rest the 67-year-old bogey of Cardiff being the only team in Wales to reach that legendary stadium. The omens were encouraging. Newcomers Swansea were innocents abroad, but Huddersfield had lost on each of their three previous visits to Wembley.

Burrows prepared his team with meticulous care and on the day he managed to strike a productive balance between defensive solidity and attacking fluency. 'Sublime Swansea glide to Victory' was one striking headline, though this scarcely conveyed the resilience which the team displayed in resisting their more physical opponents. Andy McFarlane, chosen for his mobility in attack, put the Swans ahead after eight minutes when he controlled Freestone's long free kick on his chest before scoring from a tight angle. Following a disputed corner, the Tykes equalized when Richard Logan headed home on the hour. A stalemate followed and after extra time the score was still 1–1. The Swansea penalty-takers all held their nerve. Thunderous shots by Cornforth, Ampadu and Torpey sent the Huddersfield goalkeeper diving the wrong way. Two efforts by Huddersfield were fluffed and the imperious Freestone saved another. A carnival atmosphere followed as the Welsh celebrated victory in what had been billed as the biggest game in the club's history.

Following this richly deserved success, Doug Sharpe said of Burrows: 'I think he has a lot to offer Swansea City and if everyone is patient he'll do the job for us. He is the type of person you simply cannot let go.' But coping with the chairman's mean streak was difficult and, on 2 October, probably as a result of a dispute with Sharpe over playing resources, Burrows resigned. His efforts had been undermined by the constant blood-letting and the parsimony of the board. The players, who had loved the Scot despite his idiosyncratic ways and sulphurous temper, were distraught, while angry supporters mourned the departure of a true football man.

Once more, as Sharpe desperately sought to find a buyer, the lack of planning, let alone a sense of vision, was palpable. Something was dreadfully amiss at the club and valuable time was lost in finding a suitable successor to Burrows. His assistant Bobby Smith held the fort for three months before yielding the post to Jimmy Rimmer for another six weeks. Then the managerial merry-go-round descended into complete farce. Sharpe claimed to have sold the club to Michael Thompson, a millionaire from the West Midlands of whom no one in Swansea had heard, let alone seen. In his infinite wisdom, Thompson appointed one Kevin Cullis, supposedly a youth team manager from the Midlands who had no background in professional football and who was so manifestly out of his depth that the players cringed with embarrassment. Within a week the clueless Cullis had been sent packing and Sharpe had returned from vacation to invoke a contractual clause which enabled him to call off the deal with Thompson. But no one would have been surprised had Swansea gone on to appoint a pantomime dame or even a stuffed teddy bear to manage the team.

There were serious consequences for the club. Tales of its poverty, incompetence and mismanagement did the rounds. The pressing need to balance the books meant that there were no landmark signings. Hair-raising stories were told of the lack of basic creature comforts for the players, including adequate training kit, leg and ankle strapping and overnight accommodation. Not surprisingly, several promising youngsters who dreamed of playing for their country preferred not to trust their future to such a dysfunctional club. When Wales had played Iceland on 14 October 1981, six many-times-capped Swansea players had worn the red shirt. But during the 1990s caps awarded to Swansea players virtually dried up. Worryingly, too, many home-grown products were failing to make the grade, a trend which reflected weaknesses in the scouting system and the coaching.

Manager followed manager and on 22 February 1996 the club restored some semblance of sanity by appointing a Great Dane to stave off the growing threat of relegation. The bovine Jan Molby, formerly of Liverpool, was an international star whose superb first touch and passing ability had made him a great favourite at Anfield. Sharpe hoped that he was another Toshack in the making, but he was inexperienced at this level and was unable to halt the slide into Division Three. The highlight of Molby's 19-month tenure was his valiant attempt to win promotion in a play-off final against long-ball experts Northampton Town at Wembley on 24 May 1997. On a blisteringly hot afternoon, a youthful Swansea side commanded the lion's share of possession but failed to create clear-cut chances. Deep into injury time Northampton were awarded a hotly disputed free kick on the edge of the Swansea penalty box. The kick was charged down by Jonathan Coates, but the referee ordered it to be retaken. Sod's Law then prevailed. The ball was moved a couple of feet, which allowed John Frain's second kick to fly past the unsighted Freestone into the net. There was barely time to restart the game.

Shortly after this defeat, a careworn and weary Doug Sharpe resigned after occupying the chair for 14 years. Although he deserved great credit for keeping the club afloat, he had gained a reputation for stinginess. But Sharpe had understandably become increasingly wary of trusting the judgement of his managers. He had burned his fingers as early as 1989–90 by spending over half a million pounds on five players of whom only one, Keith Walker, proved to be a valuable long-term asset. Not unreasonably, he tightened the purse-strings after this chastening experience though, unlike his Aston Villa counterpart Doug Ellis, he never became known as 'Deadly Doug'. Indeed, one of his great attributes was that he remained a genuine Swansea fan throughout his stint as chairman.

By mid-July the club was in the hands of new owners. Silver

Shield Group plc, chaired by businessman Neil McClure, represented the new corporate age of poshly-dressed executives and grand mission statements. McClure's stated ambition was to prise the club from the Sandfields and transfer it to a purpose-built 25,000-seat stadium at Morfa within a complex of shopping and leisure facilities, a hotel, a cinema, an ice rink and a fitness centre. Local cynics distrusted him, not least because he was a self-confessed Norwich City fan and also a season-ticket holder with Arsenal. More reassuringly, Steve Hamer, the new chairman of the club, was a long-standing Swansea City supporter. Yet, instability soon returned to plague the Vetch. The trigger-happy new owners sacked Molby on 8 October and once more the club found itself in managerial disarray.

Three Londoners then boarded the Swansea carousel in turn. The first, Micky Adams, presided over three defeats before packing his bags and giving way to his assistant Alan Cork, a former member of Wimbledon's Crazy Gang. His way of playing was hardly consonant with the Swansea style even though he wisely chose Alan Curtis as his assistant. Twentieth place at the end of the season was hardly what the new owners had expected and Cork fell victim to Hamer's short-termism at the end of June 1998. Unhappily, the mediocre fare served at the Vetch coincided with the demise of two of Swansea's greatest legends. Ivor Allchurch passed away, aged 67, in July 1997 and, totally unexpectedly, in February 1998 Robbie James died of a heart attack at the age of 40 while playing for Llanelli. The irony was not lost on those fans who cherished fond memories of these wonderful footballers.

Nonetheless, hope always springs eternal in a Swansea breast and on the 1 July 1998 the appointment of John Hollins, a chirpy, personable Londoner, raised spirits. Hollins's playing experience with Chelsea and Arsenal commanded respect even if his record in club management hardly inspired confidence. But at least he was a big name and one who had always been associated with attractive football. He inherited a useful squad. The evergreen Freestone was a tower of strength, centre backs Matthew Bound and Jason Smith were as rugged as any of their peers in the lower divisions, Kristian O'Leary was a versatile, tough-tackling midfielder, wingers Jason Price and Stuart Roberts were blindingly fast and tricky, Steve Watkin was an intelligent goal-scorer and Julian Alsop was the kind of no-nonsense centre forward of whom Trevor Ford would have approved. Supporters warmed to Hollins's genuine efforts to Cymricize the club. He laid great store by winning the Welsh Cup and used to drape the Welsh flag over the dugout at all away venues.

Hollins came agonizingly close to winning promotion in his first season and then, having abandoned attractive football for greater pragmatism during his second season, he achieved a feat which had eluded Swansea for 51 years: a championship title. The crucial decider was held at Rotherham on 6 May 2000. Rotherham needed to win to snatch the championship, while Swansea needed a draw to top the table. The sun beat down mercilessly on the perspiring players and when Bound scored from the penalty spot with a minute left hundreds of Swansea supporters swarmed on to the pitch. When the game resumed the home side were awarded the softest of penalties, a decision which prompted another pitch invasion, this time by the home fans. When order was restored, the spot-kick was converted, and the final whistle sounded shortly afterwards. For once, the club had made the headlines by winning a league trophy rather than by committing some off-the-field folly.

It was too good to last. For some mysterious reason, Hollins believed that his squad was sufficiently talented and robust to survive in Division Two. True, he was operating within a tight financial straightjacket, but even when a dire series of results showed very clearly that many of his charges were not up to scratch he still refused to invest in reinforcements. As a manager he lost his way and in so doing forfeited the trust of players and supporters. By May 2001 Swansea City had nosedived back into Division Three.

How had the supporters fared over the previous two

decades? For many football lovers this had been a wretchedly bleak era. There was a general slump in support, partly because of indifferent results on the pitch but also because poverty and unemployment were undermining communities in which support for the Swans had always been strong. As a consequence of Thatcherism, large-scale closures in the coal and steel industries created black holes of unemployment along the Swansea and Neath valleys, and the steelworks town of Port Talbot became known as 'Giro City'. Within Swansea itself the gulf widened between those living in wealthy parts of what was fancifully called the 'Welsh San Francisco' and the down-at-heel areas, depicted in the film *Twin Town*, where unemployment, drug abuse and violence reigned.

Crowds also dwindled because many fans were so appalled by the disasters at Bradford, Heysel and especially Hillsborough that they simply could not bring themselves to risk life and limb on crumbling terraces and in stands which were serious fire hazards. The dilapidated Vetch had become a shoddy disgrace, a testament to lack of investment and consideration for health and safety issues. Its abominable toilet facilities (sensible supporters with strong bladders took a leak before arriving at the ground), cheap but hardly cheerful pies, and poky club shop had long passed their sell-by date. The beloved pitch, a gluepot in winter and bone-hard in the spring, was plainly sub-standard. In 1990 the Taylor Report called for 'a new ethos in football' which would encompass all-seated accommodation, better facilities and greater comfort. These recommendations had important implications for clubs like Swansea. Where would it find funds to modernize the ground and was the time now ripe to relocate the club out of town, most probably at Morfa in the Lower Swansea Valley? Many hard-core supporters would sooner have parted with their wives than abandon the Vetch, but moving house to a state-of-art modern facility was bound to come.

Although plans for relocation constituted a saga littered with false starts, the arguments in favour were strengthened by the need to stamp out hooliganism. It was not unusual to hear vile racist chants and taunts, as well as see Nazi salutes, at the Vetch. Derby games with Cardiff crackled with ill will and malevolence. Many resentful Swansea fans had tired of the material and cultural benefits heaped upon a capital city which had voted against political devolution. Missile-throwing and tribal chanting by rival supporters spilled over into the rabbit warren of streets around the Vetch as terrified local residents cowered indoors. Such disorderly behaviour, though never on a large scale, sickened decent supporters and brought the club into grave disrepute. Unsuspecting fans were sometimes caught up in a melee either at home or at away fixtures. The most poignant instance occurred at Rotherham in May 2000 when Terry Coles, an entirely innocent supporter, strayed inadvertently into the path of a rearing police horse and was killed by its pounding hooves. His death was later declared by the Independent Police Complaints Commission to have been caused by a failure of duty by three police officers.

Mercifully, the combined effects of harsher sentences for convicted hooligans, closed-circuit television, and prohibiting away fans from attending derbies improved matters. In 1993 the Professional Footballers Association launched a 'Let's kick racism out of football' campaign and when managers like Yorath, Burrows and Hollins ended the tradition of white-domination at the Vetch by signing black or foreign players they were no longer greeted with monkey-noises and banana-throwing. Indeed, some of them became the firmest of favourites. The all-action style of Kwame Ampadu, the lightning speed of John Williams, the long strides of the dreadlocked winger Jason Price and the idiosyncrasies of Mamady Sidibe all delighted the home fans. Walter Boyd, a Jamaica international, even managed to achieve cult-hero status by coming on as a substitute against Darlington and being sent off after nil seconds, an achievement which is likely to remain a world record until the end of time.

Throughout this period Swansea City had to scramble and struggle to stay alive. According to its long-serving goalkeeper

Roger Freestone, who was a first-hand witness to many of the trials and tribulations, 'The club is one where there aren't any dull days'. But at the start of the new millennium prospects of survival were not at all encouraging. Having been on the crest of a wave 20 years earlier, the club was now sinking fast towards the seabed.

7

From Near Extinction to the Premiership

THE BEGINNING OF the extraordinary revival in the fortunes of Swansea City Football Club can be precisely dated to 27 August 2001. During that balmy evening, ardent and angry supporters, led by the feisty campaigner Phil Sumbler, assembled in the Patti Pavilion in Swansea not just to let off steam about the downturn in the club's fortunes but also to establish the first Supporters Trust in the history of the club. Over 600 fans pledged their support to the Trust and its aim of changing the power structure in the boardroom and gaining a voice in deliberations over the future of the club. A good deal of the groundwork had been undertaken beforehand by Richard Lillicrap, a tireless Swansea-born activist and a leading member of the board of Supporters Direct, a government-sponsored organization established in order to help supporters to found trusts. Supporters of the Swans were no longer prepared to allow themselves to be frozen out of the process of running the club or leave it in the hands of owners who did not genuinely care about its fate. Tired of mismanagement, lies and evasions, and of flirting with oblivion, they insisted that the club should be properly run as a reputable business in the interest of all the players and supporters. This bloodless revolt heralded a new era.

The summer of 2001 had been thoroughly dispiriting. On 11 July the loss-making owners Ninth Floor plc had sold their stake in the club to the former commercial director Mike Lewis for a pound, on the understanding that he would repay loans of £801,000 to the company. The supporters had no faith in Lewis and their fears were confirmed when, in October, the club fell into the hands of Tony Petty, a Londoner with business interests in Australia, once more for just a pound. Suspicion surrounded Petty and rumours soon began to circulate about his reputation for making grubby deals and his lack of any sense of financial ethics. From the outset he incensed the fans with his gung-ho, bellicose attitude. He made no secret of his scorn for 'those thick Welshies' and his personal behaviour, even in the presence of the press, was deplorable. Crassly, he almost immediately placed 15 players on the transfer list or offered them reduced terms. No one believed him when he promised to bring over outstanding socceroos from Queensland to strengthen his rapidly depleting squad of players.

Fearful that the club's affairs were descending into farce and likely bankruptcy, members of the Supporters Trust organized public demonstrations and marches to express the general sense of loathing towards the hapless chairman. 'Petty Out!' became their battle-cry and the chairman was all but burnt in effigy. Claiming the moral high ground, supporters of the Trust made it their business to run the brash intruder out of town. Local solicitor and fan Steve Penny (currently a director) offered his unpaid services to help the campaign assemble a financial package and a draft consortium agreement. In late January 2002, Petty, who was by this stage a bundle of nerves, eventually accepted a buy-out offer of £20,000 and handed over the club to a local consortium led by the former player Mel Nurse. Celebrations among the supporters were understandably loud and delirious.

The whole episode had been a striking example of fan power. A new Swansea City had been created based on a historic bond between club and community. By gaining a 10 per cent shareholding and a place on the board for Leigh Dineen, the first supporter-director and currently vice chairman, the Trust, as a not-for-profit organization, now provided a vibrant new influence which enabled the club to be administered in an open and accountable manner for the long-term good of all its supporters. From 15 February the club was placed in the hands of a management committee composed of local people – Martin Burgess, Leigh Dineen, Huw Jenkins, Brian Katzen, David Morgan and Mel Nurse – who were determined to ensure that the club would henceforth live within its means and plan sensibly for the future.

Understandably, given the circumstances, mistakes were made. In a bid to reduce costs, the manager Colin Addison and his assistant Peter Nicholas, experienced old hands who had kept the club well clear of the relegation zone following the dismissal of John Hollins, were informed that their contracts would expire in the summer. Both left at once and playing affairs for the last month of the season were entrusted temporarily to the captain Nick Cusack and senior professional Roger Freestone. A 1–7 thumping at Hartlepool did not inspire confidence in the twin caretakers, but Cusack was the club's representative with the Professional Footballers Association and had championed the players' cause admirably during Petty's reign of terror. Even though he had no managerial experience, the club felt beholden to him and offered him a twelve-month contract at the end of the season. But when the rookie manager could only register a single victory in the first nine games of the 2002–3 season, the club's confidence in him plummeted. With the club marooned in 92nd place in the Football League, Cusack was dismissed on 19 September. Learning the hard way, the management committee belatedly realized that safer hands were needed.

By this stage Huw Jenkins had begun to exercise a growing influence in the running of the club. Born in Walthamstow but raised locally, Jenkins was a former bricklayer who became a successful businessman in the local building industry. Soon to become chairman, he consistently argued that the club should not repeat the mistakes of the past by spending recklessly or by appointing inexperienced managers with little or no coaching ability. The history of the club had taught him that imprudence leads to debt, debt leads to poor decision-making, and poor decision-making leads to decay and possible extinction. Committed to establishing what he called 'a stable platform', he ensured that the club would no longer pay inflated transfer fees, run up massive wage bills or indulge in any unwarranted expenditure. Every penny would be counted and made to count, and all future managers would be expected to implement this prudent, business-like approach.

Five managers – two former Wales internationals, two Iberians and a Northern Irishman – became integral parts of the building blocks which the club put in place during the decade preceding its centenary year. During these years Swansea City climbed from the lowest place in the Football League to the dizzy heights of the Premiership by playing eye-catchingly attractive football. The club settled in a gleaming new stadium on the outskirts of the city, where its support quadrupled from around 5,000 to over 20,000 spectators. Financial probity brought rich dividends as the club's turnover increased from around a million to 56 million pounds. The transformation was as unexpected as it was heartening. The ugly ducklings had become high-flying swans. Small wonder that those who had lived through the dark days rubbed their eyes in utter disbelief.

The road to redemption began when Swansea replaced Cusack with probably the smallest manager in its history. But although Lilliputian in size, Port Talbot-born Brian Flynn had the heart of a lion and had been known in his playing days with Burnley and Leeds as the 'Mighty Flynn'. A skilful and tenacious midfielder, he had 66 international caps to his name and, most important of all, an excellent record as coach and manager of Wrexham. He had a daunting task ahead of him. Swansea were poised to fall through the trapdoor into the Nationwide Conference League but, with Kevin Reeves as his assistant and Alan Curtis as first-team coach, Flynn slowly but surely began to make his mark. Over a period of 18 months he assembled a team of wily old professionals and promising youngsters. Using his wide contacts and man-management skills to good effect, he brought in Roberto Martínez from Walsall, a classy, thoughtful midfielder who reckoned that the best football was played on grass rather than in the air. Two of his most gifted loanees were Alan Tate from Manchester United, a combustible defender who was initially thought to be an explosive indiscretion waiting to happen but who proved to be a loyal and committed servant, and Leon Britton from West Ham United, an elusive winger who would become an extraordinarily influential playmaker under future managers. Four successive 0–1 defeats in December boded ill, but the new recruits raised spirits as the club began to rally. Even so, by the end of April two victories were needed to avoid the unthinkable. The penultimate game was played at Rochdale, a nerve-shredding occasion for players and travelling fans alike, but goals by Kevin Nugent and Marc Richards secured a 2–1 victory which kept hopes of survival alive.

Then followed an emotional, gut-wrenching encounter against high-flying Hull City at the Vetch on the last day of the season, 3 May. Nothing less than three points would save Swansea's bacon and, even though the Vetch on that day was no place for the faint-hearted, the capacity crowd of 9,585 could easily have been doubled. The blunt truth was that the club was staring extinction in the face. But, cometh the hour, cometh the bravest men. Even though, as he later confessed, his stomach was in knots, Alan Curtis delivered an inspiring pre-match speech in the dressing room which left the players in no doubt about the crucial importance of the result to former players and the supporters. On the field, the Swansea striker James Thomas was determined to show that only a Morriston lad with a sweet left foot could save the Swans. When Leon Britton was tripped in the box after just six minutes, Thomas stepped forward to drill the penalty home. The roar was deafening. The din had hardly died down when two wretched errors led to two goals for Hull. Just before half-time, however, Swansea were awarded a hotly disputed spot kick. In a carbon copy of his first penalty, James Thomas coolly converted the kick and the momentum once more was with the home team. A 48th-minute goal by Lennie Johnrose eased nerves and then James Thomas sealed the victory and his hat-trick with an audacious chip. When the final whistle sounded, grown men fell tearfully into each other's arms. The Swans had survived.

During his second season in charge, Brian Flynn brought to Swansea two Merseysiders who became firm favourites with the fans. Andy Robinson was a left-sided attacker who burned on a short fuse and was capable of scoring with thunderous shots from afar. Lee Trundle was a latecomer to League football. He was 24 when he joined Wrexham in 2001 but Flynn, who enticed him to Swansea in July 2003, knew that the squeaky-voiced Scouser was a crowd-pleaser who was capable of moments of brilliance which few others could muster. By Christmas, 'Magic Daps', as he became known, had already scored 13 league goals and was well on his way to gaining cult status at the club. Alan Tate and Leon Britton became fully-fledged members of the team and prospered as the manager laid the basis for greater stability.

But the Flynn regime suffered from a major weakness. Neither Flynn nor Reeves lived locally and Huw Jenkins and his colleagues feared that standards of discipline within and without the club were deteriorating. In the absence of a code of conduct, an after-hours drinking culture was thriving. Some of the players were famous for their riotous social life and local wags reckoned that they were more likely to develop cirrhosis of the liver than win promotion for the club. Such immature behaviour was bound to affect performances on the pitch. A mid-table spot did not match the board's ambitions and on 18 March 2004 Flynn, to use football parlance, was relieved of his duties. He had every reason to feel aggrieved. He had kept the club afloat during his first turbulent season and was steadily building an attractive team. Moreover, his agreeable manner and tactical nous had helped him to develop a warm relationship with both players and supporters. But football has little room for sentiment and Huw Jenkins already had a younger manager in mind.

Like Flynn, Kenny Jackett was not a physically imposing figure, but he too had been a terrier-like midfielder, both with Watford and Wales, and was well regarded as a coach. Perky and strong willed, he was determined to do things his way and to implement a very different game plan. His mentor was Graham Taylor, a footballing guru by the 1990s and an ardent advocate of the 'long ball' game. At Watford, this direct style of play had brought rich dividends. It might not have been 'the Swansea way', but Jackett believed that direct football, or what purists derisively called 'vertical football', would set Swansea on a firmly upward trajectory in the Football League.

Relying on old heads and physical power was an integral part of Jackett's blueprint. He rightly believed that Division Three was no place to blood untried and nervous youngsters. Nor were there to be many opportunities for ball-players like Roberto Martínez. Jackett preferred to work on the collective strength of the team and to recruit and deploy strong, wholesome players with great stamina and a winning mentality. During his period in charge, there was no lack of muscle in the squad. Goalkeeper Willy Gueret, a tough, aggressive Guadeloupean, enjoyed physical confrontation both on and off the field. Kevin Austin and Sam Ricketts were no-frills defenders very much in the Alan Tate mould, and in the long term Jackett's most significant signing was centre back Garry Monk, who arrived on a free transfer from Southampton and formed a durable defensive partnership with Ezomo (Izzy) Iriekpen. Jackett swiftly realized that Monk was a genuine leader of men. As a defender, he refused to yield an inch. Strong in the tackle and in the air, he exuded defiance and over the next eight years he would prove to be a powerful voice in the dressing room and in pre-match huddles. When Monk sustained a serious knee injury, Jackett signed Dennis Lawrence, a 6' 7" Trinidadian beanpole whose matchstick legs belied his strength in the tackle. In midfield he introduced Darren Pratley from Fulham, a competitive midfielder whose athleticism and raking stride offered momentum in a key area, while strong target men like Adebayo (Bayo) Akinfenwa and, later, Rory Fallon, created room for Lee Trundle's party tricks.

The squad soon discovered that their slightly built and unprepossessing manager was in fact the toughest of taskmasters and much harder to please than his predecessor. Since he did not believe that getting legless at drinking parties encouraged team-building or togetherness, he reformed the players' drinking and dietary habits and set new standards of fitness. His arduous training routines emphasized team-shape, defensive responsibilities and set pieces. He took them to boot camps and held rigorous training sessions in cold and wet weather which exhausted the party animals in the squad and added a touch of steel to their game, though it did not prevent Lee Trundle from dating a Miss Wales, a Miss England and a Miss Great Britain in one season alone. To Jackett's great credit, he accepted Trundle's idiosyncrasies and gave him relatively free rein to showcase his exceptional gifts. Although Trundle was not the best of trainers or among the fastest runners in the team – 'Trundle by name, Trundle by nature' was the pundit Mark Lawrenson's unkind verdict – he had a wonderful repertoire of feints, dragbacks, step-overs, nutmegs and flick passes. His left foot was the stuff of legend and over a period of four seasons he scored 86 league and cup goals for Swansea, many of them quite extraordinary. Two in particular stand out. On 18 November 2005, a poor clearance by the Yeovil keeper fell to Trundle. Forty metres from goal, he took the ball on his chest and let it drop before driving an exquisite, sharply dipping volley over the head of the back-pedalling keeper. Then, on 2 April 2006, in the first few minutes of the Football League Trophy final against Carlisle, he produced another moment of magic. He cushioned a beautifully measured cross from Britton on his chest and in one movement fired a left-footed volley across his body from the edge of the box into the bottom corner of the net. It was a piece of technical brilliance of which any player in the world would have been proud. Small wonder that Trundlemania flourished.

Notwithstanding the irrepressible Trundle, the team which Jackett assembled was efficient, well-organized and durable. In his first full season at the helm, the new manager led Swansea to promotion from League Two (formerly Division Three) to League One and made off with the Football Association of Wales Premier Cup by beating Wrexham 2–1. Playing football the Watford way had brought immediate success and the club was once more a serious footballing force. But the end-of-season celebrations were tinged with poignancy. On 30 April 2005 the last league game ever to be held at the Vetch was played against Shrewsbury. A crowd of 11,469 packed into the much-loved, dilapidated stadium to cheer their heroes to victory. The winning goal by midfielder Adrian Forbes was met with a deafening roar and many fans took home as many mementos of the occasion as they could carry from the Vetch.

The time had come to leave home and tears flowed among the diehards, some of whom feared that the departure to a concrete bowl on the outskirts of the city would rip the heart out of the club. But Huw Jenkins and his colleagues were aware that the old ground now existed in a kind of time warp and was in a dangerous state of disrepair. Staying put was not a feasible option and, thanks to the generous cooperation of the city council, a brand new stadium, in which a broader range of spectators, including families, could watch their favourites in surroundings free from overcrowding, traffic congestion and hooliganism, opened its doors in August 2005. The Vetch had served as the club's beloved home for 93 years, but the latter's future would now be associated with this elegant, 20,500-seat stadium, built close to the river Tawe at a cost of £27 million. Shortly to be christened the Liberty Stadium, the new facility was appropriately built on land where reserves of coal, copper, silver, lead and zinc had once made Swansea famous. In 1912 the players had gingerly run on to a grass-free pitch, but now the splendid playing surface, in which grass seeds had been reinforced with plastic fibres, was as good as any in the land.

Kenny Jackett's men soon settled down in their new home and there were goals aplenty to relish as the likes of Trundle and Robinson enjoyed playing on the lush turf before five-figure crowds. Walsall (5–2), Bristol City (7–1) and Chesterfield (5–1) were just some of the teams dispatched by Swansea's direct, attacking play. For the second consecutive season the Swans beat Wrexham to retain the Football Association of Wales Premier Cup and, on a joyous day at the Millennium Stadium in Cardiff on 2 April 2006, goals by Trundle and Akinfenwa, brought home the Football League Trophy at the expense of Carlisle. Disappointingly, however, Swansea fell at the last play-off hurdle which would have promoted them to the Championship. Over 35,000 Swansea fans watched an enthralling final against Barnsley at the Millennium Stadium on 27 May. Although Jackett's players dominated the play and created the better chances, they suffered the agony of losing 3–4 in a penalty shoot-out. The manager had come within a whisker of fulfilling his dream.

During the following season, the board sensed that Jackett's tenure had served its purpose. Faith in his style and tactics waned. The supporters had never truly warmed to him, partly because he had brusquely dispensed with the services of loyal and much-loved players like Freestone and Martínez, but largely because his tactical approach was so alien to the Swansea ethos. Jackett himself was aware of this mood and, following a poor set of results in February 2007, he left the club by mutual consent, claiming that he 'no longer had the 100 per cent support of everybody connected with the club'. Few were sad to see him go. Nonetheless, on his departure he could boast an impressive record of success and there is no doubt that he left the club on a much stronger footing.

Huw Jenkins does not give the impression of being a gambler, but his next appointment took everyone by surprise. For the first time in its history, in recruiting former player Roberto Martínez from Chester City the board appointed a manager born and bred outside the United Kingdom. During his time at Swansea the swarthy Catalan had shown a deep knowledge of football and had behaved impeccably both as club captain and player. His good looks, natural charm and boundless enthusiasm counted in his favour, and the fans had always admired his stylish play and the pride with which he had worn the captain's armband. From the outset, therefore, there was a huge groundswell of popular goodwill towards Martínez. Even though he had no managerial experience, he was clearly an advocate of technical and tactical sophistication. His style of football was very much in the Swansea mould and over the course of two seasons he proved to be a brilliantly imaginative choice.

It is no exaggeration to claim that Martínez transformed the club. First of all, he assembled a squad of players who were comfortable on the ball and hungry for success. He retained loyal servants like Monk, Tate and Britton (who became the most beguiling playmaker in midfield), and gave every opportunity to the Dublin-born winger Tom Butler, Pratley, Trundle and Robinson to prove their worth. Two of his British-based recruits proved to be excellent long-term investments. Centre back Ashley Williams, signed from Stockport for £400,000, was a strong, competitive defender whose consistency and injury-free record proved to be enormous assets for the club and for Wales. At the opposite end of the field, facing his own goal in most games, was striker Jason Scotland, a bargain at £25,000 from St Johnstone. With his trademark dreadlocks and rippling muscles, he enjoyed the drudgery and hard knocks associated with being a target man. Although his first touch was sometimes uncertain, he turned out to be an extraordinary goal-scorer. Striking the ball with either foot and with minimal backlift, he scored 53 goals in 103 appearances.

Whereas Jackett had epitomized the British bulldog, the cosmopolitan Martínez had broader horizons. With the blessing of the board, he took the strategic decision to carry out some bargain shopping in his native Catalonia and in Holland. Scouring the Spanish market, over a period of time he brought home a rich collection of players. The best of them was Ángel Rangel from lowly Terrassa, a right back with superb technical ability and overlapping skills. His alliterative name, a gift to specialists in Welsh *cynghanedd*, prompted one over-enthusiastic reporter to ask: 'Is there a finer name in the entire football league than Ángel Rangel?' Another gifted player was Jordi Gómez, who spent a season at the Liberty on loan from Espanyol. A calm, skilful left-sided midfielder, Gómez was adept at using his upper body strength to shield the ball and unbalance opponents, and some of his free kicks were unstoppable. He scored 12 league goals in 44 appearances. Guillem Bauzá (known as 'Bussy'), formerly of Barcelona, was a skilful and intelligent goal-poacher, while Andrea Orlandi, a left winger recruited from Alaves, was an elegant attacker who sometimes flattered to deceive. Gorka Pintado, nicknamed 'El Toro', was a rampaging striker from Granada who underachieved at Swansea but who will always be fondly remembered for an eye-watering tackle on everyone's favourite villain, Robbie Savage, at Derby. Ruggedness was also associated with Albert Serrán, a central defender bought from Espanyol for £80,000. These native Catalan and Spanish speakers were joined by the Spanish-speaking Argentine left back, Federico Bessone, who came on a free transfer from Espanyol, but whose progress was plagued by injuries.

This strong Spanish contingent was also complemented by players from the Netherlands. Martínez was a great admirer of the technical ability and awareness of Dutch players. In Dorus de Vries, a former Den Haag goalkeeper whom he signed from Dunfermline in the summer of 2007, he found a confident, mentally tough player who was not only an accomplished shot-stopper but also fully able to control the play with the ball at his feet. At no time was Martínez's eye for talent better illustrated than when he snapped up Ferrie Bodde, a midfield player of the highest quality, from Den Haag for an initial fee of £50,000. Bodde was not just a fierce tackler. He could spray accurate long passes with both feet and startle goalkeepers with thunderous shots from afar. Semi-affectionately dubbed the 'Evil Genius' by Swansea supporters, he was thought to be a master of the dark arts on the field. When he sustained a long-term, career-threatening knee injury in November 2008, he was already valued in excess of a million pounds.

Nor did Martínez neglect home-grown Welsh talent. He appreciated the loyalty shown by the versatile Port Talbot midfielder Kristian O'Leary and gave every encouragement to up-and-coming youngsters like Ashley ('Jazz') Richards and Shaun MacDonald. But the brightest talent in his nursery was Joe Allen, a Welsh-speaking, Carmarthen-born midfielder who could presumably assure the Catalan contingent that his native tongue was at least as old as theirs. From the moment he joined the first-team squad and made his debut at 17, Allen showed that he possessed quality and character in abundance. His lovely touch and feel for angles meant that he could distribute the ball quickly and accurately. Snapping eagerly into tackles, he also played with a determined glint in his eye.

Never before had Swansea boasted such a cosmopolitan dressing room. Led by 'El Gaffer', it included players born in Wales, England, Ireland, Spain, the Netherlands, Argentina, and Trinidad and Tobago. It thus accurately reflected the modern globalization of football. In a short space of time, Martínez managed to blend this seemingly disparate group of individuals into an extremely well-organized unit. He was a great believer in ball retention. Controlling games by confiscating the ball for long periods became the hallmark of his team. The pattern was dictated by goalkeeper de Vries, who was instructed never to punt the ball aimlessly upfield but rather to pass or throw it to the nearest unmarked player. The back four and midfield players controlled the tempo of the game by playing simple one- or two-touch passes swiftly to feet, keeping the ball moving in neat triangles, using Jason Scotland as a point of reference and bringing dynamic runners on the flanks into play. The speed and fluency of the 4–5–1 or 4–3–3 systems adopted by Martínez bewildered tactically illiterate opponents who had been used to coping with lumpen 4–4–2 formations. The cosmopolitan Swans delightedly hogged the ball for long periods in the game and supporters at the Liberty Stadium purred with pleasure as the Spanish style came to replicate what they believed to be 'the Swansea way'. Their reaction was a firm rebuttal of Graham Taylor's claim that 'the man on the terrace is not interested in watching a team making 15 or 16 consecutive passes'. Only oafs were heard to shout 'Get rid of it!' at the Liberty Stadium.

On and off the field, habits were changed. Martínez introduced an unprecedented degree of planning. His politeness masked a steely streak, and all members of staff were expected to buckle down to their tasks. All training routines, including the warm-up and cool-down, were performed with a ball. Pre-match preparations were meticulous and feedback on performances was clinical. The players adored Martínez, and many of them would have run through plate-glass windows to please him on the field. As the fans came to understand and enjoy the highly rhythmic and attractive style of play, they serenaded the manager to the strains of 'La donna è mobile' and he, in turn, declared his undying love for the club and the community.

Martínez succeeded where Jackett had failed: his team romped to the League One title in the 2007–8 season. During the course of the season the club went on a run of 18 games without defeat. After a series of excellent performances, a 2–1 victory at Gillingham on 12 April, courtesy of a bracc by Bauzá, assured the club of promotion, but since Leeds had contested a 12-point deduction from their tally of points Swansea were not proclaimed champions until the last fixture on 3 May when Brighton were defeated. Over the season the team had won 27 games, scored 82 goals and amassed 92 points, a tally which left them ten points clear of the runners-up. Life proved much tougher in the Championship, but for long periods the team remained in the hunt for a play-off place and there was much to enthral and excite the fans as the Swans showed themselves to be the best ball-retainers in the division. There were two pulsating derbies against Cardiff, both of which finished 2–2, the team reached the fifth round of the Carling Cup (dispatching Cardiff 1–0 in the third round) and, most impressive of all, it reached the fifth round of the FA Cup, only to lose 1–2 in a replayed match at Fulham. These exertions took their toll and eventually, having drawn too many home and away games, the club finished the 2008–9 season in eighth place.

Then, completely out of the blue, came a thunderbolt. On 15 June Martínez decided to grasp Saxon gold and fulfil his ambition of reaching the Premiership by joining his old club Wigan. The chairman Huw Jenkins handled the matter with great dignity, but the fans reacted with fury. Here was a manager who had called for loyalty from his players and who had maintained that he would 'have to be forced out of here, like I was as a player'. The stench of betrayal infested the club and messages posted on websites – 'Once a God, now a Judas' and 'Never forgotten, never forgiven' – bore witness to the fact that thousands of supporters now loathed the sight of the Catalan. Clearly shaken by the volume of abuse, Martínez published a cringing letter in the *South Wales Evening Post*, but the damage could not be repaired, especially when the departed manager took his assistant Graeme Jones and his backroom staff, as well as the prolific scorers Jason Scotland and Jordi Gómez, with him.

Knowing full well that a club is bigger than its manager, Huw Jenkins was ready to move on and, if possible, maintain the refreshing Iberian influences that had made the team so easy on the eye. In the event, he appointed a cool, sophisticated, debonair figure who turned up for his first press conference in a smart grey three-piece suit, open-necked white shirt, Gucci shoes and no socks. Exuding the air of a film star, Paulo Manuel Carvalho de Sousa sported impressive credentials. He spoke five languages (four more than most managers in the Football League), had won 51 caps for Portugal, starred as a defensive midfielder for Inter Milan, Juventus and Borussia Dortmund, and been coached by the likes of Marcello Lippi, Sven-Göran Eriksson and Ottmar Hitzfeld. There was an air of self-obsession about Sousa, but he and his assistant Bruno Oliveira promised to provide continuity in their game plan and nurture a strong collective will within the squad.

The disruption caused by Martínez's departure meant that Sousa did not have a full summer to prepare. A swathe of injuries also hampered his pre-season plans. But he had inherited a harmonious group of players whose attitude and work-rate were excellent. By the end of the 2009–10 season the club had reached seventh place, its highest position for 27 years. But the irony is that, during the course of that seemingly successful season, Sousa failed to win the affection of the players and the supporters. Why was this so? Chiefly because he changed the team's playing style. He rebranded it by stiffening the players' defensive resolve and drumming into them the importance of not conceding goals. With Monk and Williams showing mental toughness as well as physical strength at the heart of the defence, and a five-man midfield providing core resilience, the flair and excitement associated with the Martínez regime disappeared. But the ultra-defensive tactics bred a negative mindset. Midfielders seldom over-committed themselves by going in advance of the ball and even winger Nathan Dyer, whom Martínez had signed for £400,000 from Southampton in early June, was prevented from showing the off-the-cuff ingenuity which was one of his great assets. The team became more resilient, harder to break down, and more functional. Only on one occasion – a 1–5 drubbing at Blackpool – was the team seriously embarrassed throughout the whole season. Sousa prided himself on having the Championship's meanest defence and a goalless draw always left him a happy man. Dorus de Vries broke Roger Freestone's club record by keeping 24 clean sheets over the season. But there was not much to excite the fans, many of whom were alarmed to see such a talented team set up to play so defensively. So long as the team was within striking range of winning promotion, they were prepared to bite their tongues, but it was noticeable that whereas the chant 'Roberto Martínez' had been heartfelt, cries of 'Sousa' were muted.

Risk-averse to the point of stubbornness, Sousa refused to liberate his attackers. Wingers were expected to track back and a good deal of harmless square passing in midfield did little to stir passions. Wingers Gower and Orlandi were converted into midfielders, but neither came close to replicating the match-winning magic of Gómez. Goal blizzards did not happen under Sousa's watch and only once – in defeating the old enemy Cardiff City 3–2 – did Swansea score three league goals at the Liberty Stadium. The team badly missed the physical presence and goal threat of Jason Scotland and his replacements starkly exposed Sousa's lack of knowledge of the quality of players in the Football League. On the surface, signing the Scotland international Craig Beattie from West Bromwich Albion for a club record fee of £800,000 in late August was a timely initiative. But even a cursory glance at Beattie's resumé would have revealed that his career had been blighted by injuries. Sure enough, he spent most of his first season on the physiotherapist's table and scored only three goals. When the experienced Finland international Shefki Kuqi joined on a free transfer in January 2010, he managed to find the net rather more often, usually with scuffed or deflected shots, but he lacked pace and guile. The shortage of firepower was also aggravated by the slow tempo of play. Keeping possession was all very well, but as the prospect of automatic promotion receded the need to win rather than draw matches became palpably clear. For instance, during a home fixture against a mediocre Ipswich on 27 March the tempo was positively funereal, even though the Swans badly needed three points. The inevitable 0–0 draw had the home fans wailing in exasperation. By failing to create many goal-scoring opportunities, the team managed to score only 40 league goals over the season.

There were also doubts about Sousa's inter-personal skills. A volatile man, given to emotional outbursts, he sometimes made unflattering comments about his players to the press. When he questioned the loyalty of Leon Britton, of all people, the player was understandably resentful and joined Sheffield United. His colleagues were mortified. Cult hero Lee Trundle was also shabbily treated by the manager and it was a mistake to allow Stephen Dobbie, a prolific scorer whom Martínez had bought from Queen of the South before his departure, to go out on loan to rivals Blackpool. Towards the latter half of the season there were strong hints of unrest in the dressing room as training routines, which had never been intense, became even more relaxed. Garry Monk was furious about the general decline in standards and the manager's bonds with the players became increasingly frayed. Sousa's relationship with the chief scout Pasquale ('Lil') Fuccillo broke down irretrievably and Huw Jenkins took umbrage when the Portuguese complained of lack of financial support from the board. There was no doubt that reinforcements were needed over the last months of the season, but Jenkins was painfully aware that Sousa's judgement in the transfer market was distinctly fallible. Signing Beattie had been an absurdly expensive mistake and there were question marks too over the wisdom of paying £600,000 for winger David Cotterill, whose arrival on loan had been made permanent. Sousa's habit of blaming everyone but himself was unappealing and even his sometimes justifiable bellyaching about incompetent referees began to grate after a while. To make matters worse, local press hawks disliked his preening self-regard and habit of turning up late for conferences. Eventually, after being comfortably placed in the play-off slots since early December, the team paid the penalty for Sousa's relaxed training schedules and ran out of steam during the last critical weeks. A victory at home in the final game against Doncaster would have guaranteed a play-off place, but the

0–0 stalemate which followed seemed to epitomize the season. As Lee Trundle complained, under Sousa the team was never encouraged to 'go for it'.

Sousa disappeared for the best part of six weeks at the end of the season and when he missed the first day of training at the end of June the air was thick with rumours of his impending departure to Leicester City. No one was greatly troubled. He had always given the impression of being a manager in transit. Unlike Martínez's departure, which was rancorously bitter, Paulo Sousa's exit aroused neither surprise nor anger. He left unlamented on 4 July and lasted just three months at the helm at Leicester.

Whatever Sousa's failings may have been, the club was still climbing up the Football League and the future looked bright, especially when Huw Jenkins appointed a rising star on the managerial circuit. One of José Mourinho's protégés at Chelsea, Brendan Rodgers had a fine reputation as a progressive coach. A native of Carnlough in County Antrim, he was a personable, thoughtful man who radiated a sense of calmness and serenity. His strong moral compass was underpinned by a powerful sense of right and wrong, justice and fair play. He immediately established a rapport with the players and, by singing the praises of the city and its environs, with the club's fan-base as well. The press and media found him endlessly obliging. His blueprint for the future fitted the Swansea mould and Huw Jenkins was convinced that Rodgers was not only the man to bring fresh ideas and firmness of purpose to the playing staff but also to serve as an ambassador for the club. Under Sousa, the club had taken a step forward, but under Rodgers it was poised to make several giant strides.

Meticulous in his preparations on the training field and before games, Rodgers set the highest standards in identifying the physical strengths and weaknesses of his players. Matters relating to nutrition, hydration and rehabilitation were given serious attention. He brought in experts to assist him. Ryland Morgans provided expertise in sports science, while

Chris Davies supplied in-depth match analyses based on GPS tracking systems of players' movements on the pitch. Nothing was left to chance.

Rodgers imposed a culture based on honest hard work, self-improvement and effective teamwork. With popular former players Colin Pascoe and Alan Curtis as his assistant and coach respectively, he enjoyed working with players who were filled with a burning desire to prove themselves at the highest level. He was fortunate to inherit a squad which had no spoiled brats or swaggering superstars. Coming to a club which was not filthy rich suited him down to the ground since it enabled him to introduce his own philosophy to a set of humble and hard-working players. True, he did bring in from Chelsea a marquee signing in left-winger Scott Sinclair, an astute bargain for less than £1 million. But Sinclair, for all his reputation as a product of the celebrity culture, was in fact an intelligent and down-to-earth player who had ambitions to fulfil. Signing him was a masterstroke. He became a goal-scoring machine, filling the void left by Jason Scotland. But Rodgers's arrival signalled not so much a change in personnel as in tactical direction and style of play.

It soon became apparent that the ultra-cautious approach of Sousa had been abandoned. Training routines, based on winning and retaining possession, were high-octane exercises which made huge physical demands on the players. Rodgers insisted that his team dictated the pace of the game. He expected his players to zip the ball around with lightning-fast accuracy, and once it was lost, to apply relentless pressure high up the pitch in order to regain possession and prevent opponents from building momentum. This *tiqui-taca* (or tiki-taka) style, perfected by Barcelona, was bright, fast and dynamic, and it bore witness to the young manager's desire to play creative, attacking football. Not that it was naïve, swashbuckling stuff. The team's success in the manager's first season was built on the solid defensive foundations established by Sousa. Although sometimes unnerved by inswinging corners,

Dorus de Vries was a brave goalkeeper blessed with safe hands and good feet. Both Ángel Rangel and newcomer, St Asaph-born international Neil Taylor, were accomplished full backs who had the pace and athleticism to launch and sustain counter-attacks on the flanks. Garry Monk, as captain, was a rock in the centre of the defence and his trusty ally Ashley Williams was both consistently excellent and remarkably injury-free. Whenever needed, utility defender Alan Tate could be relied upon to inspire the team with his heroic blocks and bone-jarring tackles, while local product Ashley ('Jazz') Richards played with the fearless drive of youth. This defensive unit ensured that the team's goals-against tally was the best in the Championship in the 2010–11 season.

But it was in midfield that Swansea were at their most eye-catching. Darren Pratley ran his heart out, his long stride, great stamina and prodigious appetite for work standing him in good stead. Joe Allen blossomed under Rodgers's direction, bringing vibrancy and forcefulness, not to mention a wide range of passing skills, into the vitally important midfield zone. The smoothness of his technique and the sureness of his touch won many plaudits and he refused to be outrun or outmuscled by bigger opponents. To universal acclaim, Leon Britton returned from Sheffield United in January 2011 and resumed playing as if he had never been away. Sharp-witted and nimble-footed, the tiny midfielder was hardly ever caught in possession or hustled into making a poor pass.

Pace and trickery on the flanks were also an integral part of Rodgers's strategy. Freed from Sousa's shackles, Nathan Dyer was transformed. His twinkling feet, darting runs and air of mischief made him a firm favourite among the supporters. On the opposite wing, Scott Sinclair produced consistently high-calibre performances, cutting defences to shreds with his acceleration and goal-scoring prowess. His 27 goals over the season proved to be absolutely critical to the team's success, especially since none of the central striking force proved capable of filling Jason Scotland's seven league boots. To fill the gap temporarily, Rodgers borrowed Marvin Emnes, a lithe and skilful striker, from Middlesbrough, worked hard on improving the touch and shooting skills of Stephen Dobbie, and then in March 2011 managed to persuade Chelsea to let him borrow Fabio Borini, a gifted young striker from Italy who was widely tipped to become a future international star. Each of these players made their mark, often in spectacular fashion.

During the first half of the season, no one expected the squad to push for promotion, especially since the team's dismal away record did not encourage optimism. Losing away against relegation-threatened opponents became something of a habit, and contrasted sharply with the successes chalked up at the Liberty Stadium. But Rodgers maintained that soccer is a game of risks and rewards. He urged his players, both at home and on their travels, to persevere with their attractive playing style, force the pace and make things happen. At their rhythmic best, Swansea were a splendid sight and were flatteringly bracketed with Arsenal and Barcelona, teams which delighted in passing the ball swiftly and skilfully. Almost like a thief in the night, Swansea crept up the table and by the end of the calendar year stood in third place with 40 points. During the second half of the season, teamwork, a collective mentality and the manager's tactical awareness maintained the momentum and raised levels of expectation. The team ran into a rich vein of form in February and, despite some woeful setbacks against lowly opposition during the run-in, eventually amassed 80 points which assured them of third place. The Swans had scored 69 goals, 29 more than in the previous season, had kept 22 clean sheets, and achieved a highly impressive average pass count of 526 per game, a total far in excess of any other side in the Championship.

As Swansea prepared for the play-off semi-final against Nottingham Forest, the city of Swansea became a bubbling pot of excitement. Both legs provided scenes of extraordinary drama. When Neil Taylor was harshly sent off within a minute of the first leg at the City Ground, Swansea fans feared the worst. But instead of sitting deep and defying Forest to prise them apart, the Swans held their shape and passed the ball so effectively that the home team were forced to chase shadows. Swansea were magnificent and fully deserved the goalless draw. The second leg on 16 May was a pulsating affair watched by nearly 20,000 supporters and a huge television audience. Taylor's earlier dismissal and the provocative demeanour of Billy Davies, the Forest manager, had ratcheted up the tension before the game, and the home fans were in raucous mood. Swansea seized the moment. A peach of a goal by Britton and a piledriver by Dobbie set them on their way before the interval and, although Earnshaw reduced the deficit in the second half, a glorious goal by Pratley from inside his own half in added time sealed a memorable victory. The primal roar which greeted the final whistle shook the Liberty Stadium to its foundations. The Swans were on their way to Wembley and a possible £90 million windfall for reaching the Premiership.

Much to the relief of every police officer and traffic controller along the M4 corridor, Cardiff surrendered meekly to Reading in the other semi-final tie, thereby ensuring that Brendan Rodgers would meet up with his former employers in the play-off final at Wembley on 30 May. Play-off final fever swept through the city and on the big day around 40,000 singing supporters made their way to the cathedral of English football. Bliss was it on that day to be part of the Jack Army. 'This is our day!' bellowed the stadium announcer Kevin Johns, and the ear-splitting roar which followed must have sent shivers down the spine of supporters of the Royals. A sensational, full-blooded encounter followed. Reading started like a house on fire, but Swansea were not to be denied and, incredibly, built up a three-goal lead. An explosion of noise greeted the first goal after 21 minutes. Dyer was scythed down and Sinclair rolled in the penalty. An even louder roar marked Sinclair's second goal, laid on by Dobbie. Five minutes before the interval, the cheers were deafening when a firecracker by Dobbie, whose farmer's gait and outlandish haircut had always somehow deflected attention from his prowess as a goal-scorer, scorched into the net.

Reading fans sat in silent disbelief, but their favourites fought back manfully in the second half and scored two headed goals from corners. A few lucky breaks (and a marvellous block by Monk) helped Swansea, and when Sinclair completed his hat-trick with another ice-cool penalty kick after 79 minutes they regained the initiative and held on to win 4–2. When the final whistle sounded, a joyous roar arose from the massed ranks of the black and white Jack Army. In their hour of triumph, the Swansea players donned T-shirts in memory of their late colleague Besian Idrizaj, a promising young Austrian striker who had died in his sleep in the previous year. Then the champagne began to flow. Swansea had become the first Welsh club to reach the Premier League and, as Barney Ronay put it in the *Guardian*: 'Who needs game 39 now? Who needs Qatar when we have Cymru?' The carnival mood in Swansea lasted for days, if not weeks. 'I'm very proud', said Brendan Rodgers. 'It's been a wonderful journey… and now it's going into a totally different stratosphere.'

The new world in which Swansea now found itself was characterized by big money, intensive media coverage, high-maintenance celebrities, greedy agents and player-power, none of which was remotely pertinent to the modestly endowed club from south-west Wales. While the rich owners of Manchester City were spending £38 million on just one player (Sergio Agüero), the Swansea board, after much heart-searching, were sanctioning a much more modest outlay of around £8.5 million on four new players over the summer. The most expensive of them was Danny Graham (£3.5m.), a proven goal-scorer with Watford, while the most intriguing was goalkeeper Michel Vorm (£1.5m.), a remarkably lithe and agile Dutch international from FC Utrecht, who replaced de Vries on his departure to Wolves. Forwards Leroy Lita and Wayne Routledge were experienced players, but both had underachieved to date and had something to prove. Steven Caulker, a strapping young centre back who arrived on a season's loan from Spurs, was a valuable addition to the squad, especially since Garry Monk had spent the latter part of the previous season playing through the pain barrier. Yet, no one among the so-called experts believed that Swansea would be more than makeweights at this exalted level and bookmakers made them odds-on favourites for relegation. London-based reporters patronized the plucky little underdogs from Wales and incensed the fans by referring to vaunted opponents having to undertake 'run-of-the-mill engagements' against them. But there were no feelings of inferiority. The Swans were determined to compete in the most demanding league in the world and enjoy their place in the sun.

One thing soon became very clear. Even though the principal aim was to avoid relegation, Brendan Rodgers had no intention of abandoning the philosophy which had brought Swansea into the top flight. From the outset he retained his 4–2–3–1 or 4–3–3 system and showcased the kaleidoscopic passing game honed over the previous seasons. To his critics he replied: 'Why change a winning formula that has served us so well?' Unfailingly positive in press conferences, he was determined not to offer fans stodgy fare or try to 'win ugly' by adopting an unfamiliar direct or physical approach. Even Rodgers, however, must have been surprised by how intense and unforgiving the new environment proved to be. Errors or momentary lapses of concentration were ruthlessly punished and chances were few and far between. Pitting themselves against a new calibre of opposition, especially the leading clubs, involved a physical and mental effort which often left the players drained of every ounce of energy.

As before, there was much to delight capacity crowds at the Liberty Stadium and up to 3,000 travelling supporters who sang their hearts out on English soil. Even in the company of the big battalions and of outstanding international stars like David Silva and Robin van Persie, the Swans were never overawed. Nor did they depart from their passing game. Michel Vorm, whose prowess as a saver of spot-kicks earned him the nickname 'the Penalty Killer', revealed excellent distribution skills with his feet and made many jaw-dropping saves. Steven Caulker provided aerial strength, Ashley Williams was phenomenally strong and authoritative, Ángel Rangel provided an outlet by making more passes than any other Premiership full back, and Neil Taylor raided profitably down the left flank. Even when visiting teams like Stoke battered and bruised the back four by employing what the home supporters derisively called 'hoof' football, the defence held firm. It was not uncommon for Swansea to command more than 60 per cent of possession and, in the pre-Christmas period, only Manchester United took home three points. At one stage in the first half of the season, Leon Britton was the only player in the Premiership with a 100 per cent pass completion rate. He and Joe Allen came of age, playing with brio and bravado against bigger players and, with the support of Kemy Agustien, a robust but skilful Dutch midfielder, controlled games by settling quickly into their passing stride. When Swansea gained a creditable 0–0 draw at Anfield, shrewd Liverpudlians on the Kop showed their appreciation by applauding them from the field. Their centre back Daniel Agger readily admitted that the visitors had made them run around 'like headless chickens'. On the flanks Nathan Dyer was a delightful, scampering trickster, while Scott Sinclair displayed the speed and sleekness of a thoroughbred racehorse. After a slow start, Danny Graham began to score goals and to show that a Geordie was fit to wear Jason Scotland's talismanic shirt. By Christmas, Swansea had accumulated 18 points and were in 14th place.

But for two critical factors, the club might have fared even better. Their progress was derailed by a string of serious injuries. Caulker suffered cartilage trouble, Agustien tore a hamstring and Tate broke his leg in a freak golfing accident. Just as alarming was the team's inability to pick up points away from home. It was only to be expected that the most affluent clubs would do them no favours and Swansea duly came home empty-handed from the Etihad Stadium, the Emirates and

Stamford Bridge. Not until 22 October did they pick up a point on their travels against ailing Wolves, but a heavy 2–4 defeat at bottom club Blackburn proved less than pleasant viewing for the travelling fans and prompted critics to question the grit and resilience of the players. But players who show bravely for the ball and trust in the manager's determination to play 'our way' do not lack mental toughness and once they had come to terms with the physical intensity of away matches things began to improve.

From New Year's Eve onwards hard work on the training ground brought a new surge of self-belief. In an enthralling match, high-flying Tottenham Hotspur were held to a richly-deserved 1–1 draw at the Liberty Stadium and on 2 January the away hoodoo was emphatically removed when goals by the twinkling wingers Dyer and Routledge at Villa Park heralded the first win on English soil. Keen to maintain the impetus, Rodgers secured the services of Gylfi Sigurdsson, a young Icelandic international who came on loan from TSG Hoffenheim in the Bundesliga. An attacking midfielder, he immediately showed that he was made to measure for the Premiership. Dubbed 'SoGoodSon', he filled that corridor of uncertainty between the attacking lines and scored some splendid goals. His debut, against star-studded Arsenal on 15 January, could not have been more dramatic. Nine years earlier Arsenal had led the Premier League, while Swansea languished at the foot of the Football League. But this was to be Swansea's day. Inspired by the dazzling runs of Dyer and Sinclair, the superlative passing of Allen and Britton, and the dogged persistence of Graham, the team outpassed and outran the Gunners in registering a 3–2 victory. Sigurdsson's introduction as substitute brought an added spark of inventiveness and a tremendous crescendo of noise filled the stadium when Danny Graham scored the winner. The pass-masters had been beaten at their own game. Chelsea very nearly became the next scalp. After Scott Sinclair had acrobatically hooked a bouncing ball with his left foot into the top corner of the net on 39 minutes, Swansea dominated play and only a fortuitous deflected equalizer in added time rescued a point for the visitors.

But Rodgers's crowning glory came on an unseasonably warm and sunny Sunday afternoon in mid-March when Manchester City, title pretenders and the most expensively assembled team in the world, came to town. In 'Swan-celona' mood, the home team, undeterred by the greater physicality of the League leaders, dominated large parts of the game in terms of territory and possession. Their neat passing triangles, composure on the ball and relentless pressing were a delight to watch. To the unrestrained joy of a packed house, substitute Luke Moore's back-post header in the 83rd minute secured the three points which capped a magnificent performance. Buoyed by this success, Swansea went to Fulham, scored three goals and, by completing one bewitching sequence of 38 consecutive passes which lasted for 1.36 minutes, even made the lugubrious soothsayers on *Match of the Day* sing their praises. With nine games left to play, Swansea were tenth and a long way from the relegation struggle at the foot of the Premiership.

As the final stages of the season unfolded, the learning process continued under Rodgers's impressive stewardship. When it became clear that some clubs were determined to stifle or neutralize Swansea's passing game by playing a pressing game high up the pitch, he devised ways and means of retaining the initiative. The adaptability of the players and their fierce commitment to him as well as to each other were always in evidence. Inspired by the manager's favourite motto – 'Per ardua ad astra' (through adversity to the stars) – they more than coped with the physical and mental demands of Premiership football. After a few scares during the run-in period, the team totally outplayed Liverpool in the final game and finished the season in 11th place with 47 points. No one, except those who knew the quality of the manager and his players, had ever expected 'little old Swansea' to survive, let alone prosper, in its first season in the Premiership.

Success on the field brought many dividends. Revenues increased substantially from merchandising and sponsorship income, and especially from terrestrial and satellite television coverage. Many games were beamed live to 212 countries throughout the world, with the result that Swansea's trademark one-touch, rat-tat-tat passing game was admired by viewers from Abu Dhabi to Melbourne and from Detroit to Kuala Lumpur. Such global attention raised the profile of the city and reminded the ill-informed that Wales does not stop at Cardiff. Higher levels of inward investment by business companies occurred and the city council and tourist operators maximized every opportunity to showcase the sandy beaches and the clear, blue waters of Swansea Bay and the Gower peninsula. Premiership football and performing on the grandest stage unquestionably helped to promote the image of Swansea as a major waterfront city.

As the club inched its way to safety in this brave new world and savoured the booming financial benefits of top-flight football, plans were unveiled to establish a much-needed purpose-built training ground for the senior squad and a youth academy at Fairwood which, it is hoped, will become Swansea's equivalent of Barcelona's La Masia. Wisely, too, the opportunity of raising decibel levels at the Liberty Stadium was also taken by outlining proposals to increase the capacity of the ground to 32,000. Over the 2011–12 season home fixtures had invariably attracted a capacity crowd of around 20,500, a total which included 16,000 season-ticket holders. Jock Stein used to say that 'football without fans is nothing' and, over the years, Swansea has learned that it cannot afford to neglect its supporters and the wider community. Its swiftly growing Jack Army – loyal, raucous and sometimes fearsome – remains the lifeblood of the club. The Supporters Trust, currently boasting over 16,000 members and a 20 per cent stake in the club, has made giant strides under the chairmanship of Phil Sumbler and its supporter-director Huw Cooze. Its influence is such that everyone involved with the club is aware of the sporting and cultural heritage of Swansea City and the family ethos which underpins its success.

One striking illustration of the symbiotic relationship between the Trust, directors, staff, players and supporters occurred in May 2011 when long queues of patient fans seeking tickets for the play-off final against Reading circled the Liberty Stadium. Leading members of the Trust took the players to meet them and distributed programmes to help them pass the time. Leon Britton took bus reservations in the travel club pod and director Martin Morgan gave a helping hand in the ticket office. As Phil Sumbler appreciatively noted: 'You wouldn't see Wayne Rooney taking bus bookings at Old Trafford or Phil Gartside selling tickets at the Reebok Stadium. We are a unique football club that I'm extremely proud to be a part of.' Inspired by the charitable work undertaken by Brendan Rodgers and Ashley Williams, the players became excellent ambassadors for the club, notably in supporting the 'one game, one community' initiative and in working with disabled supporters and children with learning difficulties. During the first season in the Premiership the reputation of Swansea as a community-based club was poignantly brought to the attention of the world when four coal miners from the Swansea Valley were tragically killed at the Gleision Colliery at Cilybebyll in September 2011. An impeccable minute's silence was observed in their memory before the home game against West Bromwich Albion. The team was carried to victory on a tide of emotion and captain Garry Monk dedicated the 3–0 win to the families of the victims and urged supporters to support fund-raising efforts on their behalf.

In a variety of unsung ways, many individuals contribute to the success and good name of the club. Ugo Vallerio ensures that an armada of buses, filled with singing supporters, travels smoothly to away grounds. Local postman Gwyn Rees not only organizes the distribution of programmes on home match-days but has also converted a room in his home into a shrine bursting with memorabilia associated with his beloved

Swans. For genuine supporters like these, the club means everything, and some of them would walk to the ends of the earth to support it. Mutual trust between the club and the fans is of critical importance and supporters have every confidence in the current board of directors. When Brendan Rodgers unexpectedly moved on to Anfield at the end of the 2011–12 season, chairman Huw Jenkins lost no time in appointing Michael Laudrup to succeed him. This lavishly gifted player had won championship medals with Juventus, Barcelona and Real Madrid and had gained extensive managerial experience at Brøndby in Denmark, Getafe and Real Mallorca in Spain, and Spartak Moscow in Russia. That Swansea had been able to attract such a celebrated footballing genius was a measure of how far the club had progressed both on and off the field over the previous decade. Most important of all, the new manager's appreciation of the importance of touch, technique, ball retention and virtuosity clearly fitted the Swansea mould to perfection.

As Swansea City Association Football Club proudly enters its second century, it is hard to imagine that this prudently run family club will ever allow itself to fall into the hands of foreign billionaires and become a multinational corporation bereft of local roots. Nor is it conceivable that the club will ever abandon its commitment to playing vibrant, attacking football in 'the Swansea way'.

Bibliography

Newspapers

Athletic News
Cambria Daily Leader
The Guardian
The Observer
South Wales Daily Post
South Wales Evening Post
South Wales Weekly Post
Sporting News and Football Leader
Sporting Post
Sunday Times
The Times
Western Mail
World of Sport

Books

Alban, J. R., *The 'Three Nights' Blitz'* (Swansea, 1994).

Alcock, Charles W., *Football: The Association Game* (London, 1902).

Bentley, Roy with Jim Drury, *Roy Wonder* (Stroud, 2005).

Birley, Derek, *Land of Sport and Glory: Sport and British Society, 1887–1910* (Manchester, 1995).

—, *Playing the Game: Sport and British Society, 1910–50* (Manchester, 1995).

Burgess, Ron, *Football: My Life* (London, 1952).

Burgum, John, *Swansea City Football Club* (Manchester, 1988).

Chapman, Herbert, *Herbert Chapman on Football* (London, 1934).

Charles, John, *King of Soccer* (London, 1957).

Charles, John with Bob Harris, *King John: John Charles* (London, 2003).

Charles, Mel with Colin Leslie, *In the Shadow of a Giant: The Autobiography of Arsenal and Wales Legend* (London, 2009).

Clarke, Stuart, *The Homes of Football: The Passion of a Nation* (London, 1999).

Conn, David, *The Beautiful Game? Searching for the Soul of Football* (London, 2004).

—, *The Football Business: Fair Game in the '90s?* (Edinburgh, 1997).

Corrigan, Peter, *100 Years of Welsh Soccer: The Official History of the Football Association of Wales* (Cardiff, [1976]).

Cowley, Jason, *The Last Game: Love, Death and Football* (London, 2009).

Curtis, Alan with Tim Johnson and Stuart Sprake, *Curt: The Alan Curtis Story* (Edinburgh, 2009).

Davies, Aneirin Talfan, *Dyddiau'r Ceiliog Rhedyn* (Llundain, [1941]).

Davies, Dai with Nic Parry, *Hanner Cystal â 'Nhad* (Yr Wyddgrug, 1985).

Davies, Dai, *Never Say Dai* (Mold, 1986).

Davies, Gareth and Michael Robinson, *Soccer: The International Line-ups and Statistics Series: Wales 1876–1960* (Cleethorpes, 1995).

—, *Soccer: The International Line-ups and Statistics Series: Wales 1961–1996* (Cleethorpes, 1996).

Davies, James A. (ed.), *A Swansea Anthology* (2nd edn., Bridgend, 1996).

Dunning, Eric, Patrick Murphy and John Williams, *The Roots of Football Hooliganism* (London, 1988).

Farewell to the Vetch 1912–2005 (Swansea, 2005).

Farmer, David, *Swansea City 1912–1982* (London, 1982).

Farmer, David and Peter Stead, *Ivor Allchurch MBE: The Authorised Biography of the Legendary Golden Boy* (Swansea, 1998).

Farmer, David, Brian Lile and Colin Jones, *The Official 'Biography' of the Swans, Town and City* (Swansea, 2000).

Fishwick, Nicholas, *English Football and Society, 1910–1950* (Manchester, 1989).

Ford, Trevor, *I Lead the Attack!* (London, 1957).

Frosdick, Steve and Peter Marsh, *Football Hooliganism* (Cullompton, 2005).

Garland, Ian, *The History of the Welsh Cup 1877–1993* (Wrexham, 1994).

Glanville, Brian (ed.), *The Joy of Football* (London, 1986).

Grandin, Terry, *Swansea City: Seasons in the Sun 1981–2 and 1982–3* (Southend-on-Sea, 2005).

Gregg, Harry with Roger Anderson, *Harry's Game: The Autobiography* (Edinburgh, 2002).

Griffiths, Ralph A. (ed.), *The City of Swansea: Challenges and Change* (Stroud, 1990).

Harding, John, *Football Wizard: The Billy Meredith Story* (London, 1998).

Harrison, Paul, *Southern League Football: The First Fifty Years* (Gravesend, 1989).

Hayes, Dean, *Swansea City Football Club: An A–Z* (Cardiff, 1999).

—, *The South Wales Derbies: A History of Cardiff City versus Swansea City* (Manchester, 2003).

Haynes, Keith, *Come on Cymru 2000! New Football Writing from Wales* (Wilmslow, 2000).

—, *Swansea City 2010/2011: Walking on Sunshine* (Stroud, 2011).

Haynes, Keith and Phil Sumbler, *Roger Freestone: Another Day at the Office* (Stroud, 2001).

—, *Vetch Field Voices* (Stroud, 2000).

Holt, Richard, *Sport and the British: A Modern History* (Oxford, 1989).

Hopcraft, Arthur, *The Football Man: People and Passions in Soccer* (London, 1968).

Hornby, Nick, *Fever Pitch* (London, 1992).

Hornby, Nick (ed.), *My Favourite Year: A Collection of Football Writing* (London, 1993).

Hughes, Charles, *Football: Tactics and Teamwork* (London, 1973).

Hughes, Chris, *John Toshack* (London, 2002).

Hughes, Stephen, *Copperopolis: Landscapes of the Early Industrial Period in Swansea* (Aberystwyth, 2000).

Hunter, Graham, *Barça: The Making of the Greatest Team in the World* (London, 2012).

Huws, Richard E., *The Football and Rugby Playing Fields of Wales* (Talybont, 2009).

Inglis, Simon, *The Football Grounds of England and Wales* (London, 1985).

—, *League Football and the Men who Made It* (London, 1988).

Jenkins, Geraint H., *Arwr Coll Wrecsam: 'Yr Ercwlff Synfawr' Leigh Richmond Roose* (Wrecsam, 2011).

—, *Cewri'r Bêl-droed yng Nghymru* (Llandysul, 1977).

—, *Yr Elyrch: Dathlu'r Cant* (Talybont, 2012).

—, *The Swans Go Up!* (Talybont, 2011).

Jenkins, Nigel, *Real Swansea* (Bridgend, 2008).

Johnes, Martin, *A History of Sport in Wales* (Cardiff, 2005).

—, *Soccer and Society: South Wales, 1900–1939* (Cardiff, 2002).

Johns, Kevin with Peter Read, *Oh Yes It Is: Kevin Johns – the Autobiography* (Talybont, 2008).

Jones, Cliff, *Forward with Spurs* (London, 1962).

Jones, Colin, *Swansea Town/City AFC: The First Comprehensive Player A–Y* (Llandybïe, 2005).

—, *The Swans 'Biography' Updated: Seven Seasons Updated Records 2000–2007* (Llandybïe, 2007).

Jones, Owain Tudur with Alun Gibbard, *Fyny gyda'r Swans* (Talybont, 2009).

Kelsey, Jack, *Over the Bar* (London, 1958).

Kuypers, Tim and Stefan Szymanski, *Winners and Losers: The Business Strategy of Football* (Harmondsworth, 1999).

Laschke, Ian, *Rothman's Book of Football League Records, 1888–89 to 1978–79* (London, 1980).

Lees, Andrew and Ray Kennedy, *Ray of Hope: The Ray Kennedy Story* (London, 1993).

Legg, Andy, *Alive and Kicking* (Bedlinog, 2009).

Lerry, G. G., *Association Football in Wales, 1870–1924* (Oswestry, 1924).

—, *The Football Association of Wales: 75th Anniversary, 1876–1951* (Wrexham, 1952).

Martínez, Roberto with Peter Read, *Kicking every Ball: My Story So Far* (Talybont, 2008).

Mason, Tony, *Association Football and English Society, 1863–1915* (Brighton, 1980).

Matthews, Brinley E., *The Swansea City Story: History of the Swansea City Association Football Club* (Swansea, 1976).

McIllvanney, Hugh, *McIllvanney on Football* (Edinburgh, 1999).

Miskell, Louise, *'Intelligent Town': An Urban History of Swansea, 1780–1855* (Cardiff, 2006).

Molby, Jan and Grahame Lloyd, *Jan the Man: From Anfield to Vetch Field* (London, 1999).

Monk, Garry with Peter Read, *Loud, Proud & Positive – My Autobiography* (Talybont, 2012).

Morgan, T. J., *Peasant Culture* (Swansea, [1962]).

Morrow, Stephen, *The People's Game? Football, Finance and Society* (Basingstoke, 2003).

Nurse, Mel with Pete Welsh, *Mr Swansea* (Talybont, 2009).

Palmer, Neil, *Derby Days: Cardiff City v Swansea City* (Skipton, 2011).

Paul, Roy, *A Red Dragon of Wales* (London, 1956).

Phillips, Gareth, *Fan's Eye City: Swansea City in the Age of the Premiership* (London, 2005).

Richards, Huw, *The Swansea City Alphabet* (Cardiff, 2009).

Rippon, Anton, *Gas Masks for Goal Posts: Football in Britain during the Second World War* (Stroud, 2005).

Risoli, Mario, *Arrivederci Swansea: How a Third Division Reject became a Serie A Superstar* (Edinburgh, 2000).

Risoli, Mario, *John Charles: Gentle Giant* (London, 2003).

Roberts, Lowri (ed.), *Canu Clod y Campau: Detholiad o Farddoniaeth y Maes Chwarae* (Llanrwst, 2009).

Rollin, Jack, *Soccer at War 1939–45* (London, 1985).

Ronay, Barney, *The Manager: The Absurd Ascent of the Most Important Man in Football* (London, 2009).

Russell, Dave, *Football and the English* (Preston, 1997).

Shepherd, Richard, *Swansea Town Football Club (1912–1964)* (Stroud, 1998).

Smith, Tommy, *Anfield Iron: The Autobiography* (London, 2008).

Sprake, Stuart and Tim Johnson, *Careless Hands: The Forgotten Truth of Gary Sprake* (Stroud, 2006).

Stead, Peter and Huw Richards (eds.), *For Club and Country: Welsh Football Greats* (Cardiff, 2000).

Sumbler, Phil and Keith Haynes, *100 Greats: Swansea City Football Club* (Stroud, 2005).

Szymanski, Stefan, *Football Economics and Policy* (Basingstoke, 2010).

Tabner, Brian, *Through the Turnstiles* (Harefield, 1992).

Taylor, Matthew, *The Association Game: A History of British Football* (Harlow, 2008).

Taylor, Rogan, *Football and its Fans: Supporters and their Relations with the Game, 1885–1985* (Leicester, 1992).

Thomas, Cyril D., *Swansea Senior Football League 1901–2001: 100 Years of Local Soccer* (Swansea, 2002).

Thomas, Dylan, *Portrait of an Artist as a Young Dog* (London, 1940).

Tooze, Andrew and Martin King, *Swansea Jacks: From Skinheads to Stone Island* (Aldwick, 2007).

Toshack, John, *Gosh It's Tosh* (London, 1976).

—, *Tosh: An Autobiography* (London, 1982).

Trundle, Lee, with Chris Wathan, *Lee Trundle: More than Just Tricks* (Edinburgh, 2010).

The Vetch Field: A People's History (Swansea, 2005).

Walvin, James, *The People's Game: The History of Football Revisited* (2nd edn., Edinburgh, 2000).

Ward, Andrew and John Williams, *Football Nation: Sixty Years of the Beautiful Game* (London, 2009).

Wharton, Gary, *From the Fourth to the First: Swansea City FC during the John Toshack Years 1978–1984* ([s.l.], 2005).

Williams, Glanmor (ed.), *Swansea: An Illustrated History* (Swansea, 1990).

Williams, John and Stephen Wagg (eds.), *British Football and Social Change: Getting into Europe* (Leicester, 1991).

Williams, Morlais (ed.), *Swansea Schools Football Association 75th Anniversary* (Swansea, 1990).

Williams, Richard, *The Perfect 10: Football's Dreamers, Schemers, Playmakers and Playboys* (London, 2007).

Wilson, Jonathan, *Inverting the Pyramid: A History of Football Tactics* (London, 2008).

Yorath, Terry and Grahame Lloyd, *Hard Man, Hard Knocks* (Cardiff, 2004).

Young, Percy M., *A History of British Football* (London, 1968).

—, *Football Year* (London, 1956).

Index

B

D

F

M

O

P

Q

R

V

W

Y

Also from Y Lolfa:

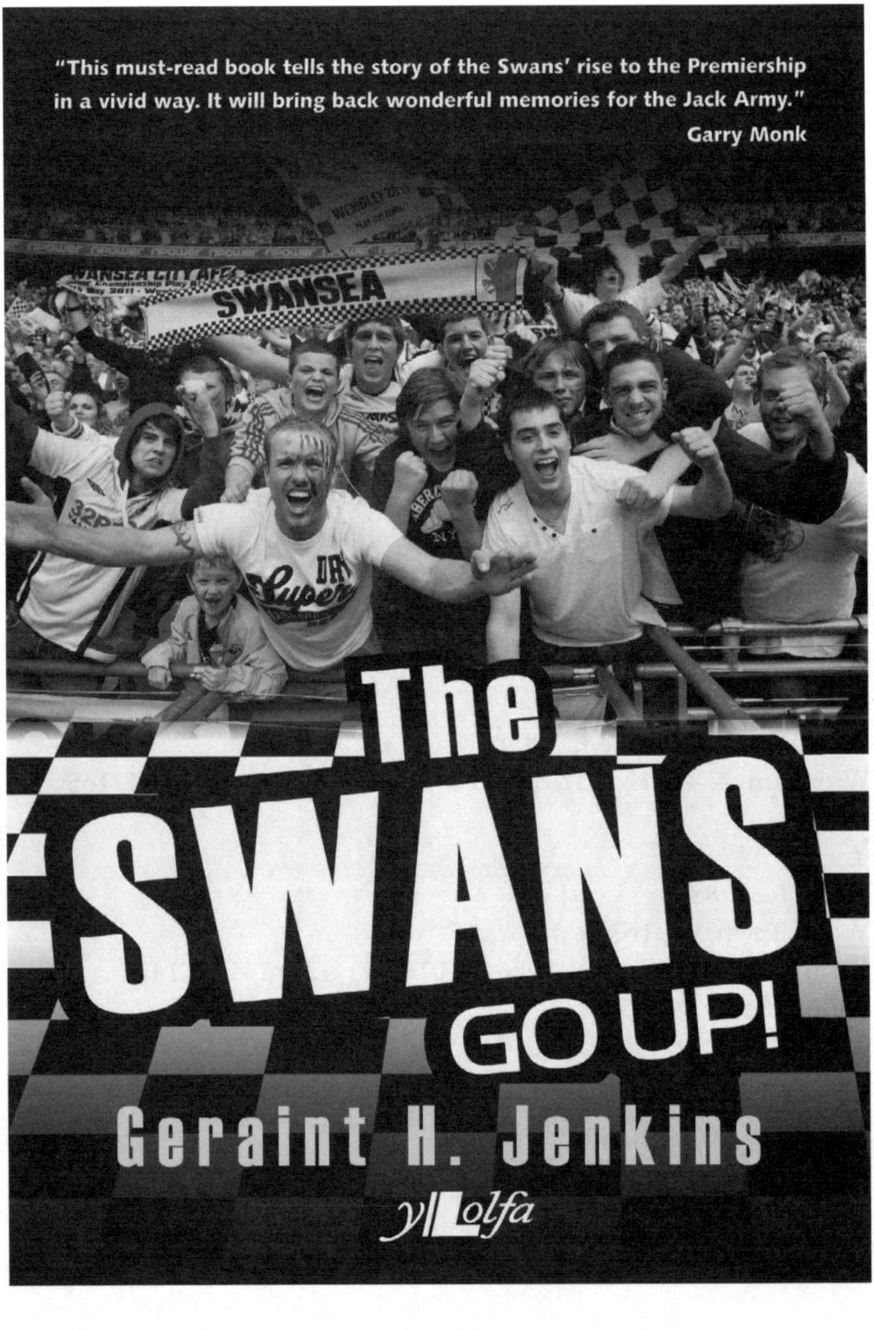

£4.95

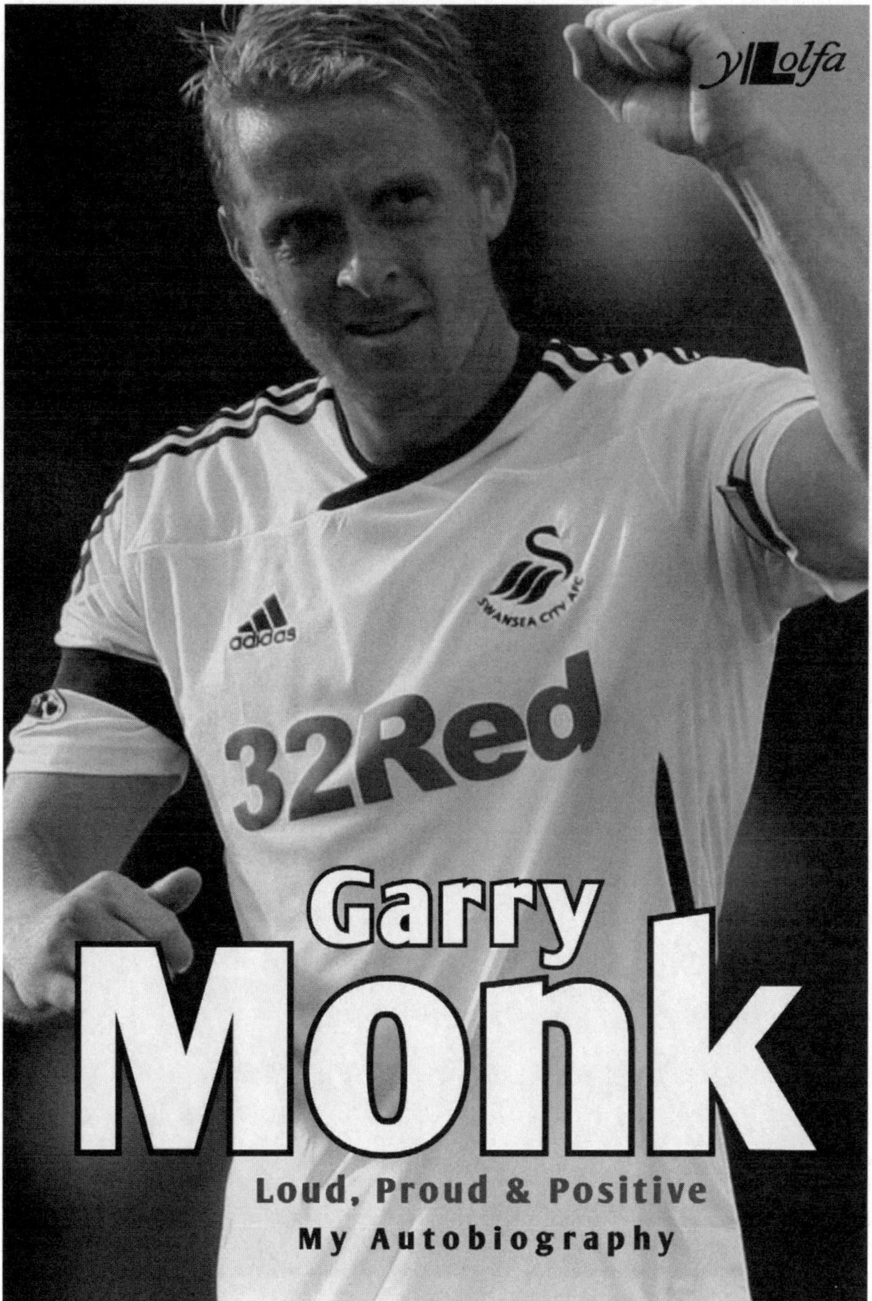
y Lolfa
32Red
Garry
Monk
Loud, Proud & Positive
My Autobiography

£9.95

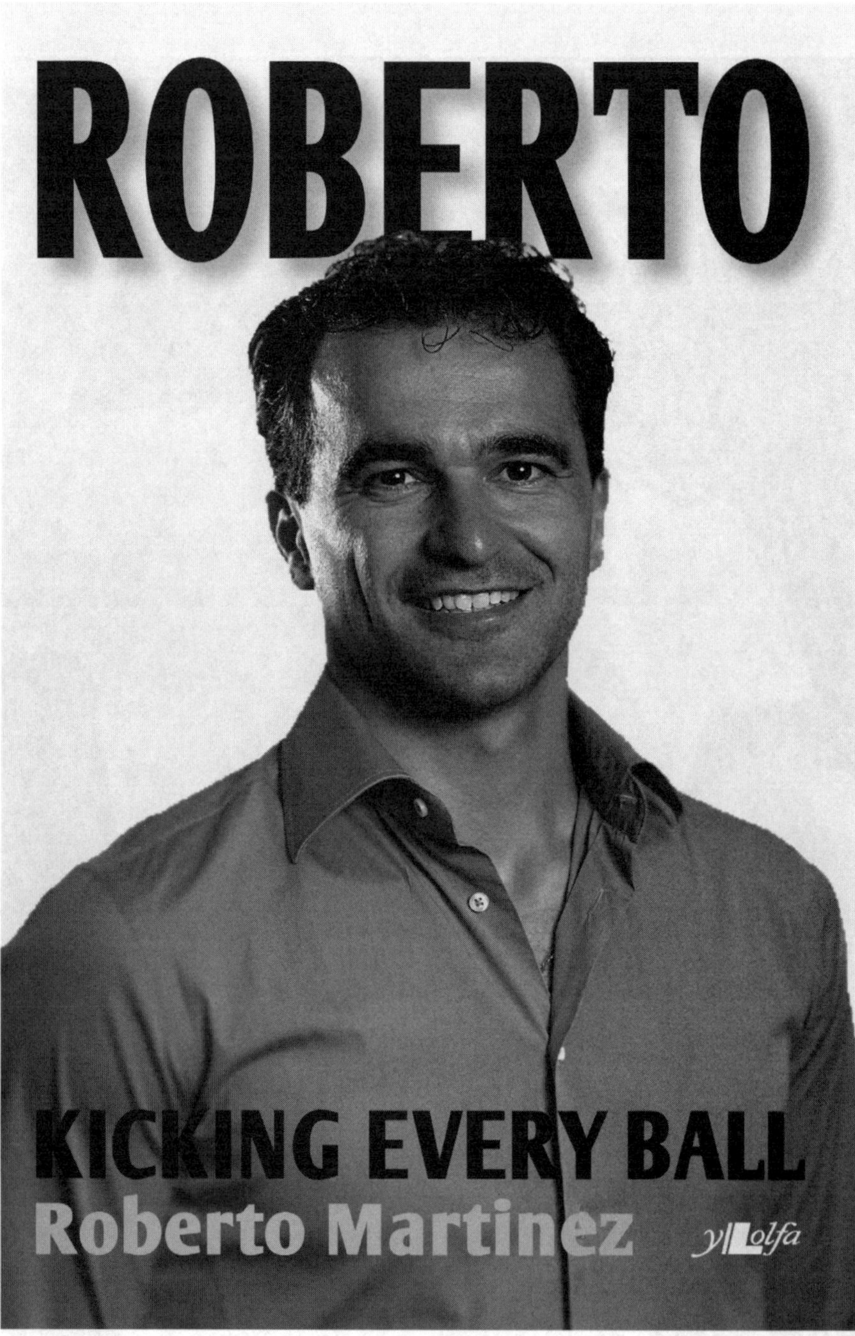

£12.95

MEL NURSE
A lifetime of football with one of the city's favourite sons
Mr Swansea
y Lolfa

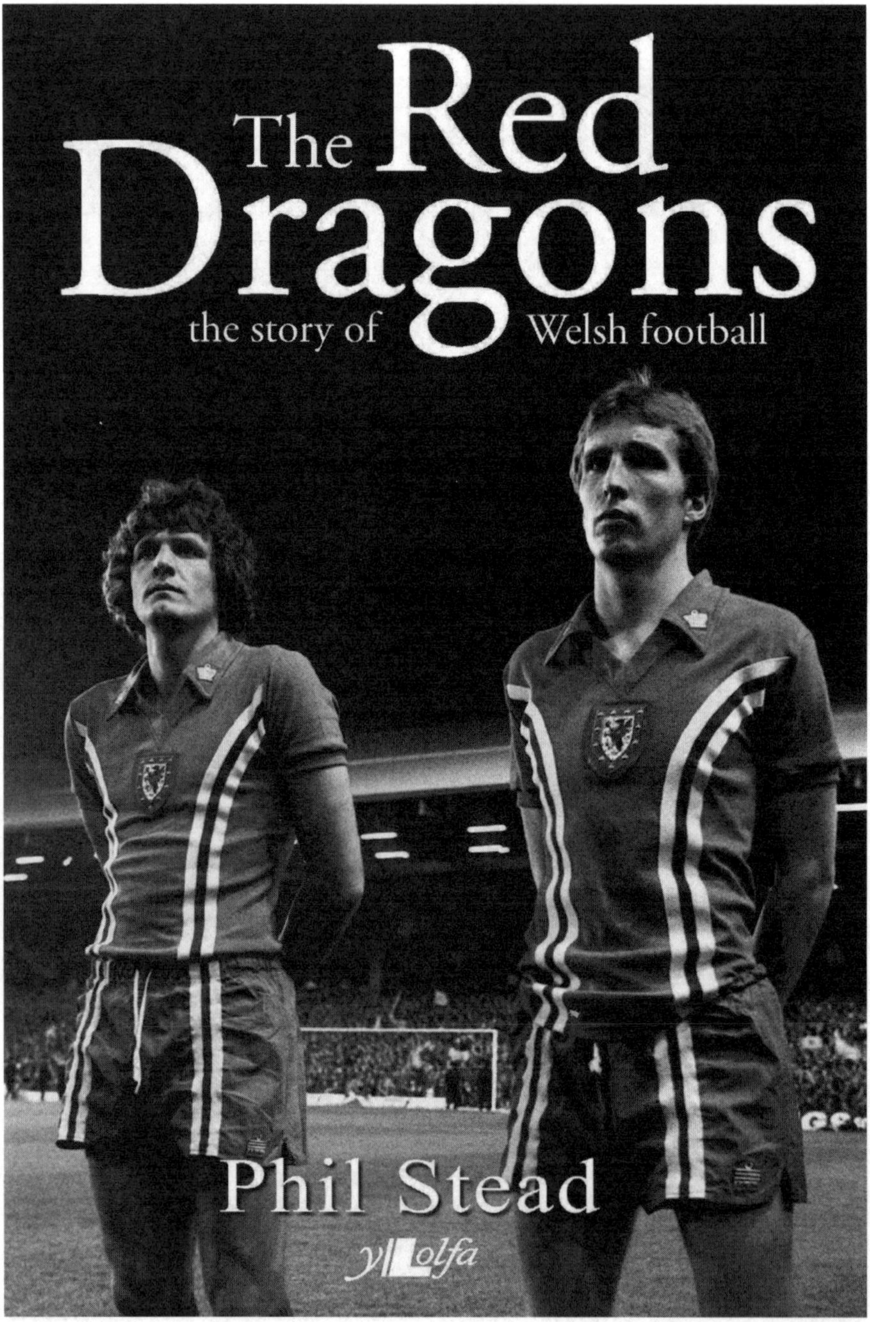

£14.95
Hardback £24.95
October 2012

y Lolfa

TALYBONT CEREDIGION CYMRU SY24 5HE
e-mail ylolfa@ylolfa.com
website www.ylolfa.com
phone (01970) 832 304
fax 832 782